Romance and the
"Yellow Peril"

Romance and the "Yellow Peril"

Race, Sex, and Discursive Strategies in Hollywood Fiction

Gina Marchetti

University of California Press
Berkeley / Los Angeles / London

The publisher gratefully acknowledges permission
to quote from "'The Mind That Burns in Each
Body': Women, Rape, and Racial Violence," in
Ann Snitow, Christine Stansell, and Sharon
Thompson, *Powers of Desire: The Politics of
Sexuality* (1983), p. 335. Copyright © 1993 by Ann
Snitow, Christine Stansell, and Sharon Thompson.
Reprinted by permission of Monthly Review
Foundation.

University of California Press
Berkeley and Los Angeles, California

University of California Press
London, England

Library of Congress Cataloging-in-Publication
Data
Marchetti, Gina.
　　Romance and the "yellow peril" : race, sex,
and discursive strategies in Hollywood fiction /
Gina Marchetti.
　　　　p.　cm.
　　Includes bibliographical references and index.
　　ISBN 0-520-07974-4 (cloth);
　　ISBN 0-520-08495-0 (pbk.)
　　1. Asians in motion pictures.　2. Race
relations in motion pictures.　3. Sex in motion
pictures.　4. Love in motion pictures.
5. Motion pictures—United States—History.
I. Title.
PN1995.9.A78M37　1993
791.43'6520395—dc20　　　　　　92-10878
　　　　　　　　　　　　　　　　　　　　CIP

Printed in the United States of America

1　2　3　4　5　6　7　8　9

Contents

Illustrations

Preface

Some readers, who do not know me either personally or by reputation, may wonder why a woman with an Italian surname would write a book dealing with Asian characters and themes. As an academic, my attraction to this subject matter needs no explanation. Shockingly few books and articles have been written about Hollywood's treatment of Asia and Asians, and no substantial study has analyzed the depiction of interracial sexual relations in the American popular cinema. This almost uncharted territory provided a research challenge too tempting to be ignored.

Throughout my scholarly career, I have been interested in cinematic depictions of gender, race, and sexuality. Working within a tradition of feminist film criticism, I have consistently tried to broaden the theoretical scope of that criticism to include ethnic, racial, national, cultural, and subcultural differences. While no one should attempt to speak for or in the place of another, a critic who refuses to engage with radically different cultures can never hope to establish any significant communication across constructed social barriers. Politically, solidarity across national and cultural boundaries is essential for any kind of concrete social change. Understanding the images used by the dominant media to erect these barriers and create social hierarchies seems like an appropriate place for any feminist scholar to begin work.

I also have a personal commitment to the study of Asian cinema and Asian themes in Western film that I have not yet explained. Although the reason behind my interest might strike some as odd, it is actually quite simple. While I was completing my dissertation on the punk and glitter youth subcultures at Northwestern University in 1982, I accompanied a friend, on a whim, to a martial arts class. Though my friend only studied for a few weeks, I continued, and I still train, on almost a daily basis, ten years later.

This interest in the martial arts led me to study the Chinese language, see countless *gung fu* films, read all sorts of fictional and nonfictional accounts of Asian culture, and cultivate friendships all around the world with diverse people with similar interests. Eventually, my involvement with Asian martial arts began to overlap with my film research. As a consequence, I helped to found the Asian Cinema Studies Society, I worked on the Asian American Film Festival in Washington, D.C., and I have written articles on Chinese, Vietnamese, and Philippine film. This book is a result, then, of both my commitment to feminist film studies and my involvement with Asian culture.

Needless to say, I am indebted to too many people to be able to acknowledge all their help here in this brief preface. However, there are a few people I must mention. The unflagging support of my mother and father has kept me from complete financial ruin. I am grateful to the University of Maryland for giving me steady employment and a very generous semester fellowship from the Research Center for Arts and Humanities in order to complete this book. Robert Kolker, chairperson of my department, has been particularly kind to read a draft of this project and give me excellent advice on revisions. My students at College Park have also been wonderful; their classroom discussions inspired many of the ideas that have found their way into this book.

I must thank my colleagues involved with the Asian Cinema Studies Society, particularly David Desser and Mira Binford, for their interest in this project. For their encouragement at various stages, I want to thank Sumiko Higashi, Marina Heung, Vivian Huang, Meng Tam, Roger Garcia, and my students Frances Gateward and Yeh Yueh-yu. I would also like to acknowledge the support of Asian American Arts and Media of Washington, D.C., which allowed me to present portions of the material here as part of their film festival program. Special thanks to Do Linh Khai for making this possible.

Jump Cut has been a constant inspiration for many years. Intellectually, this book owes its greatest debt to the associate editors of that journal, Chuck Kleinhans, Julia Lesage, and John Hess. I would never have had the heart to become involved in academic work at all were it not for the support of *Jump Cut*.

Portions of this book have been previously published in different forms in the following: parts of the conclusion in "Ethnicity, the Cinema and Cultural Studies," *Unspeakable Images: Ethnicity and the American Cinema,* ed. Lester Friedman (Urbana: University of Illinois

Press, 1991): 277–307; a part of chapter 3 in "The Threat of Captivity: Hollywood and the Sexualization of Race Relations in *The Girls of The White Orchid* and *The Bitter Tea of General Yen*," *Journal of Communication Inquiry* 11, no. 1 (Winter 1987): 29–42; a different version of chapter 6 appeared as "White Knights in Hong Kong: Race, Gender, and the Exotic in *Love Is a Many-Splendored Thing* and *The World of Suzie Wong*," *Post Script* 10, no. 2 (Winter 1991): 36–49. My thanks to all those who helped with the editorial process on these essays.

I would also like to thank everyone at the Library of Congress, the George Eastman House in Rochester, New York, and the University of California Film and Television Archive who made materials available to me for this book. My thanks go to my editors at the University of California Press, Ernest Callenbach and Edward Dimendberg, who helped to allay my terror throughout the editorial process.

For helping to take my mind off the manuscript during the critical stages of its completion, I must thank my students and colleagues at the Wong Chinese Boxing Association and everyone associated with Jimmy's and Go Lo's in Washington, D.C. I am forever in the debt of my *sifu* Raymond Wong for food, soccer, broom ball, pool, lion dancing, gung fu instruction, encouragement, and treasured companionship. My deepest thanks go to him, with the wish that a brighter day will come when we can once again enjoy such good fellowship.

1

Introduction

Hollywood has long been fascinated by Asia, Asians, and Asian themes. Mysterious and exotic, Hollywood's Asia promises adventure and forbidden pleasures. Whether in a Chinatown opium den, a geisha house in Japan, or a café in Saigon, romantic involvements and sexual liaisons unacceptable in mainstream Anglo-American society become possible. Erotic fantasies can be indulged, sexual taboos broken. However, any radical deviation from the mainstream is unlikely to be voiced openly because of the possibility of a poor box-office showing. Therefore, Hollywood's romance with Asia tends to be a flirtation with the exotic rather than an attempt at any genuine intercultural understanding.

This book dissects Hollywood's Asia by examining the cinematic depiction of interracial sexuality. Rather than look at individual characters or survey the history of Asians in film, the focus here is on the way in which narratives featuring Asian-Caucasian sexual liaisons work ideologically to uphold and sometimes subvert culturally accepted notions of nation, class, race, ethnicity, gender, and sexual orientation.

The seventeen mainstream, fictional films and television movies produced between 1915 and 1986 and discussed here do not fit into any specific popular genre but, rather, range from romantic melodramas and comedies to action-adventure and war films. Although many of the films have been popular or critical successes, others are infrequently studied, more obscure titles. Because Hollywood has favored narratives dealing with Japan, China, and Vietnam, the focus here is on texts dealing with those three nations.

1

With the exception of Eugene Franklin Wong's *On Visual Media Racism* and Dorothy B. Jones's *The Portrayal of China and India on the American Screen, 1896–1958*,[1] no book-length scholarly study of the representation of Asians, Pacific Islanders, and Asian Americans in Hollywood exists in English. Although this is not primarily a discussion of representations of Asians on the screen, the research conducted by Wong and Jones forms the bedrock of this study. Jones, for example, identifies themes involving interracial sexual relations as a key part of Hollywood's depiction of Asia. In addition to the representation of miscegenation as a threat, she notes that Hollywood also produced narratives featuring tragic love affairs and cases of mistaken identity.

Wong also notes Hollywood's interest in the theme of miscegenation. He observes that Hollywood favors romances involving white males and Asian females, while Asian men tend to be depicted either as rapists or asexual eunuch figures. By contrast, Asian females are often depicted as sexually available to the white hero. Although both Jones and Wong take important steps in analyzing the historical, social, political, and cultural importance of Hollywood's depiction of interracial sexuality involving Asian characters, neither takes up this issue exclusively. Rather, sexuality is discussed as part of the broader tapestry of Hollywood's portrayal of Asia. Here, the exclusive focus is on the construction of interracial sex and romance in the Hollywood narrative.

For the most part, Hollywood's depiction of Asia has been inextricably linked to the threat of the so-called "yellow peril." Rooted in medieval fears of Genghis Khan and Mongolian invasions of Europe, the yellow peril combines racist terror of alien cultures, sexual anxieties, and the belief that the West will be overpowered and enveloped by the irresistible, dark, occult forces of the East. Given that knowledge about Asia and Asians has been limited in Europe and America, much of this formulation necessarily rests on a fantasy that projects Euroamerican desires and dreads onto the alien other. Thus, as Western nations began to carve up Asia into colonies, their own imperialist expansion was in part rationalized by the notion that a militarily powerful Asia posed a threat to "Christian civilization."

As slavery ended and immigration to the United States increased in the latter half of the nineteenth century, the yellow peril became a flood of cheap labor threatening to diminish the earning power of white European immigrants, thereby deflecting criticism of the brutal exploitation of an expansionist capitalist economy onto the issue of race. Within the context of America's consistently ambivalent attitudes toward Native Americans, Hispanics, African Americans, and other peoples of color, the yellow peril has contributed to the notion that all nonwhite people are by nature physically and intellectually inferior, morally suspect, heathen, licentious, disease-ridden, feral, violent, un-civilized, infantile, and in need of the guidance of white, Anglo-Saxon Protestants. This concept has been ingrained in the popular imagination since the late nineteenth and early twentieth century in mass media creations like Sax Rohmer's insidious villain Fu Manchu, in the Hearst newspapers' anti-Asian editorial policies, and in Homer Lea's *The Valor of Innocence*, a 1909 treatise on Japan as an evil military giant.[2]

One of the most potent aspects of these yellow peril discourses is the sexual danger of contact between the races. Although the power of the lascivious Asian woman to seduce the white male has long been part of this fantasy, a far more common scenario involves the threat posed by the Asian male to white women. As Gary Hoppenstand points out in his essay, "Yellow Devil Doctors and Opium Dens: A Survey of the Yellow Peril Stereotypes in Mass Media Entertainment," these fantasies tend to link together national-cultural and personal fears, so that the rape of the white woman becomes a metaphor for the threat posed to Western culture as well as a rationalization for Euroamerican imperial ventures in Asia. Moreover, as Hoppenstand notes, race becomes tied to religion as a spiritual play between good and evil, sin and salvation.

> The threat of rape, the rape of white society, dominated the action of the yellow formula. The British or American hero, during the course of his battle against the yellow peril, overcame numerous traps and obstacles in order to save his civilization, and the primary symbol of that civilization: the white woman. Stories featuring the yellow peril were arguments for racial purity. Certainly, the potential union of the Oriental and white implied, at best, a form of beastly sodomy, and, at worst, a Satanic marriage. The yellow peril stereotype easily became incorporated into Christian mythology, and the Oriental assumed the role of the devil or demon. The Oriental rape of the white woman signified a spiritual damnation for the woman, and at the larger level, white society.[3]

This aspect of the yellow peril fantasy found its way into the American silent cinema through heroines threatened by villainous Asians in popular serials like *Patria* (1919), *The Yellow Menace* (1916), *The Exploits of Elaine* (1916), and *The Perils of Pauline* (1919), as well as in the numerous serials and films based on the character of Dr. Fu Manchu throughout the 1920s and 1930s.[4] Jones cites *Crooked Streets* (1920) and *Tell It to the Marines* (1926) as typical of early films that feature "the fascination of the 'Yellow Man' for the 'White Woman.'"[5] Many of these films linked the yellow peril to white slavery and the various social ills surrounding the Hollywood image of Chinatown as a world peopled by opium addicts, pimps, and fallen women. *Old San Francisco* (1927), which features a white woman saved from a life of prostitution by the San Francisco earthquake, is typical.

Along with the yellow peril fantasies of Asian rapists, there are other scenarios involving Asian-Caucasian sexual liaisons. In addition to the celebrated platonic romance featured in D. W. Griffith's *Broken Blossoms* (1919), many other silent films deal sympathetically with tragic interracial love affairs. For example, *The Red Lantern*, also produced in 1919, features the love of an illegitimate Eurasian woman (Alla Nazimova) and an American missionary. When he does not return her affection, she becomes bitter toward hypocritical Westerners who educate but still harbor racist sentiments against the Chinese. She joins the Boxer Rebellion, the 1900 uprising against foreigners in China first supported and later condemned by the Imperial court, and meets with a tragic end. Similarly, in *City of Dim Faces* (1918) Jang Lung (Sessue Hayakawa in one of his many Chinese roles) falls in love with a white woman, is shunned, becomes bitter, and finally repents before his tragic demise. The various versions of *Madame Butterfly*, including Mary Pickford's in 1915, Anna May Wong's *Toll of the Sea* (1922), and Sessue Hayakawa's "sequel" to *Madame Butterfly, His Birthright* (1918), also confer a certain sympathy to those involved in interracial romances.[6]

Occasionally, too, these interracial romances end "happily" with the union of the couple at the film's conclusion. Often, however, these narratives rationalize their endings with a plot twist that involves the revelation that the Asian partner in the romance was in reality white, for example, *Broken Fetters* (also known as *Yellow and White*, 1916), *Son of the Gods* (1929), and *East Is West* (1922, 1930). *Wrath of the Gods* (1914) is one of the few films that allowed its interracial couple to enjoy an implied future together as husband and wife (even though this bright future emerges after the total destruction of the Japanese heroine's native village).[7]

In light of the prevalence of yellow peril images springing from the press, the American government's imperialistic foreign policy and exclusionary immigration laws, organized religion's tendency to treat race allegorically, labor's fear of cheap labor, and reformers' horrific association of Asians with dirt, disease, opium, and prostitution, it seems amazing that any remotely sympathetic treatment of interracial love affairs could exist at all in Hollywood. Moreover, throughout the history of the existence of the Motion Picture Association of America (MPAA), which sought to stave off government censorship of the movie industry through self-regulation, the depiction of miscegenation was, indeed, forbidden.[8]

If Michel Foucault is correct in *The History of Sexuality* that within Western discourses on sexuality there is no dearth of material on matters that are considered the most taboo, then perhaps Hollywood's official censure and actual interest in the representation of interracial sexuality can be better understood. As Foucault points out, during the Victorian era, a time generally considered to be particularly repressive, materials dealing with sexuality—including medical, legal, and other documents—proliferated. Foucault presents many complex reasons for this *supposed* suppression that was coupled with an active interest, including the emergence of the bourgeoisie and a crisis in the legitimation of rule by blood of the aristocracy, the growth of the modern state and its interest in the regulation of the citizenry, the rise of an ideology of individualism and the challenge it presented to notions of normalcy.[9]

Similarly, Hollywood's interest in all types of taboo sexuality—in this case, miscegenation—cannot be traced to a single root "cause." Rather, Hollywood returns to this theme for complex reasons that seem to be related to economic, social, and cultural issues that have been part of the fabric of American history since well before the birth of the motion picture industry. On the most obvious and superficial level, Hollywood returns to miscegenation narratives because they sell. Beyond their commercial appeal, however, these films very efficiently use classical Hollywood narrative patterns to deal with issues ranging from racism to changing attitudes toward gender and class relations.

Perhaps most important, however, these narratives deal with that fundamental contradiction within the American psyche between the liberal ideology of the "melting pot" and the conservative insistence on a homogeneous, white, Anglo-Saxon, American identity. Although this division is usually a false one since the liberal call to "melt" presupposes a white, English-speaking "pot," Hollywood's treatment of this fundamental identity crisis featuring interracial sexuality underscores profound contradictions within American culture's conception and representation of race and sexuality. By looking at these narratives critically, a picture can begin to emerge of the way in which Hollywood sets norms and breaks taboos, offers forbidden pleasures, and maintains existing, unequal racial, gender, and class hierarchies.

Although Hollywood films have dealt with a range of interracial relationships between Caucasians and African Americans, Native Americans, and Hispanics, the industry throughout its history seems to have taken a special interest in narratives dealing with Asians, Pacific Islanders, and Asian Americans. At first, this may seem surprising because of the small population of people of Asian descent in America until well after World War II.[10] Hollywood, then, did not create these films to draw in a large and potentially profitable Asian ethnic minority audience. Nor could Hollywood be accused of making films because a growing Asian domestic population was seen as a threat (although many of these narratives certainly helped to rationalize exclusionary immigration policies). In addition, although Hollywood does export its films to Asia, a serious attempt to appeal directly to the tastes of any specific national audience in Asia never seems to have been a significant part of the industry's marketing strategy. Rather, Hollywood used Asians, Asian Americans, and Pacific Islanders as signifiers of racial otherness to avoid the far more immediate racial tensions between blacks and whites or the ambivalent mixture of guilt and enduring hatred toward Native American and Hispanics.

Moreover, Asia and the Pacific were not so far removed from the white mainstream media to be beyond topicality. In the early days of the industry, the Spanish-American War led to the acquisition of the Philippines, the only official U.S. colony. The American presence in Asia, of course, had been growing throughout the nineteenth century, after the forced opening of Japan, the annexation of Hawaii, and increased U.S. involvement in Chinese commercial and political affairs. Though strict laws virtually prohibiting Chinese immigration were enacted in the nineteenth century, immigration continued to be an issue since these laws did not as strictly limit the immigration of other Asians—specifically Filipinos, Koreans, and Japanese. With the emergence of Japan as a recognized major power during World War I and the political chaos in China and Southeast Asia during the 1920s and 1930s, Asia continued to be in American newspaper headlines. World War II, the Korean War, and the war in Vietnam, coupled with the resumption of Asian immigration into the United States after World War II, kept Asia topical and potentially profitable for the film and television industry. More recently, the popularity of films and television programs about the war in Vietnam and the surprising commercial appeal of Wayne Wang's independently produced *Chan Is Missing* (1981) and *Dim Sum* (1984) attest to the continuing draw of Asian and Asian American stories.[11]

Broadly speaking, these Hollywood narratives[12] are part of what Edward W. Said has described in *Orientalism* as "a Western style for dominating, restructuring, and having authority over the Orient."[13] They create a mythic image of Asia that empowers the West and rationalizes Euroamerican authority over the Asian other. Romance and sexuality provide the metaphoric justification for this domination. However, any act of domination brings with it opposition, guilt, repression, and resistance, which also must be incorporated into these myths and silenced, rationalized, domesticated, or otherwise eliminated. Individual texts become part of a broader narrative and thematic pattern that, in each incarnation, reproduces and reworks the same ideological problems at its core.

In this book, the classical Hollywood realist film provides the raw material for the examination of the ideology of race and sexuality. Hollywood films are *discourses*, that is, constructed objects of signification rooted in a specific social environment.[14] Their meanings spring from the institutions (both within the film industry and beyond it) and the historical, cultural, and social circumstances surrounding their production. Like all discourses, they are concrete manifestations of the ideological sphere and share in all of the struggles for power, identity, and influence political theorists like Antonio Gramsci saw as part of the construction of hegemony within any given society at any particular historical juncture.[15]

As Fredric Jameson points out in *The Political Unconscious: Narrative as a Socially Symbolic Act*, when the cultural object is grasped as part of the larger social order, "an individual 'text' or work in the narrow sense . . . has been reconstituted in the form of the great collective and class discourses of which a text is little more than an individual *parole* or utterance."[16] Thus, in order to be understood as part of a larger social formation, any given Hollywood text must be understood as linked with other discourses involving race, class, gender, ethnicity, and similar pressing social and political concerns.

The specific type of discourse Hollywood favors is the narrative fiction. As Claude Levi-Strauss points out in his essay, "The Structural Study of Myth,"[17] narratives, in the form of myths, take up actual, often irresolvable, contradictions (e.g., life and death, nature and culture) and, through the aesthetic act of creating a tale, transpose these irreconcilable oppositions into terms that can be reconciled symbolically (e.g., protagonists and antagonists). Jameson takes up Levi-Strauss's observations and goes on to conclude that the "aesthetic act is itself ideological, and the production of aesthetic or narrative form is to be seen as an ideological act in its own right, with the function of inventing imaginary or formal 'solutions' to unresolvable social contradictions."[18] In this process, as Roland Barthes points out in *Mythologies*, myth (through the narrative process) also denies that actual contradictions existed in the first place.

> It abolishes the complexity of human acts, it gives them the simplicity of essences, it does away with all dialectics, with any going back beyond what is immediately visible, it organizes a world which is without contradictions because it is without depth, a world wide open and wallowing in the evident, it establishes a blissful clarity: things appear to mean something by themselves.[19]

Hollywood films operate mythically. They take up, aestheticize, and symbolically resolve social contradictions, then deny the process by masking their ideological operations behind an apparently seamless, "invisible style."[20]

Not surprisingly, the narrative patterns that Hollywood has developed to depict interracial sexual relations have a great deal in common with more arcane mythic patterns found within the Judeo-Christian tradition and, more specifically, within American popular literature. Stories involving rape, captivity, seduction, salvation, sacrifice, assimilation, tragic and transcendent love all have deep roots within Western culture. All these narrative patterns involve questions of identity and the maintenance of that identity against threats from the outside. The development of that identity, then, is relational, not absolute. In other words, these narratives help Christians to understand why they are not pagans, Americans to understand why they are neither Europeans nor Native Americans, whites to understand why they are unlike people of color. Because sexual relations and taboos fundamentally define individual, family, clan, ethnic, and ultimately national identities, sexual liaisons with people of color pose a threat to the maintenance of white male hegemony within American society.

Rape narratives pose the danger that the "pure" but hopelessly fragile and childlike white woman will be "ruined" by contact with the dark villain. Captivity stories go a step further and threaten to make the white heroine a permanent part of an alien culture. Seduction tales offer the possibility that either the Caucasian woman or man will be tempted by the eroticism of Asia and will turn her or his back on Western Christendom. Salvation stories posit the white hero or heroine as an irresistible moral force that "saves" the Asian lover from the evils or excesses of his or her decadent culture. Sacrifice narratives justify white domination by depicting the Asian lover as willing to sacrifice his or her own culture and nation, and often to die, to maintain white American domination. Tragic love stories maintain racial divisions by forcing the lovers to separate. Transcendent romances allow the lovers to "spiritually" overcome social barriers through their love, which forces the suppression of any "aberrant" ethnic or racial characteristics. In assimilation narratives, the nonwhite lover completely relinquishes his or her own culture in order to be accepted into the American bourgeois mainstream, usually represented by the creation of a "typical" nuclear family.

Although each narrative highlights different social tensions involving race and sexuality, taken as a whole these formulas all use the interracial romance to pose certain key issues related to American identity. Since women and people of color have consistently disturbed any image of America as a harmonious melting pot of Protestant values, white bosses, capitalist enterprises, and the patriarchal family, these narratives have an enduring force within the popular media. Each chapter that follows takes up one of these narrative patterns and uses a sampling of one, two, or three films to look closely at the discursive strategies Hollywood employs in these tales of interracial romance. After analyzing each narrative pattern in more detail, a clearer picture may begin to emerge of the ideological workings of Hollywood discourses involving race, sex, and American identity.

In chapter 2, DeMille's *The Cheat* and Griffith's *Broken Blossoms* illustrate Hollywood's early interest in interracial sexuality. In both films the threat of rape forms the backdrop for the exploration of other issues involving not only racial differences but also questions of class, consumption, morality, and aesthetics. Chapter 3 looks at both the threatening and utopic aspects of miscegenation in the captivity tale by using the depression era films, *The Bitter Tea of General Yen* and *Shanghai Express*, as examples. *Lady of the Tropics* illustrates Hollywood's ambivalence toward the Eurasian seductress in chapter 4. Chapter 5 looks at cinematic interpretations of *Madame Butterfly* beginning with an in-depth look at Mary Pickford's silent version of the classic tale. Fuller's *China Gate* and the made-for-television drama, "The Lady from Yesterday," show how narratives involving Vietnam make use of the self-effacing Butterfly as a metaphor for an Asia willing to sacrifice itself for the benefit of the West.

An exploration of the themes of sacrifice and salvation continues in chapter 6 with a discussion of two films set in Hong Kong, *Love Is a Many-Splendored Thing* and *The World of Suzie Wong*. Chapter 7 focuses on pairs of star-crossed lovers in *Sayonara* and *The Crimson Kimono*. Both films applaud their protagonists' ability to transcend racial barriers, while still maintaining that tragedy necessarily follows any attempt to break with social norms. In chapter 8, the domestic melodrama, in which race is viewed as a social, political, and historical problem, is examined using two films dealing with World War II and its aftermath, *Japanese War Bride* and *A Bridge to the Sun*. Chapter 9 returns to the exploration of Hollywood's fascination with *Madame Butterfly* by looking at a film and television movie that deal with Caucasian women who masquerade as geisha, *My Geisha* and "An American Geisha." Finally, the discussion of *Year of the Dragon*, in chapter 10, illustrates Hollywood's recent tendency to use the spectacle of interracial sexuality as part of a postmodern pastiche of contemporary culture.

2

The Rape Fantasy

The Cheat and *Broken Blossoms*

The narrative pattern most often associated with Hollywood dramas involving the "yellow peril" features the rape or threat of rape of a Caucasian woman by a villainous Asian man.[1] With roots deep within the Euroamerican melodramatic tradition, these fantasies present the white woman as the innocent object of lust and token of the fragility of the West's own sense of moral purity. However, these tales often point to a contradictory suspicion that the masochistic virgin may secretly desire her defilement. Much of the raw violence of these narratives, then, involves not only the eradication of the threat of racial otherness by lynching the Asian rapist but also the brutal punishment of the white woman through both the spectacle of her assault and the humiliation of her rescue.

Two of the most notable silent feature films dealing with interracial rape are Cecil B. DeMille's *The Cheat* (1915) and D. W. Griffith's *Broken Blossoms* (1919). Although *The Cheat* xenophobically calls for the exclusion of people of color from the American bourgeois mainstream, while *Broken Blossoms* seems to ask for a more liberal toleration of some interracial relationships, both narratives use the fantasy of rape and the possibility of lynching to reaffirm the boundaries of a white-defined, patriarchal, Anglo-American culture. By looking at these two early film narratives, the nature of popular fantasies surrounding changes in both the racial composition of America and the place of women within the bourgeois patriarchy comes more clearly to the surface. However, before examining this narrative pattern in detail, it may be helpful to look broadly at the melodrama to better understand how these films operate within this specific genre.

The Film Melodrama

A prodigious amount of critical scholarship exists on the film melodrama—its aesthetic form, principal auteurs, history and politics, and ideology. Because melodramas focus on domestic life and often feature female protagonists, it is not surprising that much of this scholarship has been done by feminist critics interested in ferreting out the patriarchal ideology underlying these films. Many of these studies have attempted to reconcile the film melodrama, which is directed to a predominantly female audience, with a moral universe in which women find themselves at odds with the male status quo. However, to understand the contradictions that exist within the Hollywood melodrama, its roots within the bourgeois domestic drama must first be understood.

In *The Social History of Art*, Arnold Hauser observes that the eighteenth-century domestic drama arose as a creation of the emerging bourgeoisie to be used as "an advertisement for bourgeois morality."[2] In *The Melodramatic Imagination: Balzac, Henry James, Melodrama, and the Mode of Excess*, Peter Brooks expands on this:

> Melodrama starts from and expresses the anxiety brought by a frightening new world in which the traditional patterns of moral order no longer provide the necessary social glue. It plays out the force of that anxiety with the apparent triumph of villainy, and it dissipates it with the eventual victory of virtue. It demonstrates over and over that the signs of ethical forces can be discovered and made legible. . . . Melodrama is indeed, typically, not only a moralistic drama but the drama of morality: it strives to find, to articulate, to demonstrate, to "prove" the existence of a moral universe which, though put into question, masked by villainy and perversions of judgment, does exist and can be made to assert its presence and categorical force among men.[3]

In contrast with feudal, aristocratic tragedy, which featured elevated heroes with fatal flaws, the melodrama depicted middle-class characters, victims of fate, or a specific, corrupt social institution. Linked to a struggling, revolutionary bourgeoisie that sought to assert its legitimacy by speaking for "everyone" in society, the melodrama often elevated the poor or the powerless to central positions. The home became the battleground for the moral struggles of this newly powerful social class. The domestic world, the cornerstone of bourgeois life, came under siege from outside threats to its existence. Sentiment and emotional excess, ironic twists of fate or circumstance, became the hall-marks of these dramas in which the innocence of women was invari-ably at stake.

These dramas were set in the domestic sphere of the family rather than the public world of the court, the battlefield, or the factory for a specific reason. Since the bourgeoisie could not base its authority to rule on tradition, blood, or established feudal religious bodies, it cre-ated a secular religion out of domestic arrangements. Carefully sepa-rating the world of the family, child rearing, women, and the spiritual rectitude of hearth and home from the unscrupulous maneuverings of the public world of capitalism and the marketplace, the bourgeois pa-triarch legitimized his rule over both home and factory by pointing to the moral purity of his mate. Just as he had a "natural" right to rule his household and protect his spiritually elevated wife from any outside threat, he had a similarly unquestionable moral prerogative to rule in the outside world. Any taint from that public world could not corrupt him because of the sanctity of the domestic sanctuary he helped to pro-tect and perpetuate through the accumulation of capital. Material suc-cess and the purity of the home replaced the purity of royal blood as the emblem of rule.

As a result, issues of legitimacy within the family took on an added significance. Not only did the bourgeois patriarchy need to control female sexuality to ensure inheritance but it also needed to be able to point to the bourgeois woman as the symbol of its moral certitude, purity, and secularized spirituality. Unlike the peasant or proletarian family, the bourgeois family completely separated women from the world of production. In the realm of reproduction, they served as deeroticized maternal figures, naive and childlike, constantly threat-ened by the external world that would surely destroy them were it not for the benevolent protection of the patriarch.

However, there are many important contradictions in this picture of bourgeois domesticity. For example, bourgeois ideology, to assure a pool of "free" wage laborers and freedom from government constraints on its economic interests, preaches individual self-determination. Clearly, if this concept of individual autonomy were extended to women, the patriarchy could be threatened. Indeed, women's elevated role as protectors of morality often did provide them with a "mission" to preach, teach, and otherwise voice their wisdom in public—to the chagrin of men who came under their attack. This same ideology of in-dividualism, coupled with the disintegration of the traditional extended family as a unit of rural, domestic production, also led to the increas-ing visibility of women in the public world of production.[4]

Thus, ironically, the bourgeois family exists both as the justification of its class's right to rule and as the site of internal conflict and contradiction. The control of female sexuality, the assurance of the legitimacy and proper moral upbringing of the children, the vital separation of the world of reproduction from production, and the assurance of women's acquiescence to male rule all form an important part of the melodrama's thematic agenda. Forged in a period of intense ideological uncertainty, the melodrama has, throughout its history, been connected to a certain moral ambivalence and thinly disguised malaise about the bourgeois patriarchal family it apparently lionizes.

With the rise of cinema in the twentieth century, the melodrama continued to function as a viable vehicle for the articulation and containment of social contradictions involving class, gender, domesticity, and sexuality. Chuck Kleinhans points out in his essay, "Notes on Melodrama and the Family under Capitalism," that "in domestic melodrama we find the oppositions contained within the family, in the personal sphere, in a way that is at once dense and illusive. Repeatedly we discover very deliberately structured ambiguities in family melodrama."[5]

In fact, most recent criticism on the Hollywood melodrama has focused not on the melodrama's tendentious moralizing but on its ability to accommodate these "structured ambiguities" and to allow a certain space for the articulation of domestic discontent. In "Minnelli and Melodrama," Geoffrey Nowell-Smith, for example, summarizes the major thrust of the genre as follows:

> Melodrama can thus be seen as a contradictory nexus, in which certain determinations (social, psychical, artistic) are brought together but in which the problem of the articulation of these determinations is not successfully resolved. The importance of melodrama . . . lies precisely in its ideological failure. Because it cannot accommodate its problems, either in a real present or in an ideal future, but lays them open in their shameless contradictoriness, it opens space which most Hollywood forms have studiously closed off.[6]

Although a great deal of the critical work on the melodrama has looked at the interrelationship of class and gender within the genre and has focused on the threat feminine sexuality poses to the functioning of the bourgeois patriarchal family,[7] fewer studies of the domestic melodrama have taken up the potential threat racial differences may pose to the "typical," white, middle-class, American household. Although many excellent studies of specific melodramas do exist (including both the Sirk and Stahl versions of *Imitation of Life*[8]), much less critical attention has been paid to the representation of either the nonwhite or the interracial couple in the Hollywood melodrama.

Nevertheless, racial difference, particularly when linked to issues of female sexuality or women's economic autonomy, has consistently appeared in Hollywood melodramas as an element of disruption to the smooth functioning of the domestic order. Therefore, a serious look at how Hollywood treats interracial relations within melodramas such as *The Cheat, Broken Blossoms*, and many of the other films discussed in this study may help to reveal how the genre depicts social tensions, allows ideological contradictions to surface, and attempts to handle them symbolically through the resolution of the plot.

The Cheat and the Pornography of Lynching

In *Anatomy of Criticism*, Northrop Frye observes that a type of modern crime melodrama he labels "the brutal thriller" comes "as close as it is normally possible for art to come to the pure self-righteousness of the lynching mob."[9] Although Cecil B. DeMille's *The Cheat* (1915) is technically not a thriller, it does seem to capture the moral indignation, the melodramatic flourishes, and the invitation for arousal and catharsis necessary to bring it close to the type of fiction Frye describes. A lurid story of a bargain struck by an extravagant socialite with a Japanese merchant for cash in exchange for sex, *The Cheat* climaxes in a scene in which the white woman is branded by the Asian when she refuses to go through with the transaction. After she shoots her attacker, a trial ensues in which the socialite's husband takes the blame for her assailant's wound. Critics have noted that audiences for *The Cheat* would cry out during the famous courtroom scene in support of the mob that nearly lynches the Asian villain. A reviewer for *Moving Picture World*, for example, wrote, "One of the men that sat behind me in the Strand Theatre said, 'I would like to be in that mob.'"[10]

Indeed, the editing, cinematography, and mise-en-scène of the courtroom scene all seem to invite the audience in the theatre to adopt the perspective of the mob at the trial. Unable to control herself after her husband has been falsely convicted of shooting her attacker, Edith Hardy (Fannie Ward) becomes hysterical and rushes up to the judge's bench. She pulls down her dress to reveal the brand on her bare shoulder. A long shot of the packed courtroom stands in for the film audience. In medium close up, Edith pulls back her blonde curls to frame the brand on her pale shoulder. The film, then, cuts between shots of the violent gesticulations of Edith and medium shots of the faces of the jury, her assailant, and the anonymous, sneering faces of white men in attendance. Their looks are directed at both Edith and Tori (Sessue Hayakawa), the man she accuses of her violation, and the camera positions both as objects of scrutiny (and, by implication, moral judgment) for the film viewers.

Ironically, the "lynch mob" in *The Cheat* forms within the "halls of justice," further legitimizing the viewer's shared perspective with the angry mob. When the judge sets aside the guilty verdict, the rioting mob turns into a cheering, appreciative crowd that flanks each side of the courtroom's main aisle as Edith and her husband, Richard (Jack Dean), walk toward the camera as an iris closes in on the couple to conclude the film.

In her essay, "Ethnicity, Class, and Gender in Film: DeMille's *The Cheat*," Sumiko Higashi notes that the courtroom crowd "recalls lynch mobs that murdered blacks."[11] In light of the commercial and critical success (as well as controversy) surrounding Griffith's *The Birth of a Nation*, which was released earlier that same year, public lynchings and moral indignation over interracial sexual relations seem to have been very much a part of the narrative lexicon of the American film in 1915. Unfortunately, accusations of interracial rape and mob violence against those suspected of it were a part of the social landscape of the day as well. According to Thomas F. Gossett, at its highest point in the recorded history of lynchings, 162 blacks as opposed to 69 whites were executed outside the legal system. From 1883 to 1915, the number of blacks lynched only fell below 50 in 1914, when the number was 14. According to Gossett's statistics, ten times more blacks were lynched between 1906 and 1915 than whites.[12] In 1913, Pitchfork Ben Tillman, governor of South Carolina, publicly supported the lynching of rapists and claimed "forty to a hundred Southern maidens were annually offered as a sacrifice to the African Minotaur, and no Theseus had arisen to rid the land of this terror."[13] Although the majority of blacks lynched during this period were not accused of rape or sexual assault, lynching, in the minds of Northerners as well as Southerners, became associated with rape. The sexual nature of lynchings, too, manifested itself in the tortures inflicted on the victims by the mob before their execution. This torture involved blindings and dismemberments of various sorts, including castrations.

In her essay, "'The Mind That Burns in Each Body': Women, Rape and Racial Violence," Jacquelyn Dowd Hall discusses the complex construction of rape and lynchings in the popular imagination.

> For whites, the archetypal lynching for rape can be seen as a dramatization of cultural themes, a story they told themselves about the social arrangements and psychological strivings that lay beneath the surface of

everyday life. The story such rituals told about the place of white women in southern society was subtle, contradictory, and demeaning. The frail victim, leaning on the arms of her male relatives, might be brought to the scene of the crime, there to identify her assailant and witness his execution. This was a moment of humiliation. A woman who had just been raped, or who had been apprehended in a clandestine interracial affair, or whose male relatives were pretending that she had been raped, stood on display before the whole community. Here was the quintessential Woman as Victim: polluted, "ruined for life," the object of fantasy and secret contempt. Humiliation, however, mingled with heightened worth as she played for a moment the role of the Fair Maiden violated and avenged. For this privilege—if the alleged assault had in fact taken place—she might pay with suffering in the extreme. In any case, she would pay with a lifetime of subjugation to the men gathered in her behalf.

Rape and rumors of rape became the folk pornography of the Bible Belt. As stories spread the rapist became not just a black man but a ravenous brute, the victim a beautiful young virgin. The experience of the woman was described in minute and progressively embellished detail, a public fantasy that implied a group participation in the rape as cathartic as the subsequent lynching. White men might see in "lynch law" their ideal selves: patriarchs, avengers, righteous protectors. But, being men themselves, and sometimes even rapists, they must also have seen themselves in the lynch mob's prey.[14]

Although no actual rape or lynching is depicted in *The Cheat*, the film presents this fantasy of the violation of the white woman by a man of color in much the same way as the "Bible Belt pornography" described above. The passions exposed in the film's courtroom scene, moreover, are similarly ambivalent. This scene, in fact, seems to stand in isolation from much of the rest of *The Cheat*, which deals more with questions of consumption, female independence, changing marital mores, and the possible decay of the bourgeois family. Unlike the rest of the film, the final scene acts in a more elemental fashion as an apology for the group emotions that lead to racist acts of violence.

Even though the film pulls back from depicting an actual lynching, just as it declines to show Edith as a victim of rape, *The Cheat* still contains all the other elements associated with the public discourse surrounding rapes and lynchings at the time. The film serves, then, as a cinematic retelling of the public display and humiliation of the white victim coupled with the nearly uncontrollable rage of the white mob. Edith's husband serves as stoic patriarch and Tori functions as the rapist, finally exposed publicly, threatened with lynching, and implicitly punished suitably (i.e., legally) by the court. The mob action follows on the sexual arousal accompanying Edith's self-exposure and is, then, expressed through violence toward Tori. Rage against the woman who uses her sexuality for her own gain, outside the boundaries of the patriarchal family, turns against the man of color, who becomes the embodiment of both a sexuality and a social order out of control.

As Hall points out above, men in the audience could see themselves as both moral avenger and rapist, since all the men in the film somehow both sexually possess and punish Edith directly or indirectly. Tori both possesses and punishes Edith by branding her; Edith's husband possesses her as his wife and punishes her by forcing her public humiliation; the mob in the courtroom possesses her as spectacle and punishes her with their humiliating stares.

Given that the period from the turn of the century through World War I saw a post-Reconstruction advancement of and subsequent backlash against African Americans as well as the rise of the woman's movement demanding reproductive as well as voting rights, it comes as little surprise that stories about rapes and lynchings would become so popular. Indeed, both acts of violence are linked in the popular imagination as agents for white male control over Caucasian women and men of color. In *Against Our Will: Men, Women, and Rape*, Susan Brownmiller draws a striking parallel between rapes and lynchings:

> Rape is to women as lynching was to blacks: the ultimate physical threat by which all men keep all women in a state of psychological intimidation.
>
> Women have been raped by men, most often by gangs of men, for many of the same reasons that blacks were lynched by gangs of whites: as group punishment for being uppity, for getting out of line, for failing to recognize "one's place," for assuming sexual freedoms, or for behaviour no more provocative than walking down the wrong road at night in the wrong part of town and presenting a convenient, isolated target for group hatred and rage. Castration, the traditional *coup de grace* of a lynching, has its counterpart in the gratuitous acts of defilement that often accompany a rape, the stick rammed up the vagina, the attempt to annihilate the sexual core.[15]

Just as there seems to be an imaginative coupling of rape and lynching within public discourse, films and other fictions like *The Cheat* appear to serve the same double function as warnings to women that their independence leads to their humiliation and to blacks and other people of color that their desire to assimilate into the American mainstream will never be tolerated. Beyond these warnings, however, the discourse on rapes and lynchings in the American popular media also brings white women and men of color together as transgressors against the domination of white men. Potentially, then, these fantasies hide a

resistant core underneath their brutal surfaces. If Tori and Edith somehow recognized their similar victimizations at the trial, then the moral
universe of *The Cheat* would collapse. The tease of this possibility as
well as its violent suppression fuel the passions explored within the
film.

However, focusing exclusively on *The Cheat*'s conclusion does little
to explain other aspects of the film fantasy. The specifics of its depiction of Japanese Americans, the Long Island social set, the world of
Wall Street speculators, and the early-twentieth-century bourgeois
home also exist as somehow related to the raw image of sexual humiliation and racist rage that ends the film. Thus, it becomes necessary to
unravel how the threat of rape and the possibility of a lynching relate
ideologically to these other aspects of the fantasy in order to understand the roots of any ambivalence felt during the film's denouement.

The Japanese Villain

As Sumiko Higashi has aptly pointed out in her analysis of ethnicity
in *The Cheat*, the depiction of the assailant as Japanese was part of
the yellow peril and anti-immigration rhetoric prevalent on the eve of
World War I.[16] However, discourses on the issues of immigration,
American imperialism, race, and ethnicity promulgated by the mass
media, government, and other purveyors of ideology were highly contradictory. Such rhetoric as the "white man's burden," "manifest des-
tiny," and the "yellow peril" coexisted with the ideals of the "melting
pot," "liberty and justice for all," and the concept of the American
Dream. Because of America's peculiar relationship with Japan and
the military strength of Japan during the latter part of the nineteenth
century and the early twentieth century, fantasies involving that nation
and its people proved to be particularly complicated. For example,
although *The Cheat*'s villain was originally calculated to represent the
height of evil as a *Japanese* threat to American identity, the villain's
ethnicity was easily switched because of pressure from the Japanese
government. Thus, when America entered World War I as an ally of
Japan, the film's anti-Japanese intertitles were changed for the 1918 release print to make the villain Burmese.

This ambivalence predates World War I, however. America has had
a particularly strong and peculiarly contradictory relationship with
Japan and the Japanese since Commodore Perry forcibly opened up
the country to trade with the United States in 1853. Japan has been
seen as both a country of tremendous power, culture, and wealth with
coveted merchandise ready to be commercially exploited and as a weak
nation peopled by nonwhite, pagan, uncivilized inferiors also ripe for
exploitation by expanding American capitalism. As the Meiji govern-

ment of the late nineteenth and early twentieth century rapidly modernized the country, Japan's traditional policy of isolation and ban on emigration were lifted. Particularly after the institution of the anti-Chinese Exclusion Act of 1882, Japanese laborers immigrated to Hawaii and the West Coast of the United States in record numbers to take up the slack. Unlike the comparatively weak Chinese government, a strong Japanese position internationally enabled the country to protect its citizens abroad to a certain degree. Moreover, in order to set its citizens apart from the maligned Chinese, Japan scrutinized all potential émigrés carefully and encouraged the emigration of women to prevent the social problems associated with Chinatown's "bachelor society," for example, prostitution, gambling, opium smoking, and general vice.

Few of these measures, however, eased anti-Japanese sentiments. Particularly after Japan's stunning defeat of Russia in 1905, American observers began to worry about the expansionist tendencies of an Asian country that had not been colonized by the West yet had still managed to defeat a major European power in battle. Seeing Japan as a threat to its interests in the Philippines and Hawaii, the American government had to respond cautiously both to domestic calls for the exclusion of the Japanese from the United States and Japan's insistence on equity made from an uniquely powerful position among the nations of Asia. In 1908, President Theodore Roosevelt worked out the "Gentlemen's Agreement" with Japan that restricted the immigration of laborers to the United States. However, "picture brides," other relatives of Japanese workers already in the United States, merchants, scholars, and students were still allowed to enter, and the Japanese were not excluded altogether until 1924.[17]

This ambivalence toward Japan and the Japanese finds its way into the depiction of Hishuru Tori. Both brutal and cultivated, wealthy and base, cultured and barbaric, Tori embodies the contradictory qualities Americans associated with Japan. Like Japan itself, Tori is powerful, threatening, wealthy, and enviable; however, his racial difference also codes him as pagan, morally suspect, and inferior. Moreover, just as Japanese attempts to assimilate Western technology and material culture to strengthen itself economically and militarily during the Meiji era posed a threat to American domination of Asia, Tori's attempts to adapt to and adopt elements of Western society also pose a threat to America's conception of itself. Like any new Asian immigrant seeking to assimilate into the mainstream, Tori threatens America's definition of itself as white, Anglo-Saxon, and Protestant.

Beyond this, Tori poses a further danger to America's national identity by being able to transcend racial boundaries and move fairly easily between Japanese and American cultures, obtaining possessions and gaining status from both worlds. In the title sequence, Tori is introduced in Japanese dress with Asian-style brass brazier, poker, and ivory statuette. Key lights set off his facial features as well as these tokens of his ethnicity against the black background.[18] The chiaroscuro lighting adds to Tori's exoticism, mystery, and the implicit danger conjured up by the peculiar satisfaction he seems to get from branding his possessions.[19]

However, if Tori is associated with darkness, shadows, and the threatening exoticism of Japan in the title sequence, his introduction within the narrative itself shows him in quite a different light (literally). In the flat, high key lighting of daytime, Tori drives up to the Hardy residence in a sporty roadster. Shown in a medium long shot from a high angle, Tori looks like any other wealthy, insouciant young man in a Hollywood film of the time. Because of the distance of the camera, his racial otherness is barely noticeable. Jauntily, he gets out of the car and walks up to the house. Wearing a long duster, cap, casual tweed suit, and bow tie, his relaxed appearance belies any threat he might pose to the American bourgeois domestic sphere he enters. His body language (the self-assured way he perches on the drawing-room desk, the implied intimacy of his picking up Edith's purse and parasol) points to his ability to insinuate himself into this world with apparent ease.

An earlier title indicated that Tori was one of the darlings of the Long Island society set, and the implication is that he gained entry into this world not only from his wealth but also from this ability to "blend in" and create a certain intimacy between himself and Edith, who serves as his liaison with this otherwise racially "exclusive" society. This Americanized Tori innocently attends Edith by holding her coat and accessories, patting her hand, agreeing to help further her status in her set by hosting a charity ball, and unthinkingly grabbing her when she stumbles. Implicitly unable to find a place within the more rigidly racist society of the men on Long Island, Tori finds his niche among the women. However, although his feminization seems to confirm his symbolic castration, it also holds within it the potential threat of an ability to transgress gender along with racial barriers. Tori promises a different type of masculinity (soft, effeminate yielding, "Asian") that may displace the banal paternalism represented by Edith's husband.

When contained within his exclusively Japanese domain, Tori poses no threat, however. In the title sequence, he exists as a self-contained image of otherness outside the narrative. Similarly, when Tori appears as Edith's completely assimilated companion, he functions as what Eugene Franklin Wong has termed the Asian eunuch, an asexual, subservient foil for the white protagonists.[20] Accepted as escort, confidant, and pet in white society, Tori poses no threat to its racial exclusivity because he appears to be totally asexual. Edith's ability to take his apparently innocent loyalty to her for granted is validated by a tradition in American popular culture of emasculated, faithful Asian servants and companions.

Separation of the two spheres, Japan and the West, seems to be the ideological key. When Tori begins to embody both, to merge both into a figure that can no longer be excluded as completely alien or assimilated as impotent and harmless, he becomes a provocative villain. At the charity event held at his mansion, Tori, elegantly dressed in tuxedo, white tie, and patterned vest, moves between two worlds—the American social set of society matrons and stuffy stockbrokers all in Western attire enjoying themselves in the large ballroom and his own private study filled with a large statue of Buddha, incense, rich silks, ivory figurines, and a potted tree with falling petals resembling Japanese cherry blossoms.

When Edith steps into his parlor, she enters a world that offers the forbidden possibility of a meeting of Japan and America within the sexual realm. For a moment, the fantasy seems to be more enticing than dangerous. When Edith caresses a piece of Japanese cloth and Tori gives it to her as a gift, her willingness to be seduced by Tori's wealth and sensuality seems evident. Although Edith backs away as Tori describes the branding of his possessions, she does not leave. Perhaps this can be read as an interest in Tori's brooding, implicitly sadistic sexuality outweighing her fears.

The moment is interrupted when a stockbroker, who had talked her into gambling away Red Cross charity funds on the stock market, comes in to tell her that she has lost the stolen money. The broker leaves, Edith faints, and Tori takes advantage of the opportunity to kiss the unconscious Edith. Much has been made of rape fantasies, their appeal to women, and the sadistic sexuality of silent screen stars like Rudolph Valentino, Erich von Stroheim, and Sessue Hayakawa.[21] The fantasy has been discussed as the internalization of a patriarchal ideology that insists on female passivity and submission to male domination, as an expression of some deep-rooted masochistic desire, and as a way in which society toys with forbidden sexuality to make it acceptable as "punishment" rather than as "pleasure." Whatever the psychological roots of the rape fantasy's appeal to male and female viewers may be, it clearly both disturbs and fascinates, and it plays a key role in Hollywood's depiction of sexuality.

In this case, *The Cheat* links the crossing of racial boundaries with the rape fantasy. It plays on all the ambivalence associated with that fantasy. On the one hand, Edith seems drawn to all those things repressed in her white, American, bourgeois home, for example, open sexuality, the sensual pleasures of clothing, and other objects of consumption. In light of the rapidly changing sexual mores and life-styles of the World War I era, a certain amount of guilt and desire would likely be a part of any erotic fantasy involving a character like Tori. Tori represents indulgence of the senses, of the body, free from the Protestant denial of sexual desire. However, a willing affair with Tori would all at once completely subvert those strictures, ripping apart marriage, the bourgeois family, the Protestant ethic, as well as the racial status quo.

Although a fantasy that toys with this extreme would likely be inviting to many in the audience (women, the working classes, people of color) for a number of reasons, the pull to contain it wins out ideologically. Thus, a desired indulgence may come with the kiss, but it is still a *stolen* kiss, taken not given. As in many Hollywood narratives, forbidden desires find their fulfillment against the will of the protagonist. In this case, Edith can remain a part of the white, bourgeois family because this kiss can be read as a rape rather than the culmination of a love affair.

Moreover, while the kiss for women can be looked at as a fulfillment of secret, forbidden desires for the pleasures and freedoms promised by a love affair with a man of another race, it also marks the beginning of Edith's punishment and the turning point that moves away from any ambivalence about Tori's villainous character that may have been felt earlier. Here, Tori emerges as the archetypal "yellow peril" ravisher of white women. The object of desire, he too becomes the instrument of punishment for that forbidden desire. For male viewers, he can freely indulge sadistic desires "guiltlessly," "naturally," since he is Japanese and beyond Christian notions of morality. He can punish the wayward Edith without violating any code of chivalry, leaving her husband (and, by implication, the white men in the audience) pure. Thus, Tori's ethnicity becomes a necessary part of his ability to fulfill a number of erotic desires for both male and female spectators. His racial otherness allows him to function as a symbol of erotic indulgence and as an instrument of punishment for women's sexual self-assertion. Thus, white men can be free of the dark, brutal side of their own sexuality while maintaining the gender status quo through the threat of rape linked to the supposedly perverse sexuality of the Asian male.

However, the fantasies surrounding the Japanese villain Tori may be even more complicated than this. If Tori's sadistic, punitive masculinity functions to maintain patriarchal strictures legitimately tied to the white male authority of Edith's husband, then the subservient, eunuch-like, impotent aspect of Asian masculinity also associated with the character brings him closer to Edith's position on the social hierarchy.

Figure 1.   The sinisterly elegant Tori (Sessue Hayakawa) threatens Edith Hardy (Fannie Ward) with exposure in The Cheat *(1915). Still courtesy of the Museum of Modern Art/Film Stills Archive.*

As in many rape fantasies, this offers a peculiar invitation to women to identify with the attacker, to see themselves as pitted against the same authority that he opposes in trying to possess her.

Frightened by the apparition of her husband silhouetted on the sliding paper panel (shoji) doorway as she regains consciousness in Tori's arms and hears the confirmation of her monetary loss, Edith allows herself to be persuaded to agree to Tori's bargain. Although it is never explicitly spelled out, the assumption is that Edith will give herself to Tori sexually in exchange for ten thousand dollars. Visually on the same side of the shoji, Edith and Tori, duplicitous, self-serving, and self-indulgent, are also on the same side morally. Neither can fulfill his or her desires within the bounds of the white bourgeois patriarchy represented by the husband on the other side of the screen.

The visual and moral equivalence between Tori and Edith becomes absolutely clear during the branding and its aftermath. Not unlike the trial scene, this part of the narrative plays with the mercurial nature of the positions of victim and vanquisher in the rape scenario. Again,

Tori's costume, which combines Asia and the West with a white tie and tuxedo shirt covered by a Japanese kimono, indicates the possible transgression he represents, that is, the sensual meeting of Japan and America, the erasure of racial borders through eroticism. Edith is dressed in a black gown covered by a white wrap. The contrast not only indicates her divided, duplicitous nature but also points to the racial contrasts at issue—the dark and the light.

When Edith arrives at Tori's home, she brings the $10,000 she has finally gotten from her newly wealthy husband. Although her offer to pay Tori with money instead of herself is refused, the existence of the check places her on an even footing with him. If Tori was below Edith socially before their bargain was struck and above her financially afterward, they, at this point, have attained a certain financial, moral, and social equality.

The balance struck, the film teeters between masochistic and sadistic positions for both Tori and Edith. When Edith masochistically responds to Tori's advances with a threat to kill herself, Tori offers her a pistol from his desk. However, whether the offer is a sadistic taunt or a masochistic invitation for her to shoot him remains unclear. They struggle. Tori grabs Edith, and Edith strikes at his face and beats him with an iron poker. Tori pulls back Edith's hair, revealing her white shoulder, takes the hot poker from the brazier, and, with the camera

Figure 2.   Edith finds her own revenge as she shoots Tori—her brand clearly visible on her left shoulder. Still from The Cheat *courtesy of George Eastman House.*

fixed on his face, drives the poker down into her flesh (offscreen) and withdraws it. In a wider shot, Tori flings Edith to the tatami floor; the camera pulls back to a high angle shot of her clutching her burned shoulder. She picks up the gun and shoots Tori (offscreen). In a shot paralleling Edith's violation and fall to the tatami, Tori clutches his shoulder and falls to the floor. With this play of anger, violation, and revenge, both parties, technically at least within the narrative economy, seem vindicated. Both have been "cheated" and both have "cheated." Each has exacted revenge on the other. In fact, both find themselves in this position because of the overpowering control of the white, bourgeois, patriarchal status quo, which forbids any resolution of either Tori's desire for Edith or Edith's desire for independence, wealth, and sensualism through any means other than violence. Indeed, Sumiko Higashi views the parallel shots as a "visual example of how both characters share inferior status under white male hegemony."[22]

DeWitt Bodeen, writing on Hayakawa's performance in *The Cheat*, notes that "the effect of Hayakawa on American women was even more electric than Valentino's. It involved fiercer tones of masochism as well as a latent female urge to experience sex with a beautiful but savage man of another race."[23] Although this may be the case, perhaps the pleasure in watching Hayakawa's Tori in *The Cheat* comes, too, from both a sadistic desire to dominate a brutal man and a recognition of a status similar to that of nonwhite men within mainstream American society. Like Valentino, Hayakawa is depicted as a beautiful, engaging specular object—feminized (perhaps homoerotic) but also able to arouse the sexual interest of women because of his masochistic vulnerability as well as his sadistic mastery. Indeed, Hayakawa, here, may promise the same sort of subversive pleasure Miriam Hansen sees as part of Valentino's particular appeal to female spectators of the post-World War I era:

> In making sadomasochistic rituals an explicit component of the erotic relationship, Valentino's films subvert the socially imposed dominance/submission hierarchy of gender roles, dissolving subject/object dichotomies into erotic reciprocity. The vulnerability Valentino displays in his films, the traces of feminine masochism in his persona, may partly account for the threat he posed to prevalent standards of masculinity.[24]

By the time Edith makes her escape and her husband appears on the scene to save his wife (who has already avenged and "saved" herself), Tori has become a completely emasculated figure. Ironically, no potent Asian rapist exists for Edith's husband to vanquish. Instead, Tori appears as a fallen shadow on the shoji screen; a trickle of blood seeping through the paper signals his wound. When Edith's enraged husband bursts through the screen door, this classic gesture of the chivalrous white patriarch coming to "save" the threatened white woman from the "fate worse than death" seems empty.

Thus, although Edith is brought back into the white bourgeois patriarchy on the arm of her husband during her final march down the courtroom aisle, the foundations of male domination have already been shaken by her actions and the sadomasochistic play of the fantasy. Her husband's stoicism has been totally ineffectual. Even though Tori and her husband have both tried to punish and contain her, Edith has managed to defy both, so that the success of her reabsorption into the bourgeois family must remain at least somewhat problematic.

Wounded, exposed, and nearly lynched at *The Cheat*'s conclusion, Tori returns to his place as the emasculated Asian male. The threat he has posed to the white status quo has been obviated. However, interestingly, despite the male figures of judge, jury, enraged mob, and husband, it is the white woman, Edith, who finally acts as the instrument of his castration. Complications, then, arise. Edith may be punished for her independent decision to become involved with Tori, but she is vindicated for her equally independent actions of shooting Tori and publicly assuming responsibility for her revenge. The racist aspect of *The Cheat*, coupled with a call for female self-sufficiency, seems linked to certain elements in the suffrage movement, which pointed to the potential threat of the political power of African Americans and new immigrants from southern and eastern Europe as a reason to grant white, Protestant, Anglo-Saxon women the vote. Similarly, women viewers may look at this triumph over the Japanese villain as an apology for emancipation, since Edith's husband has been so completely ineffectual in protecting his wife, or as an acceptable expression of a desire to dominate men, to indulge in a sadistic fantasy usually denied them. From a totally different perspective, men in the audience might look at both contact between the races and female emancipation as an explosive combination that the text rightly condemns. Whether Edith's final outburst in court, then, can be looked at as an ambivalent nod toward the necessity of female independence or as a racist call for increased vigilance because of threats to the purity of the white woman seems moot.

Looked at either way, however, Edith functions as the gateway into American society that excludes those who cannot fit in because of their race or ethnicity. *The Cheat* gives the white woman this charge, then, to include and exclude the foreign, the alien, and the unacceptable through her sexuality. Thus, the text can simultaneously acknowledge, exploit, and condemn women's increased visibility in the public sphere, as well as their growing demands for sexual self-expression, by placing Edith in the shadow of the Asian villain, who both threatens and embodies all those secret desires that put the white patriarchy on unsteady ground.

Indulge: The Perils and Pleasures of Consumerism

In his essay, "Orientalism as an Ideological Form: American Film Theory in the Silent Period," Nick Browne observes, "The imaginary of the movie world linked and intermingled exoticism and consumerism . . . for cultural possession and incorporation of the ancient wealth of Asian sexual secrets and material life. The Orient served as the emblem of a deepening re-territorialization of desire."[25] As Browne notes, *The Cheat* does not stand as an isolated case of interest in Asia and Asian themes in Hollywood around World War I. Rather, the film is part of a broader interest in the "Orient" found in theater design, popular theories of the cinema, set design, as well as actual narrative themes. Also, as Browne points out, Hollywood seemed to be using this Orientalism to attempt to financially exploit and ideologically intervene in the crisis occasioned by the growth of a modern, consumer-oriented society in the first few decades of the twentieth century.

As Lary May shows in *Screening Out the Past: The Birth of Mass Culture and the Motion Picture Industry*,[26] the film industry played a key role during the silent era as a vehicle for the dissemination of a new ideology of consumption. Unlike the Victorian glorification of self-sufficiency, hard work, abstinence, and frugality for the respectable middle classes, shifts in the nature of the economy with the rise of corporate capitalism occasioned a change in values. As fewer members of the nominal middle classes owned and operated their own enterprises, the definition of the self through labor became as impossible for the bourgeoisie as it had been for the working classes previously. However, with the rise of the corporate middle classes came an increase in disposable income for a wider segment of the population, a growth in leisure time, and a redefinition of the individual through the consumption of mass-produced commodities rather than through productive enterprise. The domestic sphere began to shift from a site of small-scale production, spirituality, or reproduction to a site of leisure, consumption, and individual autonomy. Always part of a sexual economy of exchange within the patriarchy, women's importance as commodities themselves increased with a new emphasis on family life and sex as recreational. Beautiful (rather than spiritually transcendent, morally pure) women functioned as symbols of wealth and status among the bourgeoisie. Moreover, women also became the chief consumers within the household. They were placed in charge of seeing that the family maintained its status through the acquisition of commodities.

Certainly, this new role put an added burden on working class, minority, and new immigrant women.[27] Although consumption promised an entry into the American mainstream through the acquisition of the appropriate commodities, the consumer society also brought the additional burdens of an inferior economic status and the vicious cycle of working more to consume more with time to enjoy the cherished commodities less. Also, even though consumption seemed to promise acceptance into a democratic melting pot of a homogeneous mass culture, grave social divisions continued to exist. The upsurge of reactionary sentiments against women and minorities already noted above as part of a pattern that gave rise to lynching, for example, could never be countered by acquiring the *right* house, the *right* clothes, or the *right* automobile.

The cinema moved into the ideological maelstrom occasioned by these economic and social changes by providing both models for an idealized society of consumption and comforting, Victorian reassurances of the perils of indulgence and materialism. Designed to turn a profit by providing fantasies that could draw in a demographically diverse audience, these films offered elements of identification for the middle classes as well as the proletariat, for men as well as women, the old and the young, for new immigrants, people of color, and others designated as "foreign" by the American mainstream. Women, recent immigrants, and other "outsiders" played key roles in films that occasionally dealt explicitly with the tremendous social rifts within American society. Thus, another level of ideological contradictions involving the foreign and the domestic became intertwined with the contradictions arising from the legacies of Victorianism and the new consumer ideal. As May notes, "As both men and women began to question the older definitions of success and the home, they were reevaluating their relationship to foreign cultures."[28] In addition to representing a threatening assault on traditional Anglo-Saxon American values, foreign cultures also promised release from Victorian constraints and an implicit permission to indulge oneself sensually through the consumption of exquisitely exotic commodities.

During the silent era, the name of Cecil B. DeMille became inextricably linked with film fantasies that exploited the ideological contradictions arising out of the economic and social changes of the time.[29] Indeed, *The Cheat* can be looked at as one of his comparatively early forays into this territory. Dealing with the lives of the haute bourgeoisie, *The Cheat* promises a respectability and seriousness that stepped beyond the motion pictures' earlier designation as a principally working-class entertainment.[30] However, this interest in the Long Island "smart set" also offers those viewers far removed from that life-style a vicarious look at it as a model for consumption. Lavish houses, fashionable clothes, elegant furnishings, eleborate garden parties and balls, and sporty automobiles all play key roles within the mise-en-scène of the film.

Moreover, Edith provides a point of identification for all those women in the audience encouraged to look at consumerism as their vocation, while, at the same time, they are compelled to consider this consumption of commodities extravagant, frivolous, and potentially dangerous. Presented to the viewer as a beautiful commodity herself, Edith ironically gets into trouble precisely because of her desire to keep up this appearance of desirability, that is, to dress fashionably by spending exorbitant sums on clothes. Even before Tori enters the narrative, Edith's frictions with her husband are presented as stemming from her manic consumerism. In a telephone conversation, in which they are both physically and ideologically separated, Richard begs Edith to economize. A title spells out Edith's reply: "If you want me to give up my friends and social position—well— I won't." Edith's consumerism separates her from her overworked husband in a world of leisure and style that he has little part in. In fact, her acquisition of commodities threatens his authority over her because she is able to define herself and her own identity through a style created from those commodities. Thus, although Edith remains dependent on her husband for cash, consumerism gives her a certain degree of autonomy from the role of bourgeois housewife.

Later, Edith remarks to Tori, "The same old story—my husband objects to my extravagance—and you." Thus, Edith's indulgence of an interest in the foreign, in Asia, becomes equated with her self-indulgent consumerism. This link between racial otherness and the moral tensions associated with consumerism clearly has its roots outside the text. An interest in the foreign in general and in Asia in particular marked an ideological break with Victorian restraint. Moreover, this link between racial difference and consumption had overtly sexual overtones. Part of the pleasure of this display of wealth came from the exhibitionist joy of self-adornment. Through consumption, Edith becomes an envied aesthetic object herself. Unlike the prim Victorian housewife, Edith freely displays her erotic allure through lavishly feathered and bejeweled costumes. Further, Edith is "Orientalized" by her involvement with the wealthy aesthete Tori, who encourages her material indulgences. The more Edith consumes the more she becomes drawn into Tori's world of beautiful objects and the sensual pleasure offered by his collection.

Edith moves between Tori and Richard as a coveted, living possession, lending legitimacy to two different life-styles. Not only do Richard and Tori embody different styles of patriarchal domination (Richard's chivalry and paternalism in contrast to Tori's sadism and sensuality) but these different styles of masculinity appear to be linked to their different relationship to the economy. Whereas Tori offers the promise of instant gratification of desires, material opulence, and constant leisure, Richard, tied to his office rather than to his possessions, still clings to the Protestant work ethic, delays gratification, and suspects excessive indulgence.

If both Tori and Richard are part of the new consumer order, Richard represents a corrective to Tori's excesses. He acts as a mediator between the old economic order based on Victorian notions of restraint and hard work and the new consumerism linked to leisure, indulgence, and consumption. Thus, Tori and the Asian objects that surround him act as a metaphor for the suspect nature of these economic changes that seem to call for the white, Anglo-Saxon, Protestant middle classes to abandon their traditional values of thrift and self-denial and become more like the Victorian's dark image of otherness represented by Tori and his sumptuous displays of power, wealth, and eroticism. When Tori is vanquished at *The Cheat*'s conclusion, this shadowy aspect of the new economy vanishes with him, and the nouveau riche Richard is free to allow his wife to consume at will.

In *The Cheat*, sexuality and economics parallel one another and are inextricably linked together within the narrative. For example, Tori's "Oriental" extravagance not only transgresses Victorian prohibitions against self-indulgent displays of wealth but also marks him as transgressing gender boundaries by moving into a world of consumption associated with the domestic world of women. Thus, Richard's white, Anglo-Saxon, semi-Victorian, protective masculinity stands as a corrective to the imbalances in the racial, economic, and gender order Tori represents. In addition, Edith's flirtation with interracial sexuality and excessive consumption threaten the sex-gender as well as the economic system. Like Tori, she represents an excess. She confronts the Victorian values at odds with consumerism too directly. However, unlike Tori, who can be eliminated as the "other," Edith must be brought back within the bounds of the system in order to insure its continuation and legitimacy. Thus, when the "spent" Edith walks down the aisle with her husband at the end of the film, she affirms her subordinate place in the new order as the consumer held in check by the new speculative capitalist who can balance traditional values with the new consumerism.

Within patriarchal culture[31] and, as a consequence, within Hollywood films,[32] women circulate like commodities. The exchange of women affirms some social ties and forbids others. Within Hollywood films, the acquisition of the female protagonist legitimizes certain ideological positions and marginalizes or deprecates others. In *The Cheat*, Edith functions as the ultimate commodity, the ultimate token of legitimacy and desirability. From this point of view, her attraction as an object to the collector Tori seems appropriate; he allows her to "be herself," that is, a beautiful object unfettered by pecuniary concerns. When Tori brands her, however, he takes possession of her illegitimately, and she becomes stolen property. The branding acts as consumption out of control, and Edith must be repossessed as a commodity as well as reined in as a consumer in order for the economic order to continue to function. Thus, when Richard reclaims his wife, he not

Figure 3.   Cheng Huan (Richard Barthelmess) reverently caresses a Chinese gown worn by Lucy (Lillian Gish), who is enthroned in his lavish bedroom. Still from Broken Blossoms *(1919) courtesy of the Museum of Modern Art/Film Stills Archive.*

only brings a wayward woman back into the patriarchal fold but also brings the "new woman" consumer, who can assert her own identity and independence through the creation of herself in the purchase of commodities, back into a male-defined bourgeois order that still maintains an element of Victorian restraint.

For the viewer, *The Cheat* itself may promise the momentary possession of a beautiful, exotic commodity. Elegantly lighted, sumptuously decorated, sensuously displayed images excite the imagination and provide a fantasy world in which leisure and consumerism reign supreme. Perhaps seated in a movie theater itself decorated with exotic trappings, rubbing elbows with patrons from different social classes, indulging in a fantasy of cosmopolitanism, the text's sensationalism coupled with its lurid presentation of the rape-lynching fantasy might take on a certain irony.

Clearly, *The Cheat* can be looked at as a raw and direct call for racist exclusionism and a necessarily sadistic restraint of the newly independent woman for "her own good." However, the opulent and seductive world of Japanese splendor coupled with American commodity capitalism and linked to a sadomasochistic play with traditional racial and gender positions might conjure up different fantasies, creating a more ambivalent picture of the economic, social, political, and cultural order of the day.

Broken Blossoms: Sexual Perversity and Spiritual Salvation

D. W. Griffith's *Broken Blossoms* (1919) has sparked more critical interest than any other film in this study. Based on Thomas Burke's story, "The Chink and the Child," from his collection *Limehouse Nights* on the slum areas of London, *Broken Blossoms* tells a lurid tale of the love of a Chinese, opium-smoking merchant for the abused illegitimate daughter of a brutal boxer.

Given the links between American and British relations with China, the fact that an English story about the Limehouse slums should strike a responsive cord with Griffith and the 1919 film audience should come as no surprise. Since the time of Marco Polo, European trade with China has had an impact on the cultures of both the West and Asia. Tea, silk, and porcelain, in fact, put Britain so in debt to China that England encouraged illegal commerce in its opium from India to redress the trade imbalance. When the trade began to reach epidemic proportions, the Chinese imperial government launched a campaign to suppress it militarily, leading to the Opium War of 1840–1842 and the Treaty of Nanjing that forced China to concede lucrative ports and special privileges to the West. Also involved in the opium trade, American merchants benefited greatly from this blow to Chinese sovereignty. The commercial opening of China further led to increased contact more generally, and missionaries from the United States as well as Great Britain poured into China along with merchants, sailors, and a legion of bureaucrats. Ironically, the missionaries went to China to save it from the "decadence" of its pagan ways, including, of course, the opium use that the West had helped to promote.

In light of the pressure of these colonialist incursions and the internal strife occasioned by the decay of the Manchu-ruled Qing Dynasty, the impoverishment of China seemed certain, and many Chinese, particularly from the southern coastal areas, went to Britain, Australia, and America to seek their fortunes. Many went to California in search of gold and stayed on as laborers to work on the American railroads. However, owing in part to the political weakness of China internationally and racist elements within the labor movement of the latter part of the nineteenth century, the U.S. government instituted a series of exclusionary laws to keep out the Chinese. Those who did manage to stay or enter illegally tended to live isolated lives in the Chinatowns of major metropolitan areas. In Great Britain, an inhospitable climate led to similar conditions, so that the Limehouse of Burke's story would certainly strike a responsive cord with anyone familiar with Chinatown in San Francisco, New York, or in the pulp fiction of the time.[33]

Unlike the short story, however, which simply tries to sketch slum life for the prurient imaginations of outsiders, *Broken Blossoms* attempts to make a moral lesson and elevate the characters and situations of the original story into the realm of what critics have called "poetry" or "art."[34] In addition to the early praise it received as an "art film," *Broken Blossoms* has been studied seriously by film scholars interested in Griffith as an auteur,[35] Lillian Gish as a performer,[36] the production and commercial exploitation of the film as "high art,"[37] its contribution to the history of cinematography with the use of the soft focus Sartov lens,[38] the relationship of the film to melodrama,[39] the importance of the film to the history of Asian representations in the cinema,[40] as well as the film's depiction of gender relations.[41]

Perhaps the most telling studies of the film, however, have dealt with it as a tale of sexual perversity or as an example of Griffith's own well-documented penchant for young girls as objects of erotic desire.[42] Indeed, in many ways, the film can be looked at as a catalog of what society considers as sexual crimes, excesses, or perversions, including rape, incest, sadism, masochism, pedophilia, necrophilia, fetishism, voyeurism, and prostitution as well as miscegenation. In fact, given this list of sexual deviations, interracial sexuality, which remains on the

level of controlled lust and innocent affection, may be the most innocuous part of the fantasy.

Given the very thinly disguised sexual deviations depicted in the
film, approaching *Broken Blossoms* as a pornographic text seems
appropriate. Like pornography, *Broken Blossoms* uses spectacle to
arouse the sexual interest of the spectator, while narrative structure
permits, controls, and legitimizes this arousal by symbolically punish-
ing the principals (and through them the viewer who identifies with
them) for their erotic excesses. However, spectacle wins out, and the
evocation of an atmosphere, an image, a feeling that stimulates the
erotic involvement of the male viewer takes precedence over the moral
imperatives of the plot.

By looking at the erotic fantasies depicted in *Broken Blossoms* in
their rawest form, the text's ambivalent treatment of the relationship
between sexuality and race may also be exposed. The film is a contradictory mix of high-minded moralizing and lasciviousness, of racial
stereotypes and pleas for tolerance, of aestheticism and exploitative
violence.

Rape and Lynching: *The Cheat* and *Broken Blossoms*

In many ways, *Broken Blossoms* is the obverse of *The Cheat* and a
part of Griffith's post-*The Birth of a Nation* response to charges of
racism. While DeMille's *The Cheat*, like *The Birth of a Nation*, argues
for a racist exclusionism upheld by violence, *Broken Blossoms*, like
Griffith's epic *Intolerance* (1916), attempts to make a case for racial
tolerance and respect for foreign cultures. While *The Cheat* sees the
intrusion of Asia into American culture as a threat to the white,
bourgeois, patriarchal family, *Broken Blossoms* sees the Western patriarchy as a site of violence, decay, and exploitation. Rather than
lionizing capitalism and consumerism as the source of new vitality for
the bourgeois home, *Broken Blossoms* depicts the poverty and squalor
of the proletariat and subproletariat as a hopeless mire that the traditional, bourgeois, domestic virtues can do little to remedy. Ostensibly,
the film seems to present the West as brutal, violent, racist, and corrupt and criticizes it for its base treatment of women and outsiders. It
praises Asia for its elevated sense of morality and white women for
their virtue and purity.

However, underneath this plea for racial harmony and compassion
for women can be found a rape-lynching fantasy remarkably similar to
the "Bible Belt pornography" that propels the narratives of both *The
Cheat* and *The Birth of a Nation*. Like *The Cheat*, *Broken Blossoms*

deals with a relationship triangle. Like Tori, Cheng Huan (Richard Barthelmess), referred to in the credits as the "Yellow Man" and called "Chinkie" in the titles, is a merchant, associated with the forbidden sensuality and decadence of Asia. Battling Burrows (Donald Crisp), like Richard Hardy, represents the Western patriarch who is losing control of the woman in his charge. Lucy (Lillian Gish), like Edith Hardy, acts as a token of property, power, and moral legitimacy that circulates between them. Like Edith, she seeks solace from the Asian merchant because of inadequacies in her own household. Edith, however, escapes from boredom and a relatively minor shortage of petty cash, whereas Lucy tries to escape from poverty, regular beatings, and implicit sexual abuse. Just as Tori and Richard Hardy struggle to possess Edith sexually, Cheng Huan and Battling Burrows vie for Lucy.

Broken Blossoms begins with the idealistic Cheng Huan departing China to bring the message of Buddhist tolerance and passivity to the West. Yet after unsuccessfully trying to stop a fight between some American sailors while still in China, Cheng Huan seems doomed to failure from the outset. The film then cuts years later to the Limehouse district of London, where Cheng Huan has become a merchant and opium smoker. He becomes enamored of Lucy there, as she pitifully tries to stretch her meager allowance while shopping in Chinatown. When her father nearly beats her to death, she escapes to Chinatown and collapses in front of Cheng Huan's shop. He takes her in and treats her like a goddess. At one point, overtaken by lust, Cheng Huan advances on the innocent Lucy but pulls back before violating her purity. When Burrows learns of his daughter's whereabouts, he becomes enraged, takes her away from Cheng Huan's shop, and beats her to death back at his own hovel. Cheng Huan exacts revenge by shooting Burrows. He carries Lucy's body back to Chinatown and commits suicide next to her corpse.

As the basic elements of *Broken Blossom*'s plot indicate, hidden complications of *The Cheat*'s rape fantasy, buried behind a facade that denies the power of the association between the white Edith and the Asian Tori as victims of white, patriarchal power, surface in the Griffith film. Kindred spirits, Lucy and Cheng Huan, like Tori and Edith, share a bond of aestheticism and sensual delight in objects of beauty. Like Tori, Cheng Huan embodies the "feminine" qualities linked in the Western imagination with a passive, carnal, occult, and duplicitous Asia. Cheng Huan is feminized in the film not only by his close association with the world of women but also by his elaborate, exotic dress, his languid posture and gestures, and the use of soft focus and diffuse lighting to render his features less angular, more "womanly." However, while this bond is severed by the eruption of Tori's very masculine libido in *The Cheat*, the relationship between Lucy and Cheng Huan remains (as an intertitle states) a "pure and holy thing" as Cheng Huan draws back before consummating his love for Lucy.

Nevertheless, just as Tori's branding of Edith functions as a rape, Cheng Huan's ominous advance on Lucy and last minute sublimation of his desire, indicated by his kissing the hem of her sleeve rather than her lips, also symbolically marks his possession of the white woman. Battling Burrows reacts to the theft of Lucy as a rape. A title reads: "Battling discovers parental rights—A Chink after his kid! He'll learn him!" The enraged father, then, summons the aid of two of his cronies to form a "lynch mob" to avenge this wrong and retrieve Lucy. An ironic title encourages the viewer to distance himself or herself from Burrows's racist rage: "Above all, Battling hates those not born in the same great country as himself." Thus, the authorial voice of the intertitles promotes a reading that sees Burrows as a racist brute rather than as a brutal but still rightly possessive father. However, in light of Hollywood's consistent support of the rights and virtues of the patriarchy, this vilification of the parental role, no matter how excessively violent its manifestation, must conjure up a certain ambivalence for many in the audience.

In fact, it is Burrows's own sexual brutality that controls this aspect of the fantasy so that the film can make its ostensible moral point. Cheng Huan's "rape" of Lucy only loses its potential power to enrage a viewer prone to be outraged by the thought of miscegenation because Burrows also functions as a "rapist" in the text. Thus, if Cheng Huan can be looked at as the nonwhite rapist and Burrows as the enraged white patriarch, then the opposite formulation is also possible. Battling Burrows's incestuous, sadomasochistic rituals with Lucy are depicted as even more "perverse" than Cheng Huan's lustful adoration.

While the climactic scene in which Burrows hacks his way into the closet in which Lucy hides, grabs her, and beats her to death on the bed in their hovel has often been looked at as a symbolic rape, Julia Lesage has noted that the mise-en-scène of earlier scenes in *Broken Blossoms* also encourages the interpretation of Burrows's abuse of his daughter as sexual in nature. As Lesage notes,

> The first time Burrows beats Lucy, he grabs a whip from under the mattress and stands in the centre of the room, holding the whip at penis height. . . .
> Lucy tries to create a diversion by telling him there is dust on his shoes. She bends down to wipe off his shoes with her dress. Here, the

change in composition from one shot to another connotes the act of fellatio. In the long shot before Lucy wipes the shoes, the whip hangs almost to the floor. But in the close-up of her wiping the shoes, the whip's tail is at the height of Burrows's penis, and as Lucy raises her face the whip swings past her lips. As Burrows grabs Lucy's arms and throws her towards the bed near the closet, the whip is again between his legs at penis height. We see blurred, orgiastic shots of him beating her senseless.[43]

If Cheng Huan's advances on Lucy approach rape, then Burrows's abuse of his daughter also approximates rape. Just as Burrows calls together his cronies to form a lynch mob to attack Cheng Huan and retrieve Lucy, Cheng Huan also is cast in the role of avenger of the white woman when he tries to rescue Lucy from her father. As Burrows tears down the closet door to get at Lucy, Cheng Huan collects himself, gets a pistol, and goes to Lucy's aid. Crosscutting between Cheng Huan in the streets of Limehouse, Lucy pitifully running in circles in the closet and Burrows with his ax, the montage pattern established at this point brings *Broken Blossoms* close to the parallel editing associated with Griffith's "last minute rescues" in other films. However, in this case, given that Lucy has been doubly violated and that neither Cheng Huan nor Burrows can function as the avenging patriarch who can save the purity of white womanhood for the perpetuation of the Anglo-Saxon, Protestant, ruling elect, the "rescue" seems pointless. Indeed, Lucy dies before Cheng Huan can arrive.

Although Cheng Huan does manage to avenge Lucy's death by shooting Burrows, this inverted "lynching" of the white father by the Asian male loses much of its force as Cheng Huan returns to his emasculated, passive, masochistic position when he commits suicide on the floor next to Lucy's corpse. This scene, in fact, is crosscut with Burrows's buddies at the police station enlisting the help of the authorities to avenge Burrows's death. Ironically, the official authorities finally appear in the film after all the violent action has taken place. As in many rape-lynching fantasies, the legitimate agents of the government are shown to be ineffectual in keeping the racial and sexual order intact. In this case, Cheng Huan punishes himself symbolically for his transgression through suicide, usurping the role of the state and essentially "lynching" himself.

Like *The Cheat*, then, *Broken Blossoms* maintains a fundamental separation between Asia and the West played out dramatically and violently through a doomed romance in which the effeminate Asian man finds a "perverse" potency in his desire for an unobtainable Caucasian woman. Just as Tori's entrance into American high society marks a transgression of the barriers separating the races, Cheng Huan's emigration from an idyllic China of temple bells, Buddhist statues, and innocent maidens dooms him to the "hell" of Limehouse. As in *The Cheat*, it is the mixture of cultures that indicates a disturbance in the social order. Just as the American sailors wreak havoc in China in the film's opening scenes, Cheng Huan reemerges in England as a grotesque, as alien to British society as the sailors were out of place in the quaint and idealized China of the film. The intrusion of one culture into the other's domain marks the narrative disequilibrium.

In *Broken Blossoms*, the "perversity" of Limehouse is indicated by the opium den that Cheng Huan frequents "where the Orient squats at the portals of the West," as a title indicates. Interracial couples smoke opium together; drugged Caucasian women are shown in languid, sexually suggestive poses. Opium indicates the intrusion of Asia into the West as an unwelcome passivity, sensuality, mystery, and languor.

Although there does seem to be a clear line drawn between the sympathetic Cheng Huan and the villainous Burrows, it cannot be denied that both are creatures of Limehouse. As Burrows flirts and drinks with the "loose" women who also frequent the opium den and as his daughter Lucy is mesmerized by the material pleasures of Chinatown, it becomes quite clear that part of what makes Limehouse and its inhabitants disturbing and peculiar to the middle-class outsider is the erasure of social boundaries between the races. The film's ostensible call for racial tolerance becomes clouded by its insistence that any meeting of Asia and the West must somehow be either violent or "perverse." Thus, it can be argued that *Broken Blossoms*'s bleak view of Limehouse goes beyond a bourgeois suspicion of the working classes whose poverty must somehow be linked ideologically to moral inadequacy rather than to economic exploitation by the ruling order. Limehouse is not only a threat because it is a slum but also because it creates an environment in which the unprotected white virgin can be possessed by the Asian other. Burrows's dissipation and Lucy's inability to escape her father spring from this Limehouse ambience in which troubled families, prostitution, brutality, shiftlessness, and opium all become part of a "perverted," culturally and racially mixed slum.

Thus, while *Broken Blossoms* seems to praise Asian sensitivity and passivity and condemn Western callousness and violence, a closer look at the rape-lynching fantasy reveals a deeper, less liberal perspective. Stripped to its barest elements, *Broken Blossoms* still features the white virgin exposed and humiliated by contact with a man of another race, who loses his life for daring to presume he could possess her. While seeming to condemn the hypocritical white patriarch Burrows for his misplaced desire to avenge the "wrong" done his daughter through her contact with Cheng Huan, the text also allows that "wrong" to be symbolically avenged by Cheng Huan's suicide and tacit acceptance of his own culpability in loving a woman forbidden to him.

The Victorian Cult of the Virgin Child

The film makes a good deal out of the forbidden nature of Cheng Huan's love for Lucy as springing from racial differences. Burrows becomes enraged when he learns of his daughter's relationship with the Chinese merchant supposedly because he abhors Asians. However, the more obvious fact of their tremendous difference in age is never voiced in the text. Rather, pedophilia, as part of the Victorian cult of the virgin child, becomes a "natural" part of Cheng Huan's supposedly "pure and holy" attraction to Lucy.

As Ronald Pearsall notes in *The Worm in the Bud: The World of Victorian Sexuality*, this "cult of the little girl" was a common aspect of Victorian sexual life:

> The nineteenth century was especially replete with gentlemen who had for girl children an overwhelming penchant, and when these men were respectable such attachments were treated as if they were ordained by God. When these men were of the literary persuasion, the rationalization became even more involved, and the refusal to face the fact that passionate involvements with immature girls argued some personality defect resulted in some curious and tortuous thinking.[44]

While authors like Lewis Carroll and John Ruskin wrote tomes in praise of the virtues of young girls, brothels specializing in child prostitutes thrived. Some syphilitic men believed that intercourse with a virgin would provide a cure, and the trade in "virgins" (both genuine and fake) reached epidemic proportions.

In fiction, the virgin girl functions both as a passive victim, inviting her own rape and martyrdom, and as an unsullied angel, sentimentally protected and cherished by her high-minded and lascivious mentor. She is purity personified, youth untouched, and the victim of a sadistic, unchecked, male lust. Within the cult dedicated to her, she acts as a sign of spiritual transcendence through a pruriently rooted desire. Perversity becomes saintliness, and her lover's sexual passion fuels his religious fervor. Through this infatuation with the virgin child, any guilt associated with sexuality could be denied, since the girl would presumably be innocent and unaware of any sexual feelings. Moreover, the potential threats that a relationship with a mature woman might entail could be completely avoided.

Although Griffith, perhaps responding to Lillian Gish's reluctance to play the role of a child, makes Burke's thirteen-year-old heroine into a fifteen-year-old,[45] Lucy still functions in the film as the virgin child, angel and martyr, humiliated victim and elevated object of desire. True to the ambivalence of the Victorian formulation of this figure, *Broken Blossoms*'s plot alternates between sadistic and fetishistic fantasies of the violated and unobtainable virgin. As Robert Lang notes in his analysis of the film in *American Film Melodrama: Griffith, Vidor, Minnelli*, Cheng Huan represents the desire to possess the child as a fetish object, the castrating potential of sexual desire belied by his religious elevation of her image. Lang observes,

> He keeps her always at a distance, in a disavowal of knowledge, as a defense. Burrows's response to the threat she represents is sadistic; his desire is to tear the loved object apart, whereas the Yellow Man's response is fetishistic. His drive . . . is . . . to make of Lucy a representation.[46]

Having gone to Britain on a religious mission and failed, Cheng Huan finds spiritual salvation in the form of a little girl whom he worships like a saint and lusts after like a whore.

Given that pedophilia is one of society's most detested sexual perversions and that the elevation of the pure child one of Christianity's favored avenues to spiritual enlightenment, the fact that *Broken Blossoms* should teeter between the two and use a sadistic depiction of child abuse to counter the equally "perverse," fetishistic worship of the child seems appropriate. Religion and an unexplainable brutality mask the desire to sexually possess a child. As Nick Browne points out in his discussion of *Broken Blossoms* in "Griffith's Family Discourse: Griffith and Freud," religion and sexual perversity are inextricably linked within the narrative and made concrete within the film's mise-en-scène.

> The central trope through which the narrative takes on thematic significance is this religious one. It is this trope which founds the complex metaphoric system of the film. Its compostion is condensed in the contrast between two versions of a common place: this central symbolic site is the bed, the one in the Yellow Man's upstairs room which serves as an altar, and the one in her father's house on which she is attacked and dies. The central terms of symbolic expression in the film, high and low, priest and animal, ecstatic worship and incestuous violation, constitute the diacritical coordinates of the space and action of the film.[47]

The first time the film shows Lucy and Cheng Huan encountering one another is during what the intertitles describe as a "shopping trip" for Lucy—a pitiful foray into Chinatown to buy vegetables and maybe "something extra" with tinfoil she has collected. Lucy tarries in front of Cheng Huan's shop to look at a collection of dolls in his window. A title reads: "The Yellow Man watched Lucy often. The beauty which all Limehouse missed smote him to the heart." Framed by the shop window, Lucy herself resembles the coveted dolls. She is a beautiful coveted object under scrutiny, passive and fragile, framed by the window and similarly displayed. Moreover, the fact that the fifteen-year-old Lucy still craves dolls underscores her immaturity, innocence, and desire to remain a child, that is, beyond the potentially disturbing threats of adult womanhood. Earlier warned against and implicitly rejecting both marriage and prostitution, Lucy is trapped as a child, doomed to remain "pure," and fetishized like the lifeless dolls at which she gazes. To underscore Cheng Huan's supposedly "pure" interest in Lucy, the narrative introduces the character of Evil Eye (Edward Peil), who leers at Lucy out of an obviously prurient interest. As Cheng Huan steps between Lucy and Evil Eye on the street, he acts to rid the fantasy of the voyeuristic overtones of Cheng Huan's (and the viewer's) own interest in looking at the child Lucy. Paralleling the opposition between Burrows's sadistic sexual possession of Lucy and Cheng Huan's fetishistic worship, here Cheng Huan's desire to gaze at Lucy is rid of the sadistic implications of the voyeur's wish to uncover and possess rather than simply reverently look upon the beloved specular object.

Also, in this sequence, the film's titular metaphor comes into play. A title reads: "The Spirit of Beauty breaks her blossoms all about his chamber." The "broken" of the film's title conjures up the duality of the sadistic-fetishistic nature of the fantasy. On the one hand, Lucy is sentimentally equated with the beauty of the immature flower, not yet in bloom, as she tries to purchase a small bud in exchange for her tin foil. Later, Cheng Huan regales her with flowers and calls her his "White Blossom," making her an object of his aesthetic contemplation. Like the shop window dolls, the flowers help to situate Lucy in the text as a beautiful object, an appropriate image for aesthetic contemplation ostensibly superseding any forbidden erotic interest.

On the other hand, she is also a "broken" blossom—abused, humiliated, tattered, and trampled. From this perspective, Lucy can be looked on as the victimized beauty, ravaged and inviting her own inevitable destruction. In fact, the scene in which Lucy attempts to purchase her flower as Evil Eye leers at her is intercut with a scene in which Burrows counters his manager's admonitions against his drinking with the ironic line, "Wot yer expect me to do—pick violets?" In the following scene, Burrows metaphorically "picks" Lucy by beating her with his phallic whip.

The aesthetic nature of the flower metaphor, moreover, helps to situate the pedophilic fantasy within the realm of the secular religion of beauty and poetry to further mask its perverse roots. When Lucy seeks asylum at Cheng Huan's shop, a florid title interrupts the action: "Oh, lily flowers and plum blossoms! Oh silver streams and dim-starred skies!" In the two shot that follows, Cheng Huan peers into Lucy's face and holds his hands before her fallen, battered body as if in prayer. He draws his face near hers but turns his head away just before his lips touch hers. Throughout Lucy looks puzzled and a bit distressed at Cheng Huan's amorous behavior, and, later, a title points to her complete innocence: "What makes you so good to me, Chinky?"

In the struggle between pedophilic desire and religious transcendence, Cheng Huan's bed serves as both altar and battleground. Immobilized by her father's abuse, Lucy becomes one of Cheng Huan's shop window dolls on display for his visual contemplation and adoration, an object of lust and veneration. He orientalizes her by dressing her in a Chinese brocaded robe, shoes, and hair ornament, worshiping her with gifts of flowers, tea, and burning incense. He dances in the moonlight, plays the flute for her, and sleeps at the foot of her bed reverently holding one of her hands. He kneels at her bedside and looks up at her, hands clasped in prayer. In other words, he uses the child to create a narcissistic image for his own contemplation, as static, atavistic, sensuous, and dangerously inviting as any Hollywood conception of the Asian other could be. Cheng Huan gives Lucy a mirror to contemplate her own beauty and a doll to clutch, which symbolically parallels her own situation as a cherished but lifeless object.

Not only to perpetuate the religious cover to the fantasy but also to continue an indulgence in the fetishism itself, Cheng Huan must pull back before disturbing his saintly child's virginal innocence. Not to do so would break the illusion and destroy Lucy's passive potency in the text. However, not to recognize the tension would perhaps go too far in either denying a racist belief in the Asian man's supposedly innate sexual depravity or robbing the drama completely of its effect by denying Cheng Huan any internal conflict over his possession of Lucy. As Julia Lesage notes, the title that follows Cheng Huan's aborted attempt at sexual contact with Lucy confirms the erotic passion of the scene by denying it.

Significantly overapologizing for the man's sexual intent, the intertitle announces: "His love remains a pure and holy thing—even his worst foe says this." In fact the title makes no sense, because no one at the time knew that Lucy was there, and later her father and his friends just assumed that a sexual relation had taken place. Griffith seems to use the

Figure 4.   Battling Burrows (Donald Crisp) rips Lucy from her closet sanctu-ary before he kills her. Still from Broken Blossoms *courtesy of the Museum of Modern Art/Film Stills Archive.*

title to deny the sequence's visual explicitness, yet this very denial creates suspicion about and thus confirms the reality of that sexual passion which the sequence has both presented and repressed.[48]

Although the passion contained in the relationship erupts briefly here and again when the otherwise passive Cheng Huan shoots Burrows, this self-contained, distanced, aesthetic love affair finds its ultimate expression in the final suicide scene. As a lovely corpse adorned in her Asian finery, Lucy embodies both the end result of the sadistic and fetishistic aspects of the pedophilic fantasy. Thus, she has been completely destroyed physically and frozen in time as a child. She has become the perfect fetish that will never represent the demands of an adult woman, sacrificed to perpetuate a myth of transcendent innocence to deny the threatening aspect of a forbidden sexuality. Cheng Huan builds a Buddhist shrine on his bed next to Lucy's dead body. He lights incense in front of a small statue of Buddha, reads from a religious text, touches it to his forehead reverently, ritualistically, looks up at his angelic, dead Lucy, and plunges a dagger into his chest. His last pseudoreligious act of perversity, then, is necrophilic in nature. His suicide, performed with a smile on his face at the side of his beloved corpse, is orgasmic. The final shots of a Chinese monk striking a temple bell and the misty harbor of Cheng Huan's hometown contribute to the text's ostensible point that Cheng Huan has achieved some sort of religious salvation. However, this return to the spiritual cannot belie the erotic passions conjured up by the film and the inextricable link between pedophilia, the symbolic sexual possession of the white virgin child, and Cheng Huan's miraculous renewal of faith.

Made during the final days of World War I (with references to war casualties and munitions workers), *Broken Blossoms* seems to be part of the rhetoric of universalism, pacifism, and tolerance that formed part of the Versailles Treaty and League of Nations political discourses then current.[49] Given the deep-rooted hatred of the Chinese prevalent in the American popular media since the mid-nineteenth century, the fact that Cheng Huan could emerge as a sympathetic character in *Broken Blossoms* likely would be linked to this broader public interest in burying the hatchet and accepting former enemies as brothers. Thus, Cheng Huan could really be marked as an "outsider" in any respect and function in the same way in the text as the romantic, troubled aesthete saved by the sanctity of the pure, white virgin. The specifics of Cheng Huan's Chinese ethnicity and racial difference simply add a veneer of exoticism to *Broken Blossoms*, encouraging a familiar fantasy of Asia as feminine, passive, carnal, and perverse.

As in many subsequent texts featuring an interracial romance between Asians and Anglo-Americans, the "whiteness" and pure innocence of the Caucasian woman elevates and enobles the "base" qualities of the Asian other. Lucy, in *Broken Blossoms*, becomes the token
of Cheng Huan's moral salvation through the beauty of romance.
Thus, despite its critique of Western brutality and masculine cruelty,
the film remains rooted in the very Western ideology of romance
where spiritual salvation rests on the possession of the white woman
even if that inevitably means total destruction for the man of color who
loves her. The West, then, again "saves" the inferior, dependent, lost
Asian male by annihilating him.

3

The Threat of Captivity

The Bitter Tea of General Yen and
Shanghai Express

Some of the most ancient narratives that survive today feature the abduction of a woman by an alien (and expressly villainous) culture. These captivity narratives, from folktales and *The Iliad* to such films as *The Searchers* (1956) and *Hardcore* (1979), deal with a cultural tension peculiar to the sexual and racial dynamics of patriarchal relations. Linked to yellow peril discourses that connect sexual aggression to sociopolitical and cultural threats, Hollywood tales featuring the capture of an Anglo-American woman by an Asian man function in much the same way as rape and lynching fantasies. The white woman circulates among Caucasian and Asian men as a token of moral worth and as a legitimation of patriarchal power. However, even more than in films like *The Cheat* or *Broken Blossoms*, these captivity narratives often represent the white woman's potential defection to an alien culture as an appealing possibility.

Most of these Hollywood tales featuring an Asian captor seem to fall into one of two categories. One narrative formula involves the threat of "white slavery," with the captive forced into prostitution. This plot type has been common in Hollywood since the silent era and still pops up in dramas like "The Girls of the White Orchid" (1983), a made-for-television exposé of "white slavery" in contemporary Tokyo.

A second narrative type deals with a captive (usually a missionary or nurse) threatened by sexual contact with a bandit leader, warlord, or other military figure. The latter narratives were particularly popular during the 1930s when they featured Chinese warlords then ravaging China (for example, *The Bitter Tea of General Yen, Shanghai Ex-*

press). In the 1940s, the captor then became Japanese—*So Proudly We Hail* (1943) and *Cry Havoc* (1943). By the 1950s, Chinese as well as other Asian Communists now fulfilled the role of captor, as in *Five Gates to Hell* (1959) set in Vietnam. Since the 1960s, captivity stories have played a key role in Hollywood's depiction of Asia, from John Ford's *Seven Women* (1966) set in China to "Intimate Strangers," a 1980s television movie partially set in a Vietnam prisoner of war camp.

To understand the enduring power of these films, it seems necessary to begin by looking at how women function as tokens of exchange in the American captivity tale. Then two Hollywood captivity tales—*The Bitter Tea of General Yen* (1933) and *Shanghai Express* (1932)—will be used as examples of how these films use the same narrative formula to treat ideological contradictions involving race and sex.

American Popular Thought and the Captivity Tale

In her essay, "The Traffic in Women: Notes on the 'Political Economy' of Sex," Gayle Rubin summarizes the importance of Claude Levi-Strauss's work to a feminist critique of the patriarchy:

> Kinship systems do not merely exchange women. They exchange sexual access, genealogical statuses, lineage names and ancestors, rights and people—men, women and children—in concrete systems of social relationships. These relationships always include certain rights for men, others for women. "Exchange of women" is a shorthand for expressing that the social relations of a kinship system specify that men have certain rights in their female kin, and that women do not have the same rights either to themselves or to their male kin.[1]

Women, therefore, represent objects of exchange and also symbolize the necessity of exchange to maintain alliances and social bonds. If Levi-Strauss's theory of kinship is placed within the intercultural context it seems to call forth, a tension exists between exogamy and territoriality, between the necessity for exchange and a desire to maintain cultural integrity and an implicit feeling of superiority over those from other cultures.

In this light, the captivity tale can be seen as an outgrowth of two fundamental contradictions within patriarchal ideology. To deal with the threat of female autonomy, the tale acts to caution women against any act of independence by assuring them that liaisons not sanctioned and legitimated by the patriarchal family unit will only lead to violence and, even worse, oppression. In addition, the captivity tale uses women to define and strengthen cultural boundaries. The ambivalence of exogamous relations is dealt with by dividing the world into societies in which marriage exchanges are sanctioned and "enemy" nations peopled by villainous men threatening to "steal" away women without the benefit of any legitimate exchange. Thus, these tales can rationalize sexism and racism in one deft narrative movement of capture, return, and reintegration of women through socially sanctioned marriages.

Throughout U.S. history, captivity narratives have enjoyed a particularly important role in maintaining racial as well as sexual boundaries. Given the nature of the development of an American identity in contradistinction to Native American cultures here and European cultures left behind, it comes as no surprise that captivity stories achieved a popularity well out of proportion to the numbers of people actually taken captive. Issues involving the assimiliation or rejection (and subsequent annihilation) of people seen as different because of language, religion, ethnicity, or race have always occupied an important place in American popular thought. Captivity narratives highlight these issues, expose and condemn differences, legitimize racial boundaries, and allow for the rationalization of the most heinous excesses to maintain a white, English-speaking, mainly Protestant identity as the sole representation of the American experience.[2]

Captivity narratives were used not only to legitimize massacres of Native Americans, however. These same tales also helped to keep Anglo-Saxon women close to home, docile, and far from the threat of foreign influence. Because alien cultures provided different (occasionally less restrictive) gender roles, captive women could not be trusted; ultimately they might reproduce with and nurture an "enemy." The other side of the ideological coin, when expressed at all, looked quite different. African slaves and Native American women were not taken into "captivity" but were "benevolently" allowed into a Christian household to be "civilized." The use of rape to demoralize and annihilate the integrity of other races and cultures was excused, in popular fantasy, by the overpowering seductiveness and sexual desire of the alien woman. The white man also became the spiritual savior of the woman of color, who usually sacrificed herself—and, symbolically, her people—to legitimize white authority.

Recently, feminist historians and literary scholars have begun to take a second look at the historical place of both actual and fictional captivity stories in the lives of American women. Glenda Riley's *Women and Indians on the Frontier, 1825–1915*[3] is particularly astute at piecing together the ambivalent relationship that existed between Anglo-American women and native men and women on the changing frontier. Although principally concerned with the nineteenth and early twentieth century, Riley traces the roots of women's experiences with Native Americans back to the colonial period, when the earliest captivity stories (e.g., *The Narrative of the Captivity and Restoration of Mrs. Mary Rowlandson*, 1682) acted as religious allegories of sin, capture, and salvation symbolized by the captive's return to white society.

Captivity stories continue to be quite popular today, and twentieth-century captivity stories function both as cautionary tales for independent-minded women and as rationalizations of racism. In fact, twentieth-century stories seem to blend together all those things that made these tales compelling in the past: their exploration of cultural, ethnic, and racial identity; their examination of women as markers of cultural limits; and their uncanny ability to project values and vices internal to a culture onto the alien to maintain a racial hierarchy of difference.

Throughout the history of the captivity narrative, sexuality has played a key role. The threat of captivity is not so much humiliation, slavery, or torture but sexual violation. The "fate worse than death" for the Anglo-American female captives in these fantasies is rape, forced marriage, or prostitution. All those sexual crimes and mistreatments of women so prevalent in white society are denied and projected onto men of color, debauched and sexually violent Hispanics, Native Americans, Asians, and African-Americans.

Textual Ambivalences: *The Bitter Tea of General Yen*

During the 1930s, American interest in the political situation in China grew tremendously. Newspaper accounts of battles among Nationalist forces (KMT), the emerging Communist party, warlords, bandits, and the Japanese appeared regularly.[4] Later, as Japan emerged as a threat to American interests in the Pacific, sympathy for the plight of the Chinese grew, and films like *The Good Earth* (1937) and Joris Ivens's documentary *The 400 Million* (1939) appeared. However, in the early part of the decade, China principally functioned as an exotic, dangerous, and chaotic place where anything was possible.

For example, *The Bitter Tea of General Yen*, directed by Frank Capra, uses China as a land of compelling contradictions where extreme wealth and dire poverty coexist. In this case, Hollywood's China offers the depression-weary audience the possibility of escape into a distant, opulent, and beautiful world, which is also even more desperately poor and turbulent than the economically ruined United States. Given the racist roots of the captivity tale, *The Bitter Tea of General*

Yen might be expected to use its interracial romance to link economic problems to the threat of racial differences. However, the film treats a liaison between Anglo-American Megan Davis (Barbara Stanwyck) and the shadowy but seductive General Yen (played in grotesquely designed makeup by Scandanavian actor Nils Asther) in an ambivalent but ultimately sympathetic light.

Megan travels to China to marry a missionary. However, on her wedding day, she is spirited away by the warlord General Yen. While captive, Megan tries to convert Yen to Christianity only to have her efforts undermined by a growing sexual attraction to her captor. Their romance remains unconsummated, however, and the film ends with Yen's military ruin and suicide and Megan on a ship likely returning to the white community.

Although in many ways *The Bitter Tea of General Yen* is a very traditional captivity tale, the interracial liaison treated by the narrative created sufficient controversy to have the film banned in Great Britain and the Commonwealth at the time of its release. Certainly, part of the reason the film managed to be produced at all has to do with the fact that, beneath the makeup, the actual love interest in the film is between two Caucasian performers. Nevertheless, the film was also considered prestigious enough to open the then brand-new Radio City Music Hall in New York City. Capra himself called it an "art" film.[5] In the art film tradition of *Broken Blossoms*, *The Bitter Tea of General Yen* testifies to Hollywood's genius for turning controversy into cash and orchestrating textual ambivalence in such a way that a potentially scandalous theme would titillate rather than repulse the average viewer.

On the one hand, for example, the film appears to critique the accepted racial attitudes of the day in addition to investigating an unquestioned puritanical faith in sexual restraint and material well-being as a sign of spiritual grace—values a depression audience may have very good reason to question. On the other hand, this implicit social critique is quite firmly held in check by the film's ignorance of Asia and faith in Western stereotyped interpretations of Asian behavior and culture. In addition, at a time when many women were trying desperately to keep themselves fed when marriage to an unemployed man did not bring with it the traditional bourgeois dream of a happy hearth and home, *The Bitter Tea of General Yen* both questions and affirms women's dependence on men and their inability to think clearly outside of male influence. Despite this, *The Bitter Tea of General Yen*'s extremely complex and contradictory representation of racial and sexual politics takes the film beyond the cautionary moral fervor of many other captivity narratives.

However, this critical complexity does not appear in the opening scenes of *The Bitter Tea of General Yen*. The opening actually seems to link the film to the autobiographical-religious essays written by women missionaries allowed into China for the first time after the Opium Wars.[6] Set in a Shanghai missionary household in the turbulent world of postdynastic China, *The Bitter Tea of General Yen* establishes a Western moral tone and perspective at the outset, which is only questioned much later.

After several shots of turmoil in the streets of Shanghai, a shot from the interior of a European house frames the chaos outside through a doorway that sharply divides the two worlds. As guests enter to attend a wedding celebration of one of the missionaries to his New England sweetheart, China is kept at bay outside. The only indication of the house's actual location comes from a mute Chinese pianist and Chinese chorus singing "Onward Christian Soldiers" in English, in Western dress, and the occasional expressionless Chinese servant.

The image seems cliché—the light-filled American home in the midst of a dangerous, alien world outside the door, the homestead assaulted by Hollywood Indians, the pioneer family on the plains, plantation families in Africa, Asia, or Latin America—an image that visually represents American values forged in the wilderness. Bishop Harkness (Emmett Snigen), in attendance to perform the nuptials, underscores this clear dichotomy between Christian virtue and "heathen" villainy with a little anecdote about his attempts to convert a group of Mongolian tribesmen. After telling them the story of the crucifixion and heartened by their interest, the bishop later learned that a group of merchants had been crucified by those same tribesmen. Philosophic, the bishop simply observes, "That, my friends, is China," as the camera pans to a close-up of an elderly Chinese man's impassive face—a classic image of inscrutability.

The racist clichés continue to pile up. When a ricksha runner is struck down in the street, Megan's missionary companion remarks, "Human life is the cheapest thing in China." Later, Megan's hostess makes a similar comment, "They're all tricky, treacherous, and immoral. I can't tell one from the other. They're all Chinamen to me." Interestingly, even though it carefully dismantles all of Megan's claims to moral authority through Puritan values, the film still allows all these racist clichés to stand nearly unchallenged. The Chinese characters in the film invariably prove themselves to be "tricky, treacherous, and immoral." If the film does anything to combat its own avowed racism, it does so through an examination of what is missing in the cozy Victorian home of the opening scenes but happens to be present in Yen's elaborate Chinese palace—aside from the obvious wealth with which

Figure 5.   Megan (Barbara Stanwyck) finds herself surrounded by the enticing opulence of Yen's palace. For the depression era audience, the luxurious exotica on display might be more seductive because of the promise of material comfort than because of the erotic connotations of the bedroom. Still from The Bitter Tea of General Yen *(1933) courtesy of George Eastman House.*

the depression audience must have been duly impressed. That missing element found in Yen's exotic world, and in many other exotic lands conjured up in Hollywood fictions, is romance.

Yen rescues (abducts) Megan, who had been struck down in a mob trying to escape the city, and takes her to his palace in the provinces behind battle lines. The film plays on the ambiguity of Yen's action, and, in fact, the plot revolves around Megan's changing interpretation of Yen's thoughts and her own situation.

Not surprisingly, Megan has a rather difficult time figuring out Yen since he wavers between the two prevalent stereotypes of Asian men found in American popular culture. At times, Yen seems quite Western, the very picture of the knight-errant who platonically places a woman on a pedestal to worship her from afar. At other times, however, he takes on the guise of a sex-crazed demon, with only one thought on his mind—violating Megan as expeditiously as possible. As the polished mandarin, Yen hovers between the equally polished but

Figure 6.   In her dream, Megan (Barbara Stanwyck) willingly submits to the advances of General Yen (Nils Asther) grotesquely outfitted with the silk gown and long fingernails associated with Hollywood's evil mandarins. Still from The Bitter Tea of General Yen *(1933) courtesy of the Museum of Modern Art/Film Stills Archive.*

diabolical Fu Manchu and the cultivated and benevolent Charlie Chan, both popular at about the same time in Hollywood.

Running parallel to Yen's dual nature, Megan must confront her own awakening sexuality and its implications. In a unique scene, the viewer becomes privy to Megan's secret, forbidden desires through the visualization of a dream. Dressed in one of her host's embroidered robes, Megan goes out to enjoy the night air on her balcony. Images of the moon rising over a pagoda and lovers kissing in long shot, a lantern in the foreground signaling the exotic quality of their romance, prepare for the dissolve of the moon over Megan's shut eyes which conventionally marks a dream sequence.

The scene is played without dialogue, with only musical accompaniment on the sound track, like a silent film. Soft-focus cinematography and low-key shadows further distance the dream stylistically from the rest of the film. Megan sits on her satin-covered bed. A shadowy figure breaks in through her door. The figure is a grotesque Yen, sporting pointed ears and spikelike fingernails reminiscent of Murnau's Nosferatu or Ming the Merciless of Flash Gordon fame. A superimposition of Yen in military dress over the vampire-Yen makes the connection crystal clear. The camera dollies in for a closer shot of Megan's terrified face. The next shot shows her framed on the bed by Yen's long Manchu nails. Yen bends over Megan's prone body and lightly brushes her breasts with his nails. A masked man in Western dress appears at the window. His dark blazer, light pants, and collegiate hat make him appear ready to go off to the country club with the leading lady. Incongruously, the figure is masked, but, not surprisingly, he has appeared to save Megan's virtue. He strikes the unmanicured Yen, who falls back surrealistically in a process shot and disappears on impact with the wall.

Gleefully, the masked figure throws off his hat, and Megan draws close to take off her hero's mask. Without a hint of surprise, she sees that the masked man is also Yen. They look deeply into each other's eyes, and Megan falls back onto the bed. A swirling effect created by another process shot denotes her ecstasy. Yen sits on the bed next to her; he caresses her face and hair; she pulls back her head, revealing her neck in a gesture of both passion and submission; finally, they kiss. Slowly, the shot dissolves back to the sleeping Megan's face as Yen lowers her onto the bed.

At this point, the viewer may begin to realize that *The Bitter Tea of General Yen* is not a straightforward captivity narrative. The struggle principally dealt with in the film is not the struggle of two races over the body and spirit of a woman for the legitimation of a moral right to power or the assurance of cultural homogeneity. Rather, *The Bitter Tea of General Yen*'s struggle seems to be an internal one between sensuality and moral righteousness. Race, at least for the moment, seems almost secondary, since Megan's dream indicates that Yen fulfills all roles for her. He functions as her savior from the threatening aspects of sexuality, the guarantor of the blissful promises of the safety of "true love" and as the dark force of sexuality unchecked.

From this point on, Megan abandons her futile attempts to escape from Yen and sets out in the best missionary spirit to "save" him. In other words, she attempts to recoup sexuality as a possibility with a Yen unmasked as safe and gentle but still potent. In this regard, Megan sees herself as the Victorian embodiment of purity and moral goodness the "light" woman was supposed to be. Her very presence should assure Yen's eventual Christianization and domestication. This would then erase all the "dark" aspects of Yen's character and, symbolically, the dark aspects of her own sexual desires.

Just as Cheng Huan is spiritually saved by the light of Lucy's virtue (i.e., the almost magical quality Victorians ascribed to virginity) in *Broken Blossoms*, Megan may be able to "convert" Yen in a similar fashion. However, her self-consciousness seems to place her at a disadvantage. Lucy, on the one hand, is completely unconscious of the morally uplifting effect she has on others. Megan, on the other hand, tries much too hard and ends up playing a role. Yen calls her on this, pointing out her hypocrisy.

Megan, at one point, attempts to convert Yen by convincing him not to execute his disloyal concubine Mah-li (Toshia Mori). Incongruously dressed in a silk negligee, Megan seems unsuitably attired for a religious debate as she confronts Yen: "With your superior brain, your culture, how can you be so blind to spiritual greatness?" In mid-conversation, the topic quickly changes. At wit's end, crying, Megan states that her interest extends beyond Mah-li's life to Yen's soul: "We're all of one flesh and blood." Handing her a handkerchief, Yen turns the phrase away from its spiritual meaning and transforms it into a statement about race. Grasping Megan's hand, he asks, "Do you really mean that?" Repulsed and afraid, Megan draws her hand away and brings it defensively up to her throat. The gesture betrays the lie at the heart of her answer, "Of course I do." If Yen can be Megan's dream lover, in conscious life, ironically, the same values that supposedly make her interested in saving Yen force her to look at him as the enemy and an inferior being, as a threat to her virtue, in other words, the "purity of her race."

The narrative bind is classically paradoxical. If Megan is to save Yen, she must prove to him that she is not racist. However, to prove she is not racist, she must become involved with Yen romantically, and since this would taint her morally, she then could not save him. Yen, after all, represents temptation for Megan. He, because of his racial difference, symbolizes all those passions Megan has been taught to deny in herself and project onto racial others, who are then despised for those very qualities.

Recognizing the fundamental link between Megan's religion, her racism, and her sexual frigidity, Yen sets out to remove with one stroke all the obstacles that separate him from her. He remarks, laughingly, to Jones (Walter Connolly), his American assistant, "I'm going to convert a missionary." Megan agrees to be held hostage for Mah-li's loyalty. However, Yen proves himself the better judge of character. Mah-li betrays them both and runs off, leaving Yen alone and defeated.

Again dressed in her tattered wedding dress, Megan goes to Yen's quarters to "accept her fate," which she, of course, presumes to mean having to have sex with her captor. However, at this point, Yen strikes a final blow to Megan's preconceptions. Not only is she wrong about Mah-li's innocence but she is also quite wrong about Yen's presumed sadistic sexual desires. In fact, she seems to have projected her own sexual passion onto Yen, who has loved her in a presumably less carnal fashion. Insulted by the implications that he would force himself on Megan, Yen says, "Do you think General Yen could accept anything that the heart did not freely give? It was your life that you put up as a forfeit for Mah-li's loyalty." Yen goes on to throw Megan's racism in her face: "Oh torture, real torture, is to be despised by someone you love."

Here, the film, cynical about religion, becomes quite sentimental, in the most characteristically Hollywood fashion, about romance. Romantic love replaces Victorian morality, but it remains sexless, mystical, and transcendent. After so eloquently arguing against racism and prudery, *The Bitter Tea of General Yen* maintains racial divisions and denies sexuality by leaving Yen's love for Megan and her passion for him unconsummated.

If *The Bitter Tea of General Yen* meekly critiques the captivity narrative's fundamental racism, the film does nothing to diminish its sexism. As in the most traditional captivity stories, Megan here is severely punished for straying from male authority. In fact, her odyssey takes her to a point at which she comes to understand her true "place" as a woman—kneeling, subservient, passive, and broken by her own passion. By converting her from her missionary calling, based on a genuine sense of self-worth and confidence, Yen steals Megan's spirit.

In this respect, *The Bitter Tea of General Yen* uses Megan's own sexuality to perpetuate the sexist theory of an essential female masochism, a need to express sexuality through passivity and submission. Romance becomes the key to keeping women at men's feet. A fantasy of Asian sexuality, for the white male viewer, continues to be a fantasy of the domination of men over masochistic female slaves—perhaps even more insidious here because of the implication that the slave thrives on her bondage.

Rather than being outraged by this projected sadistic fantasy, *The Bitter Tea of General Yen* confirms this as true and proper sexuality for women. The viewer can enjoy the spectacle of Megan's masochism, a confirmation of the sadism and implicit moral inferiority of Asian men, and an affirmation of male dominance all in one fell swoop. Yen's convenient suicide keeps everything on a "spiritual" plane of "romance" far removed from the taint of real relations, actual oppression, and the consequences of interracial sexuality.

However, even though the film salvages those very values it supposedly despises and resurrects sacrifice, transcendence, and female masochism in the name of "true romance," *The Bitter Tea of General Yen* also leaves unresolved contradictions in its wake. After all, the film brings to light, and, at times seems almost to affirm, those things captivity narratives have for centuries denied—that there may be another side to the coin. If nothing else, *The Bitter Tea of General Yen* allows for the possibility of human feeling that may transcend racial divisions, that female sexuality may have a power of its own (outside the dark vision of rape, torture, and captivity projected onto men of color), that another culture may not simply be seductive or threatening but may have its own truth and beauty.

Taking *The Bitter Tea of General Yen* in parts rather than as a whole supports this. Megan's carnal dream of rape and salvation at the hands of the same man—her captor and suitor—highlights her sexuality in a way that makes Yen's speeches on love and the beauty of the moon seem laughably tame. The dark side of male sexuality is really not at issue here; rather the nature and power of female sexuality poses the genuine problems within the film. If nothing else, *The Bitter Tea of General Yen* voices the power of Megan's passion, her freedom to desire what her culture teaches is the most despicable degradation imaginable, sex with a man of another race, even if that freedom is eventually contained by affirmations of female masochism and allusions to the transcendence of true love.

Although the film pulls its punches by emasculating Yen through a suicide he sees as the necessary end to his romance with Megan and by leaving Megan on her knees and speechless at the film's conclusion, the ability of the fantasy to completely recoup those other moments, those other possibilities, seems limited.

Shanghai Express: Textual Excesses and the Captivity Tale

Although the majority of captivity stories focus on the imprisonment of a single individual (usually a woman) and her eventual redemption, many captivity tales deal with a group under siege eventually taken prisoner. In these tales, the relations among the captives generally take precedence over any deep exploration of the victim-captor relationship. The victims in these tales usually act as a microcosm for the culture at large, and the narrative functions to set up a dichotomy between what can be included within the group, society, or civilization and what must remain outside it as alien, dangerous, or savage. Like the captivity stories that highlight a single female protagonist, these tales also generally use female characters as tokens of exchange between these two opposing racial, cultural, and moral universes. The female characters' loyalties remain central to the ideological work of the text and to the rationalization of white, male, Anglo-Saxon dominance.

However, because these narratives are more diffuse dramatically, they employ different strategies to voice and defang the potentially threatening ideological contradictions that they conjure up. The social dynamics within the captive group serves to make concrete many of the contradictions involving race, class, nation, and gender treated by the film. In many of these tales, the captor simply functions as an unidimensional embodiment of the "other" as a threat to the definition of "free" and "equitable" American society as white and male dominated. The points contended within the narrative, that is, those elements of moral ambiguity surrounding these ideological contradictions, often find their expression within the captive group rather than in its interactions with the villain. As a consequence, these captivity tales deal with the highly problematic "purification" not of an individual soul but of an entire heterogeneous society that must be cleansed of what the film marks as "excessive" ideologically in terms of race, class, or gender.

In one such Hollywood narrative involving Asians, *Shanghai Express* (1932), directed by Josef von Sternberg, the "excessive" (morally, narratively, stylistically, as well as ideologically) wages war with those formal elements that seek to keep the dramatic and visual depiction of racial and sexual relationships within the parameters of classical Hollywood realism. A product of the uncertainties and social crises of the depression, *Shanghai Express*, like *The Bitter Tea of General Yen*, titillates the viewer with the allure of forbidden sexuality, exotic adventure, "Oriental" opulence, and decadent self-indulgence at a time when the promised security of the bourgeois home seemed like an empty illusion for the majority in the audience taunted by the very real possibilities of bankruptcy, unemployment, domestic strife, and complete moral and physical ruin. The pleasure of purging the "excessive," then, comes at a higher price than at other times when mainstream American society stands on firmer economic ground. Like *The Bitter Tea of General Yen, Shanghai Express* allows potentially disturbing ambiguities to stand. A sense of distance and irony prevails over the certainties of narrative closure.

As an auteur, von Sternberg has long been associated with a particular visual style and sensibility in which the mise-en-scène and cinematography (particularly in its pictorialization of Marlene Dietrich's body) have a force of their own, often seemingly at odds with the ostensible point of the plot. Costume, makeup, lighting, set design, spatial composition, gesture, figure movement, and camera positioning all seem to open the film to flights of fancy denied by the actual development of the story. This disjunction between the visuals and the plot allows for a number of potentially subversive readings tacitly sanctioned by these excesses. In his article, "*The Shanghai Gesture*: The Exotic and the Melodrama," Frank Krutnik sees this aspect of von Sternberg's style as part of the operation of the "exotic melodrama," a "hyper-charging of the visual field" in which the foreign becomes not only part of the film's stylistic virtuosity but part of the ideological working of the film itself.[7]

Like many of von Sternberg's other films set in distant lands, *Shanghai Express* can be looked at as an "exotic melodrama" in which style and narrative are sometimes at odds ideologically. In *Shanghai Express*, for example, the apparent narrative interest lies in the relationship between Shanghai Lily (Marlene Dietrich) and Captain Donald "Doc" Harvey (Clive Brook). Once engaged to be married, Lily and Doc have been separated for more than five years because of Doc's jealous reaction to a ploy Lily had used to test his love. They meet, by chance, on the Shanghai Express. Lily has become a "coaster," a vamp who travels along the China coast looking for men to victimize, and Doc has thrown himself into his work as a British medical officer. The main plot line revolves around their continuing romantic misunderstandings.

When they become captives of the Eurasian warlord Henry Chang (Warner Oland), Lily offers herself to save Doc. However, rather than feeling grateful, Doc misinterprets Lily's actions and assumes that she really does want to run off with Chang. With some help from the Reverend Mr. Carmichael (Lawrence Grant), who encourages Doc to look at romantic love and religious faith as similar, Captain Harvey finally acknowledges Lily's sincerity, and the couple is united at the film's conclusion.

On the surface, *Shanghai Express* appears to operate like many similar captivity narratives: a woman, who exerts her own independence, is threatened by a nonwhite captor. Through the travails of her capture, she expiates the sin of her initial disregard for the rules of the white, bourgeois patriarchy and can only then in the end be reunited with her white love. However, this simple plot structure proves to be merely the skeleton for the complications arising from a mise-en-scène that seems to take on a life of its own, at odds with the narrative.

Often, the romance between Lily and Doc appears to be distanced. The film plays with an implicit, cynical disregard for the conventional equation of heterosexual romance with religious salvation. Although Lily and Doc appear to be faithless skeptics who find themselves

Figure 7.   Shanghai Lily (Marlene Dietrich) and Doc (Clive Brook) more at odds with each other than with their captor, the Chinese warlord Henry Chang (Warner Oland), seated between them. Still from Shanghai Express *(1932) courtesy of the Museum of Modern Art/Film Stills Archive.*

through the religion of love sanctified by the Reverend Mr. Carmichael, the actors' exaggerated gestures that define their relationship—Dietrich's self-conscious poses, her wide-eyed but impassive countenance, Brook's stiff, phlegmatic posturings—indicate an "excess" that works in conjunction with these other factors to offer the jaded, depression era viewer the possibility of another sort of "escapism" beyond the parameters of the usual captivity formula.

The Ship of Fools

Writing on *Shanghai Express*, Elliot Rubenstein observes:

In its structure, the film embodies the ancient motif of the *Narrenschiff*, the Ship of Fools, which makers of motion pictures—pictures of motion—have for obvious reasons found congenial, whatever the particular mode of transportation in question. (It may at first seem peculiar to think that *Stagecoach* and *Shanghai Express* belong to a single narrative mode, but, in this sense, they do.)[8]

Actually, the analogy drawn between *Stagecoach* and *Shanghai Express* is apropos. However, unlike Ford's straightforward treatment of the myth of the American West, von Sternberg's conception of the mysteries of the "Orient" never really shakes off its threatening allure. Euroamerican civilization's symbolic descent into the "hell" of war-torn China, then, is also a journey into a peculiar sort of paradise. While *Stagecoach* can quite unproblematically kill off both internal "criminal" threats as well as the external challenge the Native Americans pose to dominant American ideology, *Shanghai Express* cannot dismiss the "other" with quite as much certainty.

However, despite these differences, *Stagecoach* and *Shanghai Express* share more than the narrative device of the ship of fools. Both films offer stories in which a "fallen woman" is saved by love, romance rises above social prejudice, people are not what they seem, and sacrifices are made to prove the superiority of Western civilization over heathen savagery. The stagecoach and the Shanghai Express train move through the hostile territory of "otherness," through a land peopled by those Hollywood posits as different racially, ethnically, morally, and sexually. In both films, racial, ethnic, and national differences are coded as immoral, duplicitous, barbaric, and dangerous to the precarious existence of white Christian civilization represented by the group on its journey. In their encounter with the savage, this microcosm of Western culture cleanses itself of any excessive, forbidden desires or moral trespasses to survive.

Both films equate the process through which the corruptions of Western civilization are uncovered and expelled with the purifying properties of romantic love. In each case, the "fallen woman," herself equated with the savage land through which the vehicle of civilization passes, is saved and rejoins the civilization that shunned her. In each film, sacrifice marks this redemption within both the principal plot and the subplot. In *Stagecoach*, Dallas (Claire Trevor) offers to sacrifice her happiness in exchange for Ringo's (John Wayne) well-being. In *Shanghai Express*, Lily offers herself to Chang to save Doc's eyesight. In both films, sacrifice delivers an acceptably "pure" heroine, rid of the taint of her potentially threatening promiscuity, to be recuperated within the patriarchy through the hero's embrace. Implicitly, Western civilization triumphs. Heterosexual romantic love, as conceived by Hollywood, confirms its right to hold white America above other races and cultures because of its unquestionable moral purity and emotional sincerity.

However, whereas *Stagecoach* neatly ties up all its various narrative threads through its denouement, *Shanghai Express* allows many of its narrative complications to remain problematic. Instead of providing a conclusion that affirms the moral triumph of the West through romance, *Shanghai Express* permits many of its "fools" to continue their deceptions, to revel in their masquerades, and to be swallowed up by Hollywood's Orient. The certainty of *Stagecoach*'s ending, in which Ringo and Dallas ride off into the sunset (albeit to Mexico rather than into a thoroughly transformed and forgiving America), has a visual weight not found in *Shanghai Express*.

Dressed in the vampish black gown, veil, and feather boa she wore at the film's beginning, Lily's final gesture is to take her lover's riding crop and gloves, the emblems of his stature within the male world of military honor and privilege, and slowly let them slip from her fingers to the ground. Although the narrative seems to assure the viewer that Lily no longer poses a castrating threat to the patriarchy, the mise-en-scène of these final images visually indicates something quite different. The power of Shanghai and Dietrich's body as spectacle, particularly this last gesture of feminine control over male privilege, seems to belie the initial ideological certainty of the narrative's conclusion.

The Captivity

Even before Chang and his agents actually take the passengers prisoner on the Shanghai Express, they already appear to be captives of the film's claustrophobic mise-en-scène. When Shanghai Lily is first introduced, she is enshrouded in her black cloak and veil; her mouth and a hint of her blond hair peek out from the shadow cast over her face to mark her race and sexual allure. Similarly, Hui Fei (Anna May Wong), Lily's Asian foil, is first shown emerging from her boxlike sedan chair. Her back to the camera, she languidly moves to board the train, then stops to turn her face briefly to the camera, before disappearing into the confines of the train car.

Associated with the mysterious exoticism of China from the outset, Lily and Hui Fei are both depicted visually as enshrouded in the decadent opulence of that world. Ambivalently presented as captives or as spiders ready to lure others into their web, they both function as tokens of the potential dangers as well as the possible forbidden pleasures associated with their sexuality. When the "respectable" passengers refuse to share a compartment with Hui Fei, Lily, finding a kindred spirit, moves in. Lily pulls down the shade, keeping the camera at a distance, creating a vague sense that their association may be somehow illicit.

The two exchange few words during the course of the film. Rather, their relationship emerges almost purely through mise-en-scène and cinematography, almost as an aspect of the train's decor. Costume,

Figure 8.   Lily and Hui Fei (Anna May Wong) trapped in a world of their own by the train's claustrophobic interior, framed and on display for the film viewer's visual pleasure. Still from Shanghai Express *courtesy of the Museum of Modern Art/Film Stills Archive.*

makeup, lighting, gesture, framing, and placement in space combine to hint at an unstated depth to their association that may be linked to their shared shadowy vocation, to their entanglement within the forbidding sensuality of their environment, or to an even more profound intimacy.

When Doc escorts Lily to her compartment, Hui Fei looks in from outside. Lily puts a jazz record on the phonograph at screen center as Doc moves off, passing between the two women. Hui Fei moves closer to Lily. She glances after Doc, then closes the compartment's window, sealing them off. Hui Fei, spatially and in terms of the organization of the gaze within this scene, positions herself as a rival to Doc, as the "dark" intimate of the sexually ambivalent Lily.[9] "It took more than one man to change my name to Shanghai Lily" hints at a disregard for the confines of traditional, heterosexual relationships, and Lily's intimacy with Hui Fei, dressed in sleek Chinese satin gowns that reveal her long, thin, boyish figure, points to another possible challenge to Doc's ability to "handle" Lily sexually.

Lily, the Caucasian blond always dressed in black, and Hui Fei, the brunette Asian always dressed in light colors, visually function as mirror images, pictorially complementing each another. Mr. Carmichael succinctly places them in the same category: "One of them is yellow and the other one is white, but both their souls are rotten." He assumes both are on the train "in search of victims," that is, in league to strengthen themselves by ruining men. Their common purpose, their castrating potential, and their intimacy all point to the threat of a lesbian romance as the structural foil to Doc's love affair with Lily.

When Chang eventually surfaces as the villain in *Shanghai Express*, he further complicates this relationship triangle. Rather than functioning as the clear antagonist to Doc's protagonist, Chang acts, in the sexually charged guise of the sadistic Asian-Eurasian potentate, as the potential violator not only of Hui Fei and Lily but of the naive and cocksure Doc as well. Exactly who must save whom from castration or rape and for what motive remains a question.

Chang's uncertain identity seems to fuel this aspect of the fantasy. He wears elegantly tailored Western suits and has an almost effeminate polish. At one point, a brash American on the train asks, "I can't make head or tail out of you, Mr. Chang. Are you Chinese or are you white or what are you?" Chang's response to the question of his racial identity puzzles the American, since the mixed-race Chang claims not to be proud of his "white blood." "You look more like a white man to me. . . . What future is there in being a Chinaman?" he queries. "You're born, eat your way through a handful of rice, and you die. What a country! Let's have a drink."

The puzzle of Chang's racial and ethnic identity seems to spill over to include his sexual identity. Chang stands as the emblem of the ideological question of difference. Neither Asian nor white, homosexual nor heterosexual, his potential threat comes as much from his existence outside the distinct, hierarchical boundaries on which Euroamerican society is based as it does from the fact that he is a vicious warlord. It is the uncertainty and the potential duplicity of Chang's existence, the possibility that rigid social distinctions based on race or gender are essentially meaningless, that creates Chang's disturbing allure.

When he finally reveals himself to be a rebellious warlord, moreover, the link between his sexuality and these other aspects of his ambiguous identity resurface. Chang brands a German opium peddler, who had been rude to him on the train and uncooperative during captivity, with a hot iron poker. Thus, instead of pursuing his sexual interest in Hui Fei, whom he had earlier attempted to rape, Chang's first victim turns out to be a man. Given the number of remakes of DeMille's *The Cheat*, this branding could be seen not only as a formulaic indication of Chang's peculiarly sadistic racial otherness but also as a symbolic replacement for rape with the invalid smuggler serving as the feminized, castrated Westerner fallen prey to the perverted Asian male. His threat to blind Doc also seems to have similar sexual overtones, particularly given Freud's interpretation of the myth of Oedipus, associating blindness with castration. Lily, in fact, takes on the role usually associated with the hero in captivity tales when she makes every attempt to rescue Doc from this "fate worse than death."

As Lily and Doc vie to save each other from Chang, Hui Fei enters the equation. She is sequestered in a shadowy upstairs room filled with fine webbing that obscures and softens the camera's gaze. It envelops her, both trapping Hui Fei and, conversely, giving her a mysterious power by visually conjuring up an image similar to that of a spider in its web. Thus, it is unclear whether Hui Fei will play the role of victim or victimizer within this associatively charged space.

The following morning Hui Fei reemerges from the depot, her hair disheveled, her gown in disarray. Lily follows the obviously violated Hui Fei into their train compartment, grabs her, and stops her before she can unsheath a dagger she has pulled from her baggage. Lily warns, "Don't do anything foolish," implying that Hui Fei's sexual violation would lead her to suicide. However, whether Hui Fei plans to use the dagger on herself or Chang remains unclear at this point. Given Hollywood's characteristic ambivalence about the inner virtue or genuine corruption of the "fallen" woman as well as its frequently voiced suspicion that the Asian woman is essentially a predatory "dragon lady," the depiction of Hui Fei with the blade of her dagger glistening in her hand may again conjure up more potent images of a potential vanquisher rather than victim.

Hui Fei, whom Lily may have saved from suicide, in her turn saves Lily from Chang's grasp. As Chang bends over to light his cigarette from the brazier he used to brand the opium dealer and threaten Doc, Hui Fei appears behind him as a shadow silhouetted against a gauze curtain. She stabs Chang in the back twice and then slowly backs away toward the doorway at the rear of the frame. In a daze, she appears at the depot's door and tells Doc, "You better get her out of there. I've just killed Chang." Thus, although she originally appeared to be a threat to Doc's hold over Lily, the violated Hui Fei becomes the instrument of their eventual reunion. However, Hui Fei still remains a potentially disturbing, sexually ambivalent figure, both vulnerable and vengeful, potent and drained of affect, self-possessed and thoroughly devastated.

When Lily returns to the train, her relationship with Hui Fei loses much of its erotic edge. Her violation has stripped her of any ambiguity associated with her gender. Moreover, as Lily has been converted through her prayers and nearly total self-sacrifice to the religion of heterosexual love, the potential threat, as well as allure, of the women's eroticized relationship has been purged from the film. Upset by Doc's continued cold treatment, Lily snaps at Hui Fei, "I don't know if I should be grateful to you or not." Hui Fei, looking down at a game of solitaire, answers phlegmatically, "It's of no consequence. I didn't do it for you. Death cancelled his debt to me." Thus, any question that Hui Fei would attempt to sacrifice herself to free Lily fades as Lily's love for Doc emerges as the corrective to any implicit lesbian relationship.[16]

Although Hui Fei is marginalized within the film, she remains part of that ideologically disturbing "excess" in *Shanghai Express* that can too easily be dismissed as part of a brilliant, but empty visual facade. Hui Fei functions as part of the exotic promise of Shanghai; she embodies its sensuality, beauty, and freedom to indulge any desire. Her existence hints, too, at the possibility that the film's "happy ending" may itself be simply another facet of that surface, drawn from the captivity story's usual insistence on racial divisions and the sanctity of heterosexual love.

Although *The Bitter Tea of General Yen* and *Shanghai Express* are quite different renderings of the captivity tale, looking at them together underscores their similarities. Perhaps one reason for the staying power of these narratives can be found in their ability to voice resistance, to allow for at least a moment the possibility that women may be right to demand independent thought and action, that other races may not be inferior, that other ways of life may have a right to exist. Here, the historical circumstances that shaped Hollywood discourses on Asia during the depression seem to determine the nature and force of this resistance to the white, male, middle-class norm, as well as the violence with which this whispered opposition is eventually hushed.

4

Passport Seductions

Lady of the Tropics

One of the more enduring aspects of the Western vision of Asia involves the East's supposedly intrinsic seductiveness. Associated with material opulence, moral laxity, sensuality, cultural decadence, and exotic beauty, this seductiveness implies a peculiar spiritual danger and often hidden threat to the Westerner. Edward W. Said's description in *Orientalism* of the late-eighteenth-century European idea of the "Orient" as characterized by "sensuality, promise, terror, sublimity, idyllic pleasure, intense energy"[1] still has a certain currency. In fact, this contradictory European perception of Asia frequently surfaces in the Hollywood interracial romance. *The Cheat, Broken Blossoms, The Bitter Tea of General Yen*, and *Shanghai Express*, for example, all include elements of this dangerously seductive aspect of Hollywood's fictitious Orient.

Feminized in the Western imagination, the entire continent becomes an exotic, beckoning woman, who can both satisfy the male Westerner's forbidden desires and ensnare him in an unyielding web of deceit. In her essay, "Gender and Culture of Empire: Toward a Feminist Ethnography of the Cinema," Ella Shohat notes,

> The Orient as a metaphor for sexuality is encapsulated by the recurrent figure of the veiled woman. The inaccessibility of the veiled woman, mirroring the mystery of the Orient itself, requires a process of Western unveiling for comprehension. . . . It is this process of exposing the female Other, of literally denuding her, which comes to allegorize the Western

masculinist power of possession, that she, as a metaphor for her land, becomes available for Western penetration and knowledge.[2]

The sadistic desire to penetrate and expose comes from a deep-rooted sexual anxiety. The fear springs from a desire or belief that Asia will entice, hypnotize, entrap, and suffocate the Western traveler, who will masochistically give up his own identity to be engulfed by what Freudians might describe as a metaphoric womb-tomb. From this perspective, Asia, as the emblem of Western otherness, becomes associated with the repressed desire to escape life, to crawl back into the womb, to obliterate the self, to die.

In interracial tales of seduction, the attractions of Asian sexuality, in fact, are usually offset by an inevitable tragic ending. The Asian seducer or seductress generally dies, and the moral lapse of the Westerner finds some suitable expiation. In Hollywood seduction tales, a Eurasian character is often cast in the role of the seducer or seductress. Thus, a single character can embody both an East-West battle of morality and the exotic sensuality associated with these sorts of stories while, simultaneously, compounding the element of deceit involved with these tales through the possibility of hiding a "tainted" racial identity.

Indeed, Eurasian characters have been Hollywood favorites since the silent era for some obvious reasons: they allow white actors and actresses to portray Asian characters with a minimum of made-up distortion to their own features; they provide the opportunity to deal with forbidden sexuality without the added threat an actual Asian actor or completely Asian character may pose to the racial status quo; and they provide an increased complexity to what may otherwise be a less interesting, more unidimensional, Hollywood character type, allowing the performer portraying the Eurasian an added element of theatrical affectation. Thus, these roles allow white performers to create their own conception of an Asian character, to produce their own fantasy of the Orient, without totally donning what has been called "yellow face" or "Asian drag." Eurasian characters (as a rule played by Caucasian performers) appear in virtually every sort of interracial romantic narrative Hollywood has produced.[3]

Eugene Franklin Wong points out in *On Visual Media Racism* that most Hollywood Eurasians have Caucasian fathers and Asian mothers,[4] symbolically naturalizing the Western male's sexual access to the Asian female. However, any given character's association with one racial identity or the other varies according to the needs of the narrative. An association with an Asian heritage often links the Eurasian character to a sinister involvement with the occult dangers of Asia, for example, *Limehouse Blues* (1934). However, Hollywood has also articulated Eurasians' pride in Asia as a positive desire to help their Asian fellow countrymen, as, for example, *The Inn of the Sixth Happiness* (1958).

As a rule, however, Eurasian characters aspire to blot out the taint of their Asian heritage through a forced acceptance by white society. Because they often appear in narratives in which their true racial identity remains hidden or somehow threatening and suspect, they resemble the African American character type Donald Bogle describes as the "tragic mulatto" in *Toms, Coons, Mulattoes, Mammies, and Bucks: An Interpretive History of Blacks in American Films*.[5] Hollywood presents these mixed-race characters as "tragic" because of their desire to be assimilated into the dominant white culture, which proves to be impossible in the narrative. This leads them invariably to an unhappy end. Even if they embrace their African American heritage, they are still forced to come to grips with their debased social position within a white-defined and dominated culture. Despite prohibitions against miscegenation, Hollywood treated this theme twice in two versions of one of the most critically discussed melodramas of the studio era, *Imitation of Life* (John Stahl, 1934; Douglas Sirk, 1959).[6]

Like the Hollywood mulattoes, Eurasian characters' tragedy lies in their desire to be accepted into white society and to put aside their vilified racial heritage. In terms of the dominant ideology, it is quite understandable that these characters should want to be classified as "white" in a world in which any other racial definition brings with it an unwelcome stigma. However, the possibility that a mixed-race character could "pass" for white in a society that defines itself in terms of absolute boundaries between the races represents a significant threat. In Hollywood, this threat surfaces in narratives that deal with Eurasian characters' sexual involvement with Caucasian characters, who may or may not know about their lovers' racial background.

Shanghai (James Flood, 1935) provides a clear example. The Russo-Manchurian hero, Dimitri Kozloff (Charles Boyer), suffers tragic consequences when he hides his Eurasian identity from his fiancée (Loretta Young). Characteristically, *Shanghai* presents an ambivalent picture of the "passing" Eurasian as both sympathetic and destructive. The ending, although somewhat inconclusive, favors an "unhappy" reading (the couple, although reunited, agree not to marry and repeat the situation that led to Kozloff's mother's suicide). Also, although the film generally presents Kozloff in a sympathetic light, the incipient threat of the Eurasian who decides to "pass" is felt during scenes in which Kozloff takes his revenge on the white society in Shanghai that rejects him.

Even in narratives that do not feature Eurasians "passing," Hollywood seems to emphasize the natal duplicity of these mixed-race characters. One plot formula features the Eurasian character trying to escape from both Asia and his or her "Asianness" by tricking the authorities into granting a passport to the West. Usually, this involves the seduction of an influential Westerner, who unwittingly agrees to aid in the plot. In these morality tales, the Eurasian's identity crisis becomes intertwined with a struggle between "true" love and the "treachery" of seduction. Whatever the eventual outcome (either a tragic death or separation or a "happy" heterosexual coupling), romantic love wins out over the ability to define the self in a racist society.

As tales of escape, these films appeal to moviegoers who enjoy exotic fictions in order to flee from what the protagonists so desperately want to escape to, namely, the quotidian life of Western society. As such, they allow the viewer an imaginative holiday, while ideologically affirming that the West is quite naturally where everyone (represented by the films' protagonists) wishes to be.

Beyond this, these seduction tales featuring Eurasian characters offer the opportunity for the exploration of issues relating to race, paternity, the patriarchal organization of the family, and the containment of female sexuality. As mentioned above, Eugene Franklin Wong has noticed that most Eurasian characters in Hollywood have a white father and Asian mother. Generally, these parents do not appear in the film. Their romances and their relationship with their children are presented in only the broadest of outlines; details remain vague. Since marriages between Caucasian men and Asian women are assumed to be rare or extremely volatile if a legitimate marriage exists at all, the Eurasian character takes on the onus usually associated with illegitimate children in Western literature. They threaten the organized continuation of patriarchal descent; they embody a suspect morality; they inherit a mysterious seductive sexuality that is seen as difficult to contain within the boundaries of patriarchal domesticity. Thus, these tales provide the opportunity to explore the edges of the patriarchal system, trying its limits, playing with the dangerous pleasures of illicit sexuality.

By looking at the ways in which these contradictory sentiments are orchestrated in one such film, *Lady of the Tropics* (John Conway, 1939), the ideological complexities of many of these treatments of race, class, nation, and sexuality can be explored. Behind an apparently clear moral vision that sympathizes with victims of racism while accepting racial stratification and that acknowledges the temptations of seduction for profit while upholding the sacrosanct place of romantic love within Hollywood cinema, this film actually offers potentially more disturbing fantasies of the penetrability of the supposedly inviolate barriers of race and class.

Deceit, Seduction, and Escape in *Lady of the Tropics*

A great deal of feminist film criticism examines the way in which Hollywood has represented female characters as mysterious, deceitful, and dangerous. In *film noir*,[7] for example, the heart of the mystery unraveled by the narrative almost invariably involves a duplicitous villainess. The mystery of the woman, her morals and her identity, propels these plots. At the conclusion of the narrative, the woman is unmasked as something other than what she seems and is either punished or rehabilitated by the hero into a "good" woman, an open book unable to do further harm.

Scholars using a psychoanalytic model of film pleasure have interpreted these plots as Oedipal fantasies involving the association of the female body with male fears of castration. Indeed, any group, separated and oppressed, will likely be viewed with suspicion by the dominant order. Guilt and paranoia intermingle to create fantasies of an evil genius lying under the servile smile of an underling. Hollywood's pale and yielding women in distress often turn out to be treacherous killers and thieves.

When race and class are added as further elements of difference in the enigmatic female, other complications must be factored in. Overdetermined in the film, the duplicity associated with femininity can be explained away with references to class or race. Female viewers can be drawn in to look down upon the suspect woman as hiding a working-class or subproletarian past or as "passing" for white. Hollywood's condensation of these multiple differences into one character does not show the connections among race, class, and gender in American society, but, rather, obscures them. Gender, racial, or class oppression do not combine to create a picture of the victim of American hypocrisy and inequality; rather, the combination hides social injustice under the cloak of a mysterious, feminine, nonwhite identity.

In *Lady of the Tropics*, the duplicity Hollywood generally associates with the threat of sexual difference seductive women pose to men is displaced onto racial difference. In this case, the Eurasian siren embodies a threat to racial boundaries and traditional morality. The Eurasian woman, when she is a simple, passive object of spectacle and speculation, is harmless. However, when she asserts her own desires, she becomes the agent of social havoc and moral ruin. Although her racial difference is highlighted in the film, the construction of her gender difference seems to take on all the trappings usually associated with the femme fatale in Hollywood seduction fantasies. Race, in this case, serves as another ideological rationalization of a fantasy of female duplicity.

The viewer first is introduced to Eurasians and their peculiar problems through a split identification with Bill Carey (Robert Taylor), the object of the seduction, and Father Antoine (Ernest Cossart), the voice of moral authority in the film. Even before Carey's tale of seduction begins, Father Antoine sets the moral tone of the film when he meets the yacht owned by the millionaire father of Carey's girlfriend as it sails into Saigon harbor. One of the passengers comments on a mixed-race child accompanying Father Antoine: "I adore half-castes. They're so vicious and fascinating." Father Antoine replies: "No, no, they're not vicious. Somehow, they remind me of, well, flying fish. Very harmless. Born to the water, they spend half their lives trying to soar above it, only to fall back again into the sea and die there."[8] He continues with his sympathetic assessment of these tragic Eurasians. He seems to put the blame on French colonialism for "creating" but not "accepting" their mixed-race children.

However, along with the apparent compassion voiced by this clerical representative of Western morality, the film offers a contradictory view that supports the idea that Eurasians are "vicious," or at least suspect, deceitful, cunning, and amoral. Father Antoine's young companion, caught stealing a scarf for his mother, returns the item with apologies only to steal it again as Father Antoine and the passengers set off for shore. Not surprised by his young friend's lack of scruples, Father Antoine seems superciliously to recognize an innate immorality among the Eurasians that he does nothing to rectify. Rationalizing their behavior as a "natural" part of their genetic inferiority, he allows the viewers to condemn their race along with their morals, while maintaining a "Christian" sense of pity.

Lady of the Tropics, here, seems to have absorbed a certain discourse on Eurasians found in French colonial fiction. Milton Osborne has noted in his essay, "Fear and Fascination in the Tropics: A Reader's Guide to French Fiction on Indo-China," that Eurasian characters, as marginal in most of the literature as they were in colonial society, fit a certain mold when they are represented in fiction:

> Up to the Second World War, the pseudoscientific view of the inferiority of Asians to Europeans then prevailing among the French in Indo-China sustained the idea that Eurasian "half-castes" were necessarily—that is, biologically—less capable than those whose European blood had not been degraded by mixture with a local source.[9]

However, Hollywood goes beyond the simple reiteration of French colonial discourses. The Indochinese setting allows the text to show America's superiority to both Europe and Asia. Just as *Lady of the Tropics* inevitably upholds Father Antoine's moral interdictions against interracial romance, it also on another level valorizes Bill Carey's "American" qualities of liberalism, open-mindedness, honest emotions, fairness, and an endearing naiveté that distinguish him from the Asian, Eurasian, and European characters that surround him.

Indeed, Bill only reluctantly gives in to temptation. In fact, it is Dolly Harrison (Mary Taylor), Bill's wealthy, reckless girlfriend, who insists that Father Antoine take them all to meet his Eurasian "flying fish" up close. He introduces them to two, Pierre Delaroch (Joseph Schildkraut), a wealthy social climber, and the object of his romantic attentions, Manon DeVargnes (Hedy Lamarr), a glamorous, former temple dancer who appears to be entirely French. (A light-skinned, brunette Austrian, Hedy Lamarr first achieved notoriety for a brief nude scene in the Czech film *Extase* [*Ecstasy*, 1932] and, thereafter, was usually associated with sensual, foreign seductresses.)

From her first close-up in *Lady of the Tropics*, Manon is coded as "glamorous" in accordance with the Hollywood conventions of the day. She appears in slightly soft-focus, light softened by pale shadows, her facial contours offset by a dark veil over her hair in contrast to the white skin revealed by her low-cut Parisian-style gown. Beginning with this initial glamour shot, close-ups of Manon punctuate the film, freezing her face as a specular object, that is, the veiled Asian woman. Hats and headdresses of various sorts play a prominent role in *Lady of the Tropics'* narrative and mise-en-scène for this very reason—the hat veils the wearer's identity, adds mystery to a half-revealed face, and acts as a fetishistic embodiment of feminine desirability and suspected malevolence.

With the establishment of Bill's own moral weaknesses (he has lost his money and now survives by drifting from one heiress to the next, charming them with marriage prospects in exchange for room and board), Manon and melodramatically fortuitous circumstances make his seduction a rather simple matter. *Lady of the Tropics* is typical of many seduction fantasies in that the seduction itself forms only a small portion of the overall development of the narrative. Given the ease of the seduction, the rest of the film takes up the possible reasons for it. The narrative enigma shifts from "Will Bill leave Dolly for Manon?" to "Is Manon more interested in Bill or a passport with a visa enabling her to go to France?" Romantic love is pitted against the desire to redefine racial identity and be assimilated into the white world. Instead of focusing on the completely love-smitten Bill, the plot takes up Manon's moral dilemma as a Eurasian woman in a white, male-defined world with Father Antoine's ambivalently sympathetic and critical opening speech haunting the depiction of Manon's involute romantic machinations.

The text shows Manon as self-consciously using her sexuality to exit Vietnam. As a consequence, she is depicted as duplicitous, since each romantic liaison is entered into with escape as an ulterior motive. Delaroch, himself Eurasian, knows this. When he cannot outwit Manon with his false promise of getting her a passport in exchange for her love, he states this explicitly: "The truth is not in you. You have the face of the West, but your soul is full of Eastern smoke. . . . We both belong to that nonrace with two heads. You dream that a passport will remove one of them by magic and leave you French, completely French. Stop dreaming, Manon."

Even though Manon has bid Bill "good-night forever" on a dock in Saigon, her seductive powers seem to have worked too well, and Bill pursues Manon on the boat she has taken on her journey to Angkor Wat to marry a local potentate. In addition to satisfying the travelogue requirement of Hollywood films set in exotic locales with stock footage of Khmer temples, barefoot dancers dressed in shimmering costumes, gongs, Buddhist monks, and elephants, this journey to the edge of the Cambodian jungle also serves to bind Manon's seductive powers inextricably with Asia and the myth of Oriental opulence.

As the cynosure of a prenuptial ceremony, Manon unquestioningly embodies the essence of what the film posits as the mysterious Orient. She is dressed in a sparkling Hollywood version of a Cambodian royal dancer's costume with a tall pagodalike headdress, upturned sleeves and earrings shaped like little bells. In opposition to the active, rational, and male West, this Hollywood version of Asia is definitely feminine. The supine figure of the seated Manon echoes the pose of a giant stone Buddha in the temple. Her femininity is associated with the apparently irrational religious and marriage rituals in which she takes part, with the natural splendor of the jungle, and with the sensuality of the material wealth that surrounds Manon and adorns her.

Manon represents a sexuality that cannot be contained. Indeed, even after her marriage to Bill, who wins her away from her Khmer fiancé, Manon's sexuality continues to be provocative. As the newlyweds sink deeper into poverty, unable to get a visa to leave because of Delaroch's malicious influence, Manon eventually gives in to Delaroch's plot to exchange sexual favors for a passport. They conspire and send Bill off to work on a rubber plantation. A final foreboding touch is added by the inclusion of a shot of three Vietnamese women, coded as "ugly" by Hollywood standards in native dress, wrapped hair,

Figure 9. In Lady of the Tropics *(1939), Bill Carey (Robert Taylor) is seduced by Manon DeVargnes (Hedy Lamarr), the feminine personification of Hollywood's opulent and mysterious Asia. Still courtesy of the Museum of Modern Art/Film Stills Archive.*

and characteristically darkened teeth from chewing betel. If Manon in Cambodia had represented the opulence and sensuality of Asia, these women symbolize its other, equally mythic aspect—Asia as destitution, squalor, and very unaesthetic despair. Bill winces when Manon tells him they were her schoolmates, reminding him of Manon's racial difference, and a supposedly "ugly" Asian interior hidden behind her apparently French exterior. Once again, racial duality is linked to gender difference. Bill winces because these Vietnamese are women, associated with his wife. Later, when Bill learns of his wife's infidelity, he lashes out, "Go back to your barefoot sisters with their black teeth."

Confronted with Bill's appraisal of her identity as inextricably bound to this dark vision of Asia, Manon, in a Madame Butterfly-like gesture of self-sacrifice, seeks to expiate her sins through her own annihilation. Manon shoots Delaroch, and then shoots herself. Bill hurries to his wife. He forgives her and tries to expedite their escape; however, she dies in his arms before they can use her ill-gotten passport. Father Antoine voices the elegy: "She goes where there is no East or West, and she will be judged by One who alone knows how great or how little her sin." Self-annihilation means the end to her identity crisis and moral dilemmas.

With typical Hollywood ambivalence, the film remains reluctant to assign blame. On the one hand, Manon cannot be blamed for the "sins" of her parents who created her nor can she be blamed for wanting to obliterate her Asian identity, since the film itself presents that identity as "ugly," "pagan," and "immoral." On the other hand, *Lady of the Tropics* never quite assigns complete culpability to French colonialism and racist exclusionism. The film presents Manon as an isolated individual, who makes very particular decisions when faced with moral choices. Sharing certain similarities with other Eurasians in the film, she still never becomes emblematic of a more generalized, institutionalized oppression.

Likewise, her "salvation" is pictured as a personal choice, a tribute to the all-consuming nature of heterosexual romantic love promoted by Hollywood. Indeed, Hollywood's secular religion of heterosexual romance supercedes any Catholic dogma prohibiting homicide or suicide. The camera tracks down from a two shot of Bill with his head buried in Manon's breast to linger on a close-up of Manon's passport, fallen just out of reach of her hand. It reads: "Manon Carey. Nationality— French. Profession—housewife." Ironically, it legitimizes the identity Manon had hoped to attain and that Hollywood takes for granted as both ideal and the norm. It not only officially makes Manon white by legitimizing her French paternity but domesticates her and brings her into the bourgeois fold as Mr. Carey's "housewife." Imaginatively, her death obliterates any challenges to the sanctity of these roles of legitimate daughter and domesticated wife her other Asian, seductively feminine identity might pose. Unable to be both wife and exotic love object, European and Asian, "true" to her nature and "true" to her American husband, Manon must self-destruct. Like similarly ambivalent Hollywood films, *Lady of the Tropics* is both suspicious of and enthralled by female sexuality, appalled and fascinated by interracial sexuality, and unable to reconcile a liberal desire for individual freedom with that racist fear of contamination that rationalizes exclusionism.

5

The Scream of the Butterfly

Madame Butterfly, China Gate, and "The Lady from Yesterday"

"Madame Butterfly" stories are among the most common interracial romances found in Hollywood.[1] In these tales, a Caucasian man, far from home and its morally moderating influences, falls in love with, and often marries, a young girl from another race and culture. He leaves his young bride, and, back in the West, marries another. When he returns, he discovers his nonwhite wife has had a child, whom he and his white wife adopt. Abandoned by her husband, sacrificing her own happiness for the "good" of her child, the cast-off lover kills herself.

This basic tale offers a number of points of identification for the audience. While ostensibly confirming an absolute separation of the races, it also allows for the possibility of assimilation through the adoption of the mixed-race child. Even though the West misunderstands and mistreats those it marks as "different" racially and culturally, the tale takes the West as the norm, subject to moral lapses and blind spots, but still inevitably the victor in any battle for the heart of a woman or a nation.

Although a distance exists between the viewer and the figure of the ignorant, ingenuous, young bride, this character's martyrdom is the focus of the narrative. Her innocent faith in her Western husband counters his callousness and hypocrisy, and it is through her marriage to him that the Butterfly character converts to Western notions of marriage, morality, and the religion of love. Moreover, Butterfly tales ennoble female sacrifices of all sorts. They argue, in support of dominant male notions of the social order, that women can be morally "superior" to men by sacrificing themselves completely for the patriarchy. The tales may state that men are, indeed, insensitive beasts, but, ironically, it is only through total submission to men and complete faith in their superiority that women can fulfill themselves and express a "genuine" (i.e., masochistic) femininity.

The Butterfly character may be a fool, but she represents a spiritually transcendent folly that transforms her into a saint. Although a Western man destroys her, she must submit to the authority he wields because of his race and his gender. The tale offers few other options. The Butterfly becomes a scapegoat for the excesses of men and for the abuses of the West. Thus, she both conjures up uneasy feelings of guilt and purges them through her self-sacrifice, presented as tragic but necessary in most versions of the narrative. Although the West may be insensitive and unfair, the Butterfly's suicide legitimizes its authority by allowing the heroine to martyr herself for its continuing domination.

In Hollywood, the Butterfly character has been Latin, Native American, Polynesian, mulatto, and, of course, Asian. Versions of the Butterfly tale have been set in China (*Toll of the Sea*, 1922), Vietnam (*China Gate*, 1957), Chinatown (*Daughter of the Dragon*, 1931), and, of course, Japan, the setting of the original tale and the preponderance of its successors. (There have even been male versions of the Butterfly—for example, *Limehouse Blues* [1934].) Conveniently, the Butterfly serves not only as a rationalization of American attitudes toward Japan; in her various guises, she also represents the necessary sacrifice of all people of color to assure Western domination. In addition, she provides a model for all women, white and nonwhite. Her example instructs them in their true mission within the Western patriarchy to sacrifice themselves for their men. Romantic love promises compensation for the loss of themselves.

Female sacrifice narratives can be traced back to biblical tales like the story of Ruth, who gives up everything for the sake of her husband who has a culture and religion different from her own. In America, Pocahontas tales, which call for the sacrifice of the woman of color for the sake of white men, have been common. However, the Japanese Madame Butterfly has become the best-known modern manifestation of this type of narrative. In *Japan versus the West: Image and Reality*, Endymion Wilkinson notes,

> In recent centuries the rich tradition of Oriental exoticism took a new form as colonial conquest and rule provided the opportunity in the form of readily available girls, and encouraged Europeans and Americans to think of the West as active and masculine and the East as passive and feminine.[2]

Building on this observation, it can also be argued that Japan became a particularly inviting setting for these stories because it defied Western military and economic encroachments for so long. Even after its forced opening by the United States to trade, Japan remained defiant and beyond the colonial domination of the West. The nation existed as a political affront to the West's notion of itself as innately superior to Asia. As Japan gained in military strength throughout the later decades of the nineteenth century, tragic, interracial love stories set there gained popularity in Europe and America. From this point of view, Japan perhaps "needed" to be trivialized, marginalized, mocked, and emasculated within the Western imagination, and these tales fulfilled that need within popular fiction.

The Butterfly narratives represent Japan as a fragile, powerless woman, who cannot resist the attractions of the West embodied by her American husband, but who self-destructs as a consequence. Although likely a reaction against Japan's growing military power in the later decades of the nineteenth century, these stories continue to be popular, not only because of the West's continuing ambivalent relationship with Japan and the Japanese but also because these tales come to grips with so many other contradictory sentiments surrounding race, sexuality, gender, and ethnicity.

Wilkinson traces Butterfly stories back to the writings of Julien Viaud, a French naval officer who wrote under the pen name of Pierre Loti. His novel, *Madam Chrysanthemum* (*Madame Chrysantheme*, 1887), was inspired by a visit to Nagasaki in 1885. As one of the few ports isolationist Japan kept open to foreign traders, Nagasaki had a reputation as a safe harbor for Dutch, Portuguese, and other European traders. While there, sailors could benefit from the services of a variety of Japanese prostitutes, geisha, and other types of female companions. Stories like the one about Will Adams, the sixteenth-century Englishman who settled in Japan and married a Japanese woman (this romance became the basis for the novel *Shogun*), were well known in Loti's day.

In his short story, "Madame Butterfly," published in 1898, John Luther Long took up Loti's theme, transforming the naval officer into an American. In 1900, with Long's assistance, David Belasco brought the story to the stage, where it became a tremendous success in both the United States and England. Giacomo Puccini saw the play in London and immortalized the story in one of his most highly regarded operas. Indeed, Puccini is credited with taking the pathetic story of a simple, ignorant girl, treated as a doll-like object speaking comically mangled English in the short story and play, and turning it into grand tragedy with Butterfly as the noble defender of her honor brought down by the cruelties of her fate. The story has been filmed on many occasions; the 1915 version with Mary Pickford and the 1932 version with Cary Grant are perhaps the best known. In 1988, Henry David Hwang won accolades for his *M. Butterfly*, a contemporary retelling of the tale with a Chinese transvestite spy as the title character.

In Long's story, Butterfly attempts suicide but is rescued by her maid; otherwise, all versions of the tale end with the heroine's ultimate sacrifice. In some variations, Butterfly is a geisha; in others, she is simply a teenager encouraged to help her parents by marrying a wealthy foreigner. In most versions, Butterfly's conversion to Christianity figures prominently as the motivation for her estrangement from her family and culture as well as her willingness to die to defend her newly acquired Western sense of "honor." In all versions, the American Lieutenant B. F. Pinkerton fails to take his Japanese bride seriously. In some tellings, he repents—too late, of course. In most versions, Butterfly gives up her baby to be raised by Adelaide, Pinkerton's white American bride.

Beginning with Belasco's suicide scene at the end of his play and continuing with Puccini's emphasis on Butterfly's tragic end, the story has had a dark side. With all the racism inherent in the condescending treatment of this Japanese innocent, there is an ambivalence in the narrative that goes beyond its surface critique of Western hypocrisy. Although in some versions Adelaide symbolizes the morally uplifting qualities of late Victorian womanhood and, in a few versions, Pinkerton himself feels remorse, the preponderance of Butterfly stories fail to provide the reader or viewer with a clear moral focus since they depict the heroine as a fool and the hero as a cad.

The Butterfly story, as unsavory as it may be in its depiction of both Japan and women, then, is far from an unproblematic affirmation of the ideological status quo. Rather, the narrative reveals the callousness of men who take the sexual double standard for granted as well as the horrific consequences of not only Western moral hypocrisy but also the West's racist disregard for the values and emotions of those who live outside its domain. Although it may appear to criticize only those who break taboos against miscegenation, the tale also, on a deeper level, critiques that very morality which causes a trusting convert to destroy herself. Butterfly may be a fool, stigmatized by her racial difference, but she also rises to become a heroine, who is ironically destroyed by the Western values that elevated her to the status of martyr. Whether those values are strengthened by her death or whether her suicide forces the audience to reexamine its own notions of moral excess remain arguable.

The focus here is on the 1915 version of *Madame Butterfly*, directed by Sidney Olcott, with Mary Pickford as Cho Cho San. In 1915 Pickford enjoyed enormous popularity and, undoubtedly, her star persona

Figure 10.   Mary Pickford in the title role with Marshall Neilan as Pinkerton in Madame Butterfly *(1915). Still courtesy of George Eastman House.*

added a unique dimension to the Butterfly character. Although primarily thought of today as an actress who played prepubescent roles into her thirties and became a millionaire as well, Pickford actually played a variety of roles—many of them tragic—which accentuated her sensuality and ability to break many Victorian taboos under the guise of her angelic, childlike face and long curls.[3] Given that she is so often associated with a tomboyish independence and spunk, the Butterfly role may seem out of keeping with her star image. However, the year before *Madame Butterfly*, Pickford starred in a similar vehicle, *Hearts Adrift* (1914), in which she gives up her love to another woman and ends up throwing herself into a volcano. Moreover, on a number of occasions, Pickford played nonwhite heroines, adding a certain exotic dimension to her image as "America's Sweetheart," and, perhaps, freeing herself somewhat from the constraints of that characterization.

Pickford's Butterfly, for example, allowed the star to explore a certain sexuality out of keeping with a Victorian sensibility. Although the film did not attain the critical success of so many of her other starring vehicles and Pickford herself referred to the film as "Madame Snail" because of its slow pace,[4] the fact that Pickford took the role helped to take the Butterfly character further away from her origins as the almost comic simpleton found in the original short story. However, the Pickford persona also likely brought the character down from its associations with Puccini and grand, operatic tragedy into the world of Pickford's favored working-class heroines. If anything, Pickford's Butterfly mediates between these two extremes by emphasizing the sentimental aspects of the character. Neither too grand nor too lowly, the Pickford Butterfly can function as a flexible point of identification for the star's primarily female middle and working-class fans.

The character first appears as an emblem of many of the contradictions that are explored throughout the film. As customary in many silent films of the period, the players are introduced before the actual narrative begins. Within these introductory shots, a star can be solidly identified visually with the character to be portrayed and can provide the viewer with a thumbnail sketch of that character's principal attributes. The film introduces Mary Pickford as Cho Cho San by showing her kneeling, directly facing the audience, her eyes lowered. She wears a kimono and Japanese wig, and she kneels quietly in front of a Japanese screen. However, after bowing solemnly to the audience, she raises her head, smiles, laughs, and then demurely covers her face with the long sleeve of her kimono. Although she may first appear to be the model embodiment of the Western notion of the Japanese woman as passive, elegant, imperturbable, implicitly obedient, and yielding, underneath the mysterious exterior her smile and laugh betray the better-known Pickford persona of carefree, childlike innocence coupled with mischief. If Pickford's Cho Cho San has the doll-like quality and the erotic objectification associated in the West with Asian femininity, then she also contains the ostensibly paradoxical qualities of the Victorian innocent. She personifies the contradictory extremes of "pagan" sensuality and "Christian" virtue, embodying qualities associated with both the madonna and the whore within the patriarchal imagination.

By adopting "yellow face" for her role, Pickford frees herself from certain Victorian prohibitions against sexual display while maintaining a sense of innocence (since the film assumes that Japanese women are "different" and not subject to the same sexual restraint associated with the Protestant West). Like Lucy in *Broken Blossoms*, Cho Cho San embodies both sentiment and sexuality as the child-woman, an object of lust generally devoid of sexual feelings herself. The Butterfly allows female sexuality to be expressed and explored, because the heroine is punished by death for any taboos she may have broken. Thus, drawing in the female viewer with the force of emotion as well as a fantasy of sexual expression, this Butterfly can more freely explore what the Victorians may see as an illicit link between emotion and sexuality displaced onto the taboo realm of interracial romance.

A Martyr to the Religion of Love

Much is made in the Butterfly tale of the opposing notions of sex and love taken by Japanese and Western cultures. In Japan, sexuality, divorced from romance, is subject to contractual arrangements among men. Conversely, in the Christianized West, love is presented in religious terms with marriage as a sacrament and divorce a fall from grace. The tragedy of the Butterfly story revolves around Cho Cho San's misrecognition of the sexual double standard by which her husband Pinkerton can live as a Western man, adopting the Japanese customs that suit his erotic desires. Inadvertently, Pinkerton wins the Butterfly over to the Western religion of love, which she embraces with a passion that ultimately causes her self-destruction.

Although this fatal misunderstanding can be read as an ideological condemnation of miscegenation and a warning not to cross racial barriers, it can also be interpreted as a tragedy of gender differences, as a tribute to women who suffer from the sexual double standard by which men can do as they please at the expense of women's honor. At this time around the First World War, when women's roles were constantly changing and sexual mores were bending, this latter interpretation may have been the underlying reason for the female audience's interest in *Madame Butterfly*. Pickford, as a star, prided herself on her particular appeal to her female fans.[5] This Butterfly tale, then, of a fundamental misunderstanding between men and women likely had particular potency for those Pickford fans negotiating uncertain emotional waters in 1915.

The Butterfly tale provides only one instance of the countless reworkings of the tragic beauty of impossible romance found in Euroamerican literature. In *Love in the Western World*, Denis de Rougemont uses the story of Tristram and Isolde as the basis for his discussion of the descent of courtly love, with its quasi-religious links to spiritual transcendence and death, through its modern manifestations within the Western literary tradition. As in the courtly tales, modern works often deal with the self-destructive aspects of love made impossible by social conventions or other external forces. However, the seeds for this tragedy really spring from an internal misunderstanding. Thus, de Rougemont argues that love represents a narcissistic "false transcendence" that makes a happy, romantic union between men and women impossible:

> The history of passionate love in all great literature from the thirteenth century down to our own day is the history of the descent of the courtly myth into "profane" life, the account of the more and more desperate attempts of Eros to take the place of mystical transcendence by means of emotional intensity.[6]

In *The Second Sex*, Simone de Beauvoir writes eloquently on how women adopt romantic love as a religion, pinning their hopes for material, emotional, and spiritual transcendence on a godlike lover:

> Since she is anyway doomed to dependence, she will prefer to serve a god rather than obey tyrants—parents, husband, or protector. She chooses to desire her enslavement so ardently that it will seem to her the expression of her liberty; she will try to rise above her situation as inessential object by fully accepting it; through her flesh, her feelings, her behavior, she will enthrone him as supreme value and reality: she will humble herself to nothingness before him. Love becomes for her a religion.[7]

Although in the 1915 film version love as religion is an implicit rather than explicit theme, John Luther Long's story does expressly link Cho Cho San's romantic emotions to religion. When her Buddhist relatives disown her because of Pinkerton's impossibly rude behavior and she can no longer turn to her own religion for spiritual definition, Pinkerton places himself as her god: "To her, he was a god . . ." "a new religion, if she *must* have one."[8] Whereas the Long story creates a sense of ironic detachment from both the cad Pinkerton and the gullible Cho Cho San, the 1915 *Madame Butterfly* underscores sentiment, heightens emotion, and works within the melodramatic tradition to elevate its heroine's plight rather than ridicule or denigrate it. More than a pathetic fool, Pickford's Butterfly is an angelic martyr who willingly and nobly sacrifices herself for her American god.

In fact, this version of *Madame Butterfly* portrays Pinkerton as well as Cho Cho San in a less ironic, more sympathetic light. Instead of contracting with a marriage broker for any available young girl to be his Japanese wife, this Pinkerton (Marshall Neilan) meets Cho Cho San by accident when their rickshas collide. The lieutenant apologizes, and their romance begins with an act of chivalry as Pinkerton shows his concern for Cho Cho San's safety.

In a series of flashbacks to this original meeting, the discourse seems to emphasize a mutuality of sentiment not found in the callously exploitative Pinkerton of other versions. The use of parallel flashbacks, from both Pinkerton's and Cho Cho San's perspectives, indicates a commonality of thought, an equal attraction between the lovers. The film makes concrete its protagonists' subjectivity, that is, their dreams, reveries, memories, and desires, to bring the emotional element of their romance into the foreground and to downplay its convenience or Pinkerton's lust for any easily available woman. Their physical sensuality, then, is linked to an interior, psychological realm that connotes romantic emotions.

Interestingly, although this *Madame Butterfly* seems to take Cho Cho San's sentiments more seriously than some previous versions, it also robs the tale of much of its satiric bite by softening Pinkerton, showcasing his sentiments, and making him the unhappy victim of a love triangle. Ironically, while Pickford's Cho Cho San struggles to transcend the flat, one-dimensional image of the Japanese doll-woman, that same process makes Pinkerton more sympathetic. Thus, while this film moves away from much of the cynicism of the earlier story, it does not allow any critical seeds condemning either racial or gender inequalities to germinate. Rather, the operations of fate and the tragic mysteries of romance take the place of any attempt at an understanding of what might go beyond a sentimental rendering of the heroine's plight.

Moreover, whereas the Adelaide of the Long story is presented as a fittingly callous companion for Pinkerton, calling Cho Cho San a "pretty . . . plaything,"[9] in this film version Adelaide provides a properly maternal Victorian foil to her husband's childlike Japanese bride. Instead of appearing at the end of the narrative, as she does in the original story, Adelaide is seen much earlier in the film in a sequence that crosscuts between her wedding ceremony in the United States and a meeting in Japan with Cho Cho San, the marriage broker, and Cho Cho San's prospective new husband, Prince Yamadori (David Barton). Playing with her new baby, Cho Cho San confidently states, "In America no one can get divorce except in large courthouse full of judge." Ironically, the next shot shows the newly wedded Pinkerton and Adelaide driving away from the church. Their marriage is sanctioned by the laws Cho Cho San invokes, while hers is a figment of her own wishful thinking. Faithful to her American husband, Cho Cho San ridicules Yamadori and avoids his advances.

Believing in the Western religion of love, Cho Cho San has become an unwitting martyr by adhering to its sanctions against polygamy. When the nearly penniless Cho Cho San goes to the American Council to invoke the laws that she believes operate in her interests, she cuts a pitiful figure. She becomes the cinematic embodiment of what de Beauvoir has identified as the abandoned, sacrificial victim of romance:

> The abandoned woman no longer is anything, no longer has anything. If she is asked how she lived before, she does not even remember. She let her former world fall in ashes, to adopt a new country from which she is suddenly driven; she forswore all the values she believed in, broke off her friendships; she now finds herself without a roof over her head, the desert all around her. How begin a new life, since outside her lover there is nothing? . . . There is nothing left but to die.[10]

Cho Cho San's plight bears a similarity to many other melodramatic plots that feature abandoned women. Trapped in her home by her love for Pinkerton, several shots show Cho Cho San at the window waiting for her husband to return from his ship. Night falls, and midnight arrives. Chiaroscuro lighting with a key light on Cho Cho San's face against the window, the rest of the room in shadow, visually expresses the somber emotions associated with the heroine's abandonment. A series of fades marks the passage of time. As Cho Cho San's eyes begin to close, her total abandonment becomes a certainty. A point-of-view shot shows that Pinkerton's ship has left the harbor, and Cho Cho San's silent scream breaks the spell of waiting.

This extended dramatization of Cho Cho San's waiting underscores the emotions and qualities associated with her abandonment—masochism, passive acceptance, misplaced faith, saintlike endurance. She represents, too, all the ambivalence associated with those qualities and emotions—the utter stupidity of her belief in men, her foolish gullibility, the foreigner's ignorance of American perceptions and prejudices. Her situation both elevates her as a model for female behavior and places the viewer above her as intellectually and culturally superior. As in many melodramas featuring emotional excess, the viewer can identify with a character's unfortunate plight and still remain at a safe distance as either morally superior or simply luckier than the victim in the fiction. In this case, Cho Cho San's racial difference from most of the audience makes this distancing even easier.

Butterfly represents the impossible, masochistic passion of romantic love, while Adelaide embodies the safety of a socially sanctioned marriage, the "true" legitimacy of the white American family. Thus, Adelaide helps distance the viewer from the excesses of Cho Cho San's for-bidden passion for her American husband. Adelaide is the voice of reason, beyond the emotional excesses associated with Cho Cho San: "Think of your baby's future. His father can do better by him." Cho Cho San comes to recognize this when she gives up Pinkerton's son to Adelaide.

The contrast between Adelaide and Cho Cho San helps to explain away many of the film's more disturbing social contradictions. Her de-sire to adopt Pinkerton's half-Asian son responds to any question of racism by showing the bourgeois American home, and by extension the entire country, as willing to assimilate the racially, ethnically, or cul-turally "other." Moreover, her "happy" marriage to Pinkerton helps to alleviate any implicit criticism the tragedy might otherwise conjure up of the unhappy, unequal relationship between men and women within the patriarchy. Her appearance, then, helps to quell any threat Pinker-ton's racism or sexism might otherwise pose to white, male, American, bourgeois hegemony. The American home must truly be the ideal, it can be reasoned, because Adelaide still has faith in her husband and is willing to help him rectify his past mistakes.

By shoring up the white American ideal, Adelaide offers no solace, however, to the outsider Cho Cho San. The Butterfly becomes the emblem of excess—emotionally, sexually, culturally, racially—that cannot be recuperated into this picture of domestic tranquillity. Moreover, her death marks her absolutely as the embodiment of an essential female passivity and masochism. Thus, as Pinkerton, Ade-laide, and her son drop out of the picture, the Butterfly transcends the material world of the bourgeois home to become a patron saint of female submissiveness, a martyr to Western romantic notions of love.

Before Cho Cho San wades out into a lake to drown herself, she turns back to Buddha and her ancestors for solace, but her last thoughts are of the man-god Pinkerton: "O my ancestors! Never let that honorable Pinkerton know what I am going to do for him!" A medium long shot lingers on Cho Cho San as she slowly stretches out her arms so that her sleeves float up to the top of the water, As she sinks deeper and deeper, a title underscores the poignancy of Cho Cho San's act: "Could one give up more for love than did little Cho Cho San!" Victorian regard for sentiment could only save Cho Cho San spiritually and not physically, exacting a heavy price for her nonwhite, exotic femininity.

Certainly, Pickford's Cho Cho San could represent "every woman" to her female fans at a time when female sexual self-expression and Victorian notions of the power of sentiment were vying for ascendancy in women's daily lives. In a male-defined world, where the sanctity and limited, often illusory sanctuary of the bourgeois home was being assailed on many fronts, women, encouraged to give up all for their men, likely could see the perils of their situation in the Butterfly tale. This story of a martyr to the religion of love, who could not be saved by the strength of her sentimental attachment to her husband and child, probably struck a responsive cord. While Cho Cho San is praised for her selfless devotion, she must die for her love, purging it of its sensual and passionate excesses. While Pinkerton may suffer only a twinge of guilt as he makes the arrangements to take his son, Cho Cho San loses everything. Her spiritual apotheosis may provide a certain narrative equilibrium, but this tale of female masochism cannot cleanse itself of all the ambivalent feelings Cho Cho San's death may conjure up for those who see her tragedy not as the justified consequence of miscegenation but as the unfair sacrifice of a woman's desire.

Pocahontas in Vietnam: *China Gate*

Before the Butterfly appeared in American popular culture, Pocahontas served a similar function as a symbol of white, Anglo-American hegemony over people of color. The early-seventeenth-century Powhatan princess still epitomizes the self-sacrificing qualities of the nonwhite heroine that have long been used to legitimize white male domination of an expanding American domestic and, later, international frontier. According to Captain John Smith's records, Pocahontas saved him from execution by physically placing her head over his to sacrifice her life, if need be, to spare his. However, both Smith and Pocahontas were spared. She, then, helped to establish a trade relationship between her people and the British and taught Smith about Native American customs and survival techniques. Pocahontas converted to Christianity, adopted European dress, and was even presented at the British court. Spurned by Smith, however, she married another settler, John Rolfe, to cement her alliance with the English.

Within the white American mythos, Pocahontas has been elevated to the level of a mystic seer, who, through her sexual liaisons with two white men, came to realize the moral right of Christianity and the inevitable conquest of her own supposedly backward and inferior people by the self-professed superior civilization of Europe. Her marriage represents the establishment of a new American identity, forged by a union of the noble savagery of the wilderness with the revitalized civility of Europe, based on the metaphoric feminization and symbolic sexual capitulation of the nonwhite world. She sacrifices her own people and her love for Smith to solidify her commitment to this newly defined "America" and its new citizenry legitimized by her aristocratic nobility in her marriage to Rolfe. Also, by marrying Rolfe, Pocahontas's image changes from sexually aggressive, native temptress to legitimate wife and symbolic mother of a new American nation.

To this day, Pocahontas, the beatified traitor, continues to function within the popular imagination as a complex and contradictory symbol of the origins of the American state. Philip Young, for example, has identified her as both the "mother of us all" and an "imperialistic icon."[11] In her essay, "The Pocahontas Perplex: The Image of Indian Women in American Culture," Rayna Green emphasizes the contradictory sexual aspect of her image:

> Both her nobility as a Princess and her savagery as a Squaw are defined in terms of her relationships with male figures. If she wishes to be called a Princess, she must save or give aid to white men. The only good Indian . . . rescues and helps white men.[12]

In *Pocahontas's Daughters: Gender and Ethnicity in American Culture*, Mary V. Dearborn notes that beyond this white, male-defined vision of Pocahontas as princess-squaw, madonna-whore, traitor-savior, temptress-sacrificial lamb, Pocahontas also makes concrete some of the unobtainable dreams found in fiction written by ethnic women in America. If Pocahontas has a certain mythic significance for white, male America, she has a different but complementary meaning for those outside mainstream culture because of race, ethnicity, or gender. As Dearborn observes,

> Intermarriage between white men and ethnic women becomes a symbolic literalization of the American dream, both in terms of success and of love: variously, it suggests an assertion of melting-pot idealism, of the forging of a "new man," of Cinderella success, of love "regardless of race, creed, or color," of the promise of America itself.[13]

Thus, Pocahontas can be viewed as a metaphor for the promised, melting-pot assimilation of the alien woman into the benevolent paternalism of American society or as the enticingly sexual, maternal, self-sacrificing, fertile, and mysterious native woman who acts as an icon for America's conquest. As Dearborn has pointed out, Pocahontas stands at the fulcrum of the precariously balanced issues of racial, ethnic, and gender identity.

Many Hollywood narratives featuring romances between Anglo-American men and Asian women follow the Pocahontas paradigm. These stories bear a striking similarity to Butterfly narratives with an overtly political dimension. An Asian woman, member of a bellicose nation or ethnic group, betrays her people and sacrifices herself out of love for her white American lover. Through marriage or through the bearing of the white American's baby, the Asian woman solidifies her commitment to the dominant white culture and leaves her own behind by dying or going to live with her child or Anglo-American husband.

Thus, according to the popular mythos, she is saved either spiritually or morally from her own "inferior" culture, just as she physically saves her lover from her own people. Ideologically, the narrative can be looked at as either a liberal call for assimilation or as a portent of the annihilation of a conquered people. In either case, these stories legitimize Anglo-American rule over a submissive, feminized Asia. For women (particularly women further marginalized by class, race, or ethnicity), they promise the American Dream of abundance, protection, individual choice, and freedom from the strictures of a traditional society in the paternalistic name of heterosexual romance.

China Gate (Samuel Fuller, 1957), for example, can be looked at as a fairly standard retelling of the Pocahontas story within an Asian context. Set in northern Vietnam near the Chinese border in 1954, before the fall of Dien Bien Phu and French capitulation to Vietnamese forces, *China Gate* deals with a commando unit of French legionnaires assigned to blow up an ammunitions depot held by the Viet Minh. To accomplish this mission, the legionnaires must enlist the aid of a Franco-Chinese alcoholic saloonkeeper—the notorious femme fatale, Lia, known also as Lucky Legs (Angie Dickinson). Since she has close contacts with the Viet Minh commander, Major Cham (Lee Van Cleef), and knows the border area from running whiskey behind enemy lines, the French choose Lia as their guide, confident of her loyalty because she wants her young son to be given safe passage to America.

Unfortunately, this deal nearly collapses when Lia learns that her former husband, Johnny Brock (Gene Barry), is part of the expedition. Years earlier, after their son had been born with Asian features, the racist Brock abandoned mother and son. Yet determined to send her son to America, Lia finally agrees to go on the mission with Brock and the others.

However, before the unit can accomplish its mission, these men must be ideologically cleansed of what the film posits as the West's only handicap to legitimate world rule, that is, its open racism. During the course of the mission, Lia repeatedly proves her loyalty to the Allies by using her sexual allure to sneak past or destroy Viet Minh outposts. Gradually, clothed in army fatigues rather than the revealing *cheong sam* she wears at the opening of the film, the deeroticized Lia becomes "one of the boys," that is, an accepted part of the little microcosm of the West represented by the combat unit. When the men of

Figure 11.   In a rare moment, Lucky Legs (Angie Dickinson) and Johnny Brock (Gene Barry) embrace. Still from China Gate *(1957) courtesy of the Museum of Modern Art/Film Stills Archive.*

the unit discover her marriage and Brock's attitude toward her and their son, they shun Brock. Eventually, after a series of conversations with Lia and other members of the combat group, Brock recants and agrees to reconcile with his wife and accept his child.

This comes too late for Lia, however, who has had to act as a spy so as to infiltrate the China Gate ammunition depot. Romanced by the committed Communist, Major Cham, who wants Lia and her son to join him at an officers' school in Moscow, Lia cannot extricate herself from Cham before the sabotage is discovered. Menaced by Cham, Lia manages to push the major off the balcony and detonate the charges herself, dying in the explosion.

Of the original unit, only Brock and Goldie (Nat King Cole), an African American Korean War veteran, return to base alive. Given that *China Gate* was produced three years after the French defeat, the fact that the Americans are the only survivors of the international mercenary unit does more than simply presage the emergence of America after World War II as the single dominant Western military, political, and economic power in Asia. Reunited with his son and cleansed of his racism, Brock leaves the foreign legion to fulfill Lia's last wish of an American future for the boy. Goldie remains behind, singing the title song, as Brock and his son walk off together amid the rubble of the town. With the French literally out of the picture (i.e., the film frame) at the end of *China Gate*, America stakes a legitimate claim to rule in Vietnam (symbolically represented by Brock's recognition of his son's legitimacy).

China Gate's resemblance to the story of Pocahontas is striking. Lia acts as the nonwhite madonna-whore, both abandoned by and married to a white man. Brock functions as both Smith and Rolfe in the tale, accepting and rejecting his paramour. Betraying her own people, Lia aids the Western cause, showing Brock how to defeat the Viet Minh and survive in the Indochinese jungle. She sees a brighter future for her child in America, just as Pocahontas intuits a Euroamerican future and the inevitable collapse of Native American culture. Moreover, through the course of the narrative, Lia's threatening sexuality is tamed, just as Pocahontas is eventually domesticated by her marriage to Rolfe.[14] Though Pocahontas survives her offer to sacrifice herself for her white lover, Lia does not, and the foundation for the future international domination of the Anglo-American way rests on her corpse.

Like Pocahontas, Lia legitimates white Western imperialism by allowing herself to be conquered willingly by the sexual prowess of the Caucasian male. However, just as Pocahontas continues to stand as a highly contradictory figure within the American consciousness, Lia, too, cuts an ambivalent figure in *China Gate* as both noble princess and whore, traitor, and patriot. At one point, the priest who performed Lia and Brock's marriage verbally expresses this ambivalence: "They say . . . she lived like a princess and lived like a prostitute. They say she's a traitor to France. They say she's a traitor to the Chinese Reds." Although Brock suffers the brunt of the film's moral outrage for abandoning his wife and child, *China Gate* also contains a threat represented by Lia, who embodies the wild excesses of sexuality.

Like Pocahontas, Lia represents a closeness to the wilderness and to the threatening savagery of nature so often associated with female sexuality in Western thought. When racial difference is added to this coupling, another dimension is added to the masculine imaginative conquest of nature through the sexual conquest of a woman. As an untamed barbarian, the nonwhite, "natural" woman absorbs both the projected sexual wantonness and the coveted maternal fertility of the white male imagination. Both Pocahontas and Lia point the way for a masculine domination of the wilderness and its peoples through force of arms sugar-coated by romance and Christian righteousness.

From her first appearance in *China Gate*, Lia's identity as both sex goddess and madonna is made clear. Inside the bombed-out ruins of Lucky's Bar, the camera dollies up from a pair of high-heel shoes, one bare leg sporting an ankle bracelet, and a pair of thighs peeking out from the slit of a Chinese-style cheong sam. The camera's slow dolly and use of the scope frame seems to elongate her legs, the emblem of her sexual allure. Lia, like a Titian Venus or a Matisse odalisque, lounges horizontally. A shiny necklace, shoulder-length dark hair, and low-cut gown further accentuate her pale skin. The camera slowly reveals her full form as an object of specular contemplation. As "Lucky Legs," she has a certain fetishistic power to command men's attention. Later, as Lia, she must be scrutinized so that her racial identity and political loyalties can be fathomed along with the threat and promise of her sexual allure.

She holds a liquor bottle in one hand and seems to be in an alcoholic haze. However, when her son comes up to point out the downing of a plane with provisions for her, she attends to him swiftly, dropping her bottle to run out to forage for food. The portrait of the reclining Venus with her Cupid can be interpreted as a picture of the Madonna and her Child. As Rick Berg points out in his essay, "Losing Vietnam," Lia functions as both a sexual and racial enigma. "She is the monstrous unknown 'other' whose looks tell us nothing more than that looks deceive."[15]

Yet even if Lia's appearance is deceptive, her loyalty to the Euroamerican world, like Pocahontas's, never comes into question. Although *China Gate* positions Lia physically and figuratively between two contending worlds, her choice has been predetermined. She rejects devastated, colonial Vietnam and the innocent barbarism of her native highlands, turning away from what the film posits as the excessive stoicism of Asian communism as well as its opposite extreme, Asian decadence and sensuality. She embraces Catholicism (e.g., she saves the priest who performed her marriage to Brock from certain death at the hands of the Viet Minh) and the promise America offers her Amerasian son. Even when she confronts her own American husband's open racism, she does not waver, confident he can be cleansed of his prejudice through romance. When presented with the opportunity to marry Cham, who offers acceptance, social advancement, and security under communism, she mysteriously chooses America as less violent, and, if undeniably racist, more likely to change. The fact that America, primarily represented by Brock, is no less bellicose and far more closed-minded in its racial attitudes than the Viet Minh, represented by Cham, never surfaces.

Moreover, as in the case of Pocahontas, Lia's genuine sense of Christian morality and commitment to her marriage never come into question. Although it codes Lia as openly sexual, implicitly a prostitute, and gives her Hollywood's stereotypical potential for Eurasian duplicity,[16] the film never grapples with the obvious challenge the appearance of her Asian son might pose not to Brock's racism but to his masculinity. Clearly, Lia's son could look Asian because he has an Asian father; the licentious Lia may have been unfaithful to the cuckold Brock. The film carefully explains (on more than one occasion) that Brock abandoned Lia not because he thought her son did not belong to him but because he could not accept his legitimate child's appearance. Still, as in many Hollywood treatments of interracial sexuality and mixed-race characters, the taint of illegitimacy and the threat of female sexual expression outside the strictures of patriarchal laws remain as unvoiced disturbances. This further complicates the film's ostensibly antiracist stance by potentially displacing the question of Brock's racism onto one of masculinity and patriarchal descent.

As a result, Lia's Eurasian eroticism becomes an even greater burden, since her sexuality challenges both racial divisions as well as patriarchal hierarchies. If the narrative can accommodate the former within a discourse of benevolent American assimilation, it cannot tolerate the threat to the patriarchy posed by Lia's feminine sexuality. As a consequence, Lia's eroticism and independence lead to her self-destruction.

China Gate inextricably binds gender and sexuality to an affirmation of Western culture and its American military champions in a scene in which Goldie chides Brock for abandoning his family. In addition to directing Brock's transgression away from questions of racism toward the problem of patriarchal obligations, the scene serves to link the American bourgeois family with male identity. Thus, it indirectly explains Goldie's impassioned commitment to his mercenary vocation as a substitution for his unfulfilled American Dream of the bourgeois nuclear family as the prerequisite to psychological well-being.

Goldie's family situation bears a certain similarity to Brock's dysfunctional family unit. Wounded in the foot while pursuing a young boy in league with the Viet Minh, Goldie returns to camp to be nursed by Brock. In a tight two shot, Goldie addresses Brock, whose face turns away from the camera, so that Goldie's can remain the focus of attention.

> I always wanted a kid, Brock. When my wife was told we couldn't have one, I put in papers to adopt one. But my wife got sick . . . eaten up in-

side not being able to have one . . . just eaten up. She died feeling sorry for me. That's how much she knew I wanted a kid. I'll tell you one thing. Lucky Legs is going through hell for your son. And, if something happens to her on this job, he'll still get to the States, even if I have to crawl all the way back with him on my back.

Up to this point, Goldie's dissatisfaction with Brock's attitude toward Lia and her son could be interpreted as his own abhorrence of white racism. Instead, this monologue reveals that Goldie's reaction to Brock's treatment of Lia comes from his commitment to a patriarchal ideal of the nuclear family rather than any deeply felt feelings of racial injustice. Through this personal revelation, the film robs Goldie of any threat he might pose as the voice of the emerging civil rights movement. Goldie's commitment to America—and, by implication, to the dominant white forces that rule the United States—does not come under scrutiny. He never questions Brock's authority in the unit; he never doubts that his "proper" place must put him in a subordinate position to Brock; he sees nothing of his own plight in the struggle of the Viet Minh; and his identification with Lia comes not from a shared experience of racism but from a frustrated desire to live the American Dream through the bourgeois nuclear family.

If *China Gate* appears to condemn racism, it never questions the racial hierarchy but shores it up by affirming traditional notions of masculinity. An infantalized, emasculated, black "buddy" in Brock's paternal care, robbed of his sexual potency, Goldie legitimizes white male rule by insisting on the perpetuation of the traditional American family. If the Viet Minh boy in the jungle represents the nonwhite world gone astray, then the plight of Brock's son represents the potential for America to "save" Vietnam from itself.

Rather than looking at the war in Vietnam as a conflict between competing political ideologies or economic systems, *China Gate* pictures the Franco-Viet war as a paternalistic struggle over a childlike people who must be brought under the protection of their "legitimate" Western patriarch. Communism is pictured as dark, malevolent, and amoral. Montagnards ignorantly sing the "Marseillaise" under the implicitly illegitimate, paternal gazes of portraits of Ho Chi Minh, Mao, and Stalin. Just as Ho Chi Minh wants to be the "father of his country," Cham wants to be the father of Lia's child and bring him under Communist protection.

In fact, compared to Brock, Cham seems an unlikely villain. Unlike Brock, Cham is well educated, a former teacher who speaks seven languages. Whereas Brock despises racial differences and, particularly, Asian features, the Eurasian Cham cherishes them, remarking to Lia,

"We're both half-castes, but I'm more fortunate than you. I have Chinese characteristics, you don't." Cham welcomes Lia's son and has no problem with his appearance. Unlike the cynical mercenary Brock, Major Cham has a genuine commitment to communism, believes his cause will win, and proudly boasts of the responsibilities of his command.

Only the occult properties of romantic love can save *China Gate* from the obvious possibility of allowing viewers to read Major Cham as the actual hero of the film. Despite everything, Brock, standing in for an America purified of its racism, must be proven right and Cham condemned because Lia, who embodies both worlds and all sides in the struggle, loves only Brock. As Lia circulates between the two men, her recognition of Brock as her legitimate husband (i.e., married by a Catholic priest and never divorced) and his acceptance of their son as his legitimate heir become linked ideologically to the acknowledgment of white America as the "true" father of Vietnam. To make her romantic commitment absolute, Lia makes the ultimate sacrifice, killing herself and Cham, wiping away any threat her mercurial existence might pose to the ideologically absolute barriers between Asia and the West, Communist and capitalist, nonwhite and white, female and male.

The "Voice of God" in *China Gate*: Ideology and Film Style

China Gate appropriates the Pocahontas myth for a specific political end. The film conjures up an Asian Pocahontas in the figure of Lia as an undisguised call for increased United States involvement in Vietnam. As such, the film slides between narrative and propaganda, using myth to elide the two.

To this end, the film borrows many of the strategies associated with documentary filmmaking to create an impression that the image is the "truth," that a particular perspective cannot be contested, and that the text simply states the "facts" of the matter. To establish its authority, *China Gate* opens with an elaborate montage of images accompanied by a "voice of God"—off-screen narration. Disembodied and apparently omniscient, this forceful male voice actually serves as a guide to the proper interpretation of the images shown. In part, this voice states,

> This motion picture is dedicated to France. More than three hundred years ago, French missionaries came to Indochina to teach love of God and love of fellowman. Gradually, French influence took shape in the

Vietnamese land. Despite many hardships, they advanced their way of living, and the thriving nation became the rice bowl of Asia. Vast riches were developed under French guidance until 1941 when Japanese troops moved in and made the rice bowl red with blood of the defenders. In 1945, when the Japanese surrender was announced, a Moscow-trained, Indochinese revolutionist, who called himself Ho Chi Minh, began the drive to make his own country another target for Chinese Communists. Headquartered in the north, he called the new party Viet Minh. With the end of the Korean War, France was left alone to hold the hottest front in the world and became the barrier between communism and the rape of Asia. Members of the foreign legion imported from North Africa fought valiantly under the French flag.

The voice-over goes on to introduce the China Gate ammunitions site, which will become the central plot problem, the northern village under Viet Minh siege, the airlifting of supplies from America that assures the survival of the town, and the precise year, day, and time. This leads to the introduction of Lia's son, clutching a puppy, which the voice-over tells us is the last animal left alive in the village. The child, who remains unnamed in the film to better symbolize the country in general, represents the vulnerability of the childlike Vietnamese and serves as a link between the combat story and the romance between Brock and Lia. Thus, the introductory voice-over attaches the history of Vietnam to the fiction of *China Gate*, documentary to narrative, the combat genre to the romance, and politics to personal life.

As Sarah Kozloff points out in *Invisible Storytellers: Voice-Over Narration in American Fiction Film*, "voice of God" narrators "who speak for (or rather *as*) the image-maker, are particularly likely to provide guidance concerning what conclusions the viewers should draw. They tend to voice the ideological and/or moral agenda behind the film."[17] In the case of *China Gate*, this opening voice-over becomes a critical part of fixing not only the signification of the images that accompany it but also the contradictions present in the rest of the narrative, that is, the voice-over rationalizes Lia's choice of Brock and America over Cham and communism. The pseudodocumentary and the Pocahontas myth converge for a very clear propagandistic end.

As a mythic apology for American involvement in Vietnam, *China Gate* works to rationalize this myth by drawing on documentary reportage and stark drama to create a fairly obvious Cold War political statement that can act as a "realistic" depiction of the "truth" of the war in Vietnam. Given the uncertain settlement of the Korean War, the war in Vietnam provides an opportunity for reaffirming American post-World War II military and political sovereignty. Moreover, the image of the American mercenary in Asia also reaffirms a white male identity challenged at home by the civil rights movement and the ghost of the independent, wartime, working woman.

Although the dedication of *China Gate* to the French may seem like faint praise to a defeated power, the film still insistently sides with the French, subsuming any contradictory rhetoric of democratic self-determination and national liberation under the guise of the "Red Menace." The Americans, Brock and Goldie, emerge not so much as a slap in the face to the defeated French but as representatives of a new, neocolonial world order based on a cleansed, color-blind, democratic, and potent America. Although France and Western capitalism can tag along, the tale of this Vietnamese Pocahontas remains a distinctly American affirmation of its own legitimate right to world domination.

Pinkerton's Story: "The Lady from Yesterday"

Although *China Gate* was among the first Hollywood treatments of American military involvement in Indochina, its Pocahontas story line has not often been used subsequently in fictional treatments of the Vietnam War. Most of the better-known feature films on America's involvement in Vietnam deal with combat, for example, *The Green Berets* (1968), *Apocalypse Now* (1979), *Platoon* (1986), *Rambo* (1985), and *Full Metal Jacket* (1987). Fewer films, such as *Coming Home* (1978) and *Gardens of Stone* (1987), have dealt with the war's impact on soldiers' personal lives and domestic relations. Beyond the occasional subplot or passing allusion, romantic relationships between soldiers and Vietnamese women during the war almost never receive serious treatment within these features.

Perhaps the frustrated love story in *Good Morning, Vietnam* (1987) explains a more general trend. In this film, the Vietnamese woman's links, through her family, to the Viet Cong taint any question of romance with suspicion and possible danger. Unlike the passive, defeated, Butterfly-like Japanese women of the post-World War II era, the Vietnamese women in Hollywood today still conjure up the troubling prospect of Vietnam as a potent, unvanquished, threatening nation with its women linked to the possibility of castration.

In general, Vietnamese women (regardless of the political affiliations of the character with the NVA, VC, ARVN, or no one) have served as disposable tokens of the cruelties of war. A recently popular narrative theme involves the murder mystery formula with a Saigon setting. It features the slaughter of Vietnamese prostitutes by some unknown, insane, presumably American G.I. The feature film *Off Limits* (1989) and episodes of "Miami Vice",[18] "China Beach," "Tour of

Duty," and "Magnum P. I." have all exploited this plot line. Rather than exploring the intercultural dynamics that a more traditional love story might allow, these narratives silence the Asian woman from the outset, making her a beautiful corpse for the visual contemplation of the camera. This confirms the passivity of Vietnam metaphorically, while allowing the exploration of other themes open to historical revisionism—for example, interracial male bonding, the rationalization of American atrocities during the war, and the symbolic solving of the "mystery" of Vietnam's ability to defeat America.

As this example shows, television seems to have taken up the issue of interracial sexuality within the context of the Vietnam War to a greater degree than the feature film industry. However, although interracial sexuality has been dealt with in various Hollywood cinematic and televisual treatments of the war, the romantic bond between men and women, so important in other wartime fictions, has been generally eclipsed in television programs about Vietnam by another narrative pattern—the search for and legitimation of a soldier's estranged progeny, taking up the theme established in *China Gate*.

However, unlike Lia in *China Gate*, the mother of the child in these dramas plays a very minor role. Although she may appear, it is the child who serves to justify the father's role in the war and its existence rationalizes America's continuing claim to "father" the infantalized, helpless, misdirected Third World embodied by the Amerasian child. The feature film *Braddock: Missing in Action III* (1988), the made-for-television movies "Green Eyes" (1976), "The Girl That Came Between Them" (1990), "The Lady from Yesterday" (1985), and episodes of the television series "The A-Team," "Magnum, P.I.," and "China Beach" all have dealt with either the search for or the acceptance of Amerasian children by their soldier fathers. Like *Uncommon Valor* (1983), *Rambo*, and *Missing in Action* (1984), these narratives allow their American heroes another opportunity to fight the Vietnam War and win, this time, by staking a patriarchal, blood claim to Vietnam's children. The absorption of the Amerasian children of war into America argues against any residual charges of American racism, cruelty, or heartlessness. Dramatic representations of children rescued by their American fathers from the excesses of communism replace documentary images of children, clothes burned off by napalm, fleeing in terror from their American "protectors."

Not surprisingly, many of these tales of lost children, with or without their Vietnamese mothers in the fiction, have been produced for television broadcast. Whereas action-adventure dominates cinema screens, the living room television tends to privilege the domestic in its search for the female consumer and the "family" audience. Motion pictures sell the spectacle of combat and the promises of that almost exclusively male world to the young men who make the most ticket purchases. Television, however, brings the war into the living room for housewives, mothers, their children, and husbands. Here, melodrama dominates, and emotions, subjectivity, interpersonal relations, and familial order all become critical parts of Vietnam narratives.[19]

"The Lady from Yesterday" (Robert Day, 1985) provides an example of this type of story. However, unlike many of the other similar narratives that either eliminate completely or virtually exclude the role of the Vietnamese wife, lover, and mother from the plot, this television movie allows the Asian woman, to whom the title refers, to have a key role in the drama. Because of this, it comes closer than any of the other dramas involving murdered prostitutes, missing children, female guerrilla fighters, or fleeting romantic liaisons to addressing an interracial romance seriously within the context of the Vietnam War.

Produced ten years after the fall (or liberation) of Saigon, "The Lady from Yesterday," like many made-for-television movies,[20] relies on the topicality of its subject matter to draw in an audience. In this case, documentaries on Vietnam, an upsurge in the popularity of film and television fiction on the war, and a general postwar reassessment of America's involvement in Vietnam appeared around the same time. However, like these other dramas, "The Lady from Yesterday" finds its "topicality" in memory, nostalgia, and the desire to somehow rewrite the history of America's defeat in Vietnam.

"The Lady from Yesterday" shifts its attention from the war itself, its political expediency, and its morality to the aftermath of the war. If America had set out to win the "hearts and minds" of the Vietnamese and failed, shows like "The Lady from Yesterday" attempt to prove the contrary position. Thus, the war fades from view, and the problems of the "boat people" (mainly ethnic Chinese, many of whom were merchants or small-scale industrialists who fled Vietnam during the flare-up in tensions between mainland China and Vietnam over Cambodia in 1979) move to the foreground.

However, these dramas do not deal with the real problems of the Indochinese diaspora (separated families, political exiles, refugee camps, ridiculously low immigration quotas, diplomatic impasses, the economic exploitation of new immigrants, etc.). Rather, they combine popular sentiments linked to American involvement in the war with the increased visibility of Indochinese immigrants in the United States to come up with a formulaic explanation for what revised histories claim as a "noble" defeat in Vietnam. Any echoes of American political manipulation of the country, reports of bloody massacres, and the unnecessary suffering of women and children fade. In these narratives, the helpless and hopeful new immigrant, totally committed to American jingoism, fairly easily overcomes whatever racial or cultural barriers may stand in the way to attain the American Dream.

Ironically, these stories do not use the Vietnamese refugee as the central protagonist. Rather, the American "white knight" war veteran, victimized by some unspeakable angst linked to his involvement in the war, becomes the principal hero of the tale. Often, these narratives displace what nonfictional accounts and more critical materials on the war associate with returning soldiers' guilt or ambivalence about their participation in an undeclared war of dubious legality, morality, and efficacy onto the more concrete and possibly reconcilable problems of interpersonal relationships, romance, and domestic life. Bringing the Vietnam War into the living rooms of America for a second time, melodramas like "The Lady from Yesterday" domesticate it. National guilt becomes personal anguish. The bittersweet memory of a doomed romance replaces the devastation of defeat. The unspeakable atrocities of the war metamorphose into questions of domestic duties and patriarchal rights.

Clearly, the emotions and ethical consequences of fathering Amerasian children are more easily digestible than the far more controversial issues of the legitimacy of the war itself. Indeed, by not mentioning these issues, these narratives can quietly reconcile them by transposing them into the problem of the legitimacy of a child rather than the legality of a war.

"The Lady from Yesterday" uses melodramatic strategies to displace, transform, personalize, domesticate, and, ultimately, resolve the perplexities of the war. The war becomes not a deep national crisis of governmental legitimacy but, rather, a personal crisis of patriarchal rule within the domestic sphere. The tensions played out involve generational rifts, strained marriages, and questions of inheritance. Although American racism is broached, its relationship to the war is never addressed (as, for example, America's willingness to fight the cold war in Asia against the "yellow peril" rather than in Caucasian Europe, the disproportionate number of nonwhite minority troops involved in the war, and America's insensitivity to former nonwhite allies after 1975). Rather, racism becomes a family affair. Its solution results from the narrative resolution of the plot, with the symbolic assimilation of all people of color, including the Amer-Viet child, into the American melting-pot family embodied by the bourgeois, patriarchal home.

"The Lady from Yesterday," despite the promise of the title, does not highlight the trials and sacrifices of Vietnamese women victimized by the war. Rather, it tells America's story, and a flawed, defeated America cleans its own house to reabsorb the victims of its own racist and imperialistic excesses. Although in many ways this drama retells, yet again, the story of Butterfly and Pinkerton, with the Butterfly sacrificing herself and her desires to perpetuate and legitimize American domination in Asia, the emphasis has shifted considerably. No longer is the tragic Cho Cho San at the heart of the story; rather, Pinkerton is now the protagonist, elevated from a cad to the morally troubled but genuinely righteous champion of American hegemony. The Butterfly fades into the background as Pinkerton emerges to symbolize a tainted America that rationalizes its old imperialistic mission through a new telling of an old story.

The Renewal of the American Dream: The Butterfly and the Crisis of Bourgeois Patriarchy

"The Lady from Yesterday" begins with a picture of American domesticity in crisis. Class, generation, and gender are aspects of this crisis that this television movie implicity links to the national turmoil of the Vietnam War. The voice-of-god narrator booms before the credit scene rolls in the teaser, which introduces the drama in a nutshell to the viewers, whetting their appetite for sensationalism: "Two worlds collide for the man trapped between the good life and the lady from yesterday." As this introduction makes clear, the central conflict of the narrative involves its male protagonist's internal struggle over maintaining his class standing or giving in to his desire to reassert his potency, that is, to express the forbidden, repressed urges embodied by the woman of the title. The narrative, then, attempts to reconcile these conflicts, rid itself of the disturbances represented by a taboo sexual liaison, and reestablish the hero, and, by implication, the American nation he represents, as the legitimate heir to a family's (and a nation's) material riches and class privileges.

At first, Craig Weston (Wayne Rogers), the model "yuppie," would seem to be a figure who would alienate a large segment of the audience (e.g., the working classes, women, nonwhites), despite his envious position and power. Thus, another vantage point seems necessary to draw the viewer into this narrative of a world of advantage and privilege inaccessible to most although held up as an ideal for all. The drama, then, takes up the problem of assimilating the marginal (the dispossessed, the feminine, the racially other) into the American mainstream in order to morally rationalize the continuation of this bourgeois "good life" as a model for all those excluded by it.

In order for the "lady from yesterday" to be able to make inroads into this "good life" and for the viewer to see Craig as something other than a rich, self-satisfied emblem of an impossible dream of success, the contradictions contained within this representation of the American bourgeoisie first must be voiced. As most in the audience might secretly suspect or desire, this apparently perfect world must have its flaws, that is, the rich cannot possibly be wealthy, happy, morally upright, and untroubled at the same time.

Thus, even before the enigma of the presence of the Asian woman can be addressed, internal tensions associated with the reproduction of the bourgeois family rise to the surface. J. C. Bartlett (Pat Hingle) calls Craig into his office. Both boss and father-in-law, J. C. wields enormous power over Craig's professional and personal life. He undercuts Craig's interest in expanding the company's involvement in the Third World by refusing to deal with nonwhite contractors and laborers "south of the border," and he goes on to criticize Craig's treatment of his family. J. C. represents an old-line patriarchal presence (Southern, bellicose, obviously racist, and overly possessive of his daughter) that the drama implies is passé, while Craig represents a new image of masculinity (Californian, pragmatic, a "sensitive" father who is implicitly amenable to change).

The struggle between the two men for control over the business as well as the family provides the fuel for working out what can be looked at as a classic Oedipal scenario. Thus, J. C. must be done away with so that the castrated son Craig can emerge as the new patriarch with legitimate control over his wife and children. With his success, a newly revitalized American bourgeoisie also emerges, cleansed of its obvious racism and committed to "progress" for the ostensible betterment of all.

Craig's relationship with his wife Janet (Bonnie Bedelia) points to the depth of his gender crisis. As J. C.'s daughter, Janet is associated with her father's privilege, wealth, and power. Thus, Craig's masculinity comes into doubt on all fronts. His father-in-law controls his ability to provide for his family. His wife, still under the tutelage of J. C., fails to acquiesce to Craig's authority over their home and children. Moreover, she literally robs him of his sexual potency by icily distancing herself from him in bed. Underneath the image of the powerful executive lies a defeated Vietnam veteran whose gender role as husband, father, and provider has been seriously threatened by what the drama presents as the "excesses" of the bourgeois, patriarchal system that created him.

Lien (Tina Chen), the "lady from yesterday," appears in the narrative not only as a disruptive sexual force breaking into this oppressive "model" world of bourgeois domesticity but as a corrective for its excesses. As an icon of sexuality, she returns Craig's potency to him, bringing with her what the television movie indicates is "missing" from his relationship with Janet. In contrast to the deeroticized, castrating Janet, the elegantly dressed Lien embodies the Hollywood conception of Asian femininity as alluring, provocative, and mysterious as well as passive, yielding, and vulnerable. Her deep red lipstick accentuates the sensuality of her mouth; her blue eye shadow highlights the racial difference that marks her taboo desirability; and her simple white jacket and quiet gestures (hands folded in her lap, the way she gingerly alights on chairs and benches) give her an almost ethereal fragility. She is, indeed, the "lady" of the title, able to be both erotic and pure, apparently reconciling the impossible duality of femininity as both unobtainable madonna and sexually available whore.

As a war victim rather than victor, Lien represents a feminized Asia that can potentially shore up the shaky masculinity of Craig and, through him, the threatened international ascendancy of the United States. A "boat person" who has relocated to Hong Kong and is now in need of help, Lien gives back to Craig the role he played in Vietnam as white knight, idealistically there to act as an interpreter to "help" the Vietnamese rather than harm them as a combatant. She conjures up memories of their romantic involvement during the war as an idealized past, free from his wife and oppressive father-in-law.

Lien represents the "ideal" woman, the new Butterfly, that is, supportive, demure, self-effacing, self-sacrificing, and disposable, who has quietly faded into the background so that Craig could return to his legitimate wife and children. Craig recalls her to one of his friends:

> You know, out there in Saigon, we were free. I knew it was crazy, and she was sane. She was warm. She gave. She loved without claims, without promises . . . and she knew I was going to leave. She knew one day . . . that I would leave and come home. . . . All that seemed like a dream. Saigon was a fantasy.

For ten years, this "dream" woman remained silent about herself and her concerns, allowing Craig to fulfill his American Dream of success with his white wife and family. Lien's self-sacrificing disposability makes her the perfect erotic object; her racial otherness can rationalize Craig's sexist insensitivity.

Lien also represents a defeated Vietnam, an American military and moral fiasco, that somehow must be brought back within the orbit of American power and prerogatives. The Butterfly may sacrifice herself because of her involvement with an alien nation, but she cannot sever all ties that inevitably bind her to America. Just as earlier versions of the tale ideologically rationalized America's mission to rule paternalistically over Asia by allowing Pinkerton to recognize and adopt the Butterfly's child as his own, "The Lady from Yesterday" offers up Lien and Craig's illegitimate son as the symbolic emblem of America's continuing paternalistic right to rule over the infantile and helpless citizens of Vietnam. Quan (Bryan Price) acts as the symbolic marker of the hope of American liberalism. He acts as a token of the dream of assimilation of the nonwhite into mainstream American society. The narrative works, then, to enable Quan's assimilation into the bourgeois suburban home to act as a corrective to any threats to male, bourgeois, American hegemony in either the domestic or public spheres.

Although the drama initially toys with the possibility that Lien may be a "bad," modern woman who simply no longer wishes to be unfairly burdened with single parenthood, she quickly regains her nearly saintly status when she reluctantly reveals that she will soon die. Her last wish is for her son to be with his American father, to be part of his American Dream. Lien's death by natural causes, moreover, frees Craig from any hint of the guilt that taints Pinkerton in the other versions of the tale. Her death, without any strings attached, allows Craig to assert himself and prove the true worth of the liberalized, American, bourgeois patriarchy.

At first, Craig is reluctant to take Quan. Lien attributes this to Craig's subordination to his wife and her father. She chides him, "The man I loved in Saigon was a free man. He was a happy, loving man. . . . The man I loved in Saigon wasn't trapped and afraid." Ironically, during the war, Craig enjoyed the unrestrained expression of his masculine desires; any fear of death, moral equivocations, or any other physical or psychological burdens seem not to have been at issue. Rather, Craig's family proves to be his battleground. The bourgeois home and office threaten his masculine identity, and Vietnam becomes a nostalgic place of genuine self-expression and liberty.

The television movie contains here the seeds of a potentially subversive reading by posing the possible questions, Why did Craig go home to be miserable? Why did he leave his Asian lover? Why doesn't he return to Asia? Why doesn't he run away from the strictures of American capitalism? Although Craig claims to love Janet, Lien's imminent death completely closes off the possibility that Craig might turn his back on America, its racism, the oppressiveness of its familial and economic structures and return to the lost dream of his wartime euphoria. Just as Saigon no longer exists, the absolute impossibility of Craig's return to a utopic land, removed from the castrating burdens of the American suburban home, forces the narrative to work to reconfigure the ideologically troubled image of mainstream domesticity.

The movie goes about this by eliminating what it marks as "excessive" ideologically. In other words, it does away with the power of the two characters on the ideologically opposed poles of its moral

spectrum—Lien and J. C. Lien, as the symbol of an impossible feminine ideal, tragically tainted by her racial otherness and association
with America's defeat in Vietnam, must die to cleanse the text of any
residual guilt associated with Craig's and America's inability to fulfill
their role of paternalistic protector in Vietnam. J. C., too, must also be
eliminated to show that a failed America has changed.

With no sympathy for the plight of the boat people recently driven
from the fishing industry in Texas by acts of white supremacist ter-
rorism,[21] J. C., who refuses to "have an Asian kid in this family," embodies the excessive racism the movie works to soften by juxtaposing
that racism with Craig's paternalistic concern. The old patriarch's control over his daughter's life is also presented as excessive and implicitly
perverse (he encourages her to leave Craig rather than accept his
illegitimate son, thus breaking up the "sanctified" nuclear family, and
he gives her a frilly, childish, organdy dress so that she can physically
fulfill his desire to see her as a dependent girl rather than a woman).

In contrast, Craig represents the "new" patriarch. The movie legitimates this authority by equating it with "natural" heterosexual romantic love rather than the implicitly incestuous attachment Janet has to her
father. By requiring Janet to choose between himself and J. C., Craig,
in terms of the ideological operations of the narrative, cleanses the
movie of any excesses associated with racism, incest, potential female
independence, or any bending of class or gender roles. When Janet returns to her husband at the end of the tale and accepts his illegitimate
son into the family, she returns to a rejuvenated patriarchy, liberalized
and above reproach. The possibility that Janet would leave both Craig
and J. C. is never offered as an alternative.

As in all other versions of *Madame Butterfly*, Pinkerton inevitably
wins everything in the end. He has conquered the heart of Asia while
remaining true to the American bourgeois ideal of the white-defined
and dominated patriarchal home. His son's filial devotion proves his
altruistic disregard of color, while the elimination of the Butterfly en-
sures that racial otherness will be kept under control and the sexual
excesses of interracial romance will not be sanctioned.

In "The Lady from Yesterday," the Butterfly figure reaches its
pathetic extreme. Under the veneer of the self-possessed, educated,
articulate "lady" lies the fading, self-sacrificing, self-effacing shell of
the naive but vibrant Butterflies of other versions. In this case, Lien,
perhaps more than the others who preceded her, can be easily and
guiltlessly eliminated, without any nagging doubts occasioned by
suicide or illicit hopes attached to her survival. As the embodiment of
a racial and sexual otherness that cannot be accommodated within
bourgeois, patriarchal ideology or within the parameters of this televi-

sion movie, Lien simply fades away as a ghost who has sacrificed her existence for the perpetuation of a post-Vietnam, American dream of domestic bliss rid of any ugly taint of racism or xenophobia. With Lien, the disturbing consequences of the Vietnam War and its impact on veterans also fade into the background, and the rejuvenated American patriarch reemerges in the fiction to exercise his prerogative to rule over women, children, and all people of color.

In *China Gate* and "The Lady from Yesterday," the Pocahontas and Butterfly myths converge to create a metaphoric image of Vietnam that legitimizes American rule. Seduced by the promise of the American Dream, a feminized Vietnam sacrifices herself for the possibility of future assimilation into the American mainstream. Thus, the myth endures and continues to function not only as a romantic justification for traditional female roles within the patriarchy but also as a political legitimation of American hegemony internationally.

6

White Knights in Hong Kong

Love Is a Many-Splendored Thing and The World of Suzie Wong

The myth of romantic love and the myth of the romantic hero are inextricably intertwined in Hollywood fiction. These two popular myths often come together in stories that feature the rescue of a woman from the confines of a stifling family situation, romantic relationship, or job. When set in Asia, the romantic hero functions as a white knight who rescues the nonwhite heroine from the excesses of her own culture while "finding" himself through this exotic sexual liaison. Although these films may promise a social critique, they actually deliver a conservative adherence to the racial and gender status quo.

The figure of the "white knight" has its roots in both the myth of romantic love and the myth of the antiestablishment romantic artist. Romantic love promises spiritual transcendence, emotion winning out over social stigma, while actually delivering female passivity, domesticity, and a rationalization of women's subservient role. Hollywood's romantic hero, like Byron, Rousseau, Goethe, and his other late eighteenth- and early nineteenth-century ancestors, also champions the belief in individual transcendence in the face of a closed, corrupt, aesthetically, morally, and emotionally bankrupt bourgeois society. At the same time, this myth presupposes a male artist in pursuit of a female muse. This "genius" may pity the poor and oppressed, but he has no need to do anything about the conditions he deplores. Although both myths are about breaking taboos and crossing social boundaries, neither myth allows for social change. The fantasy promises the pleasure of imaginatively breaking conventions while maintaining the inevitability of the dominant culture's right to rule.

The exotic figures prominently in both myths, because it allows for the exploration of these taboos at a distance from daily life, where any potential threat to the social order will be negligible. For Hollywood, Hong Kong has long been one of those privileged exotic locations. Like Paris, Casablanca, or, more recently, Saigon, it is a city that promises romance, adventure, and a pleasurable respite from the boredom and constraints of the everyday. It can be argued that, even for Hong Kong residents, Hollywood's version of their city promises the same mystery. The Hong Kong of these films is Hollywood's Hong Kong, constructed out of the American imagination and decidedly unlike even the Hong Kong film industry's vision of its own city.[1]

The myths of romantic love and the romantic hero surface in two post-World War II melodramas set in Hong Kong. *Love Is a Many-Splendored Thing* (Henry King, 1955) and *The World of Suzie Wong* (Richard Quine, 1960) use Hong Kong's exoticism to shore up these myths. However, not only does Hong Kong provide a distant location to explore the forbidden in relative safety but it also provides a space for the examination of more topical issues. It is a place where a postwar American identity can be defined against an emerging Asian communism and the decay of European colonialism. This is a cold war Hong Kong—poised between post-1949 Chinese communism and the decay of the British Empire. As such, it provides an ideal place for America to assert and legitimize its presence in Asia as an "enlightened" Western power opposed to British colonialism and promising a neocolonial prosperity in the face of socialist leveling.

In fact, Hong Kong provides a place where all sorts of social and ideological oppositions can be played out in fiction—East-West, Communist-capitalist, white-nonwhite, rich-poor, colonizer-colonized, European-American, Asian-American, progressive-conservative. Within the context of the Hollywood love story, moreover, all these oppositions can be addressed using the cinematic vocabulary of that fundamental opposition between male and female. By using the romance to examine these other ideological sore points, Hollywood can make any boundaries between nations and races appear as natural as the differences between men and women. Relationships between nations or races can be seen as the male-female romance writ large, with its patronizing sentimentality and inherent inequality left intact.

Both films open with elaborate wide-screen crane shots of the Hong Kong skyline, immediately situating their stories within a world of both sampans and skyscrapers. The opening long shots themselves visually prepare for the conflict between the foreign and the Chinese, between the modern and the traditional, while, at the same time, promising the exotic and, via established cinematic conventions, implying the romantic and erotic.

Set against this backdrop of Hong Kong exoticism, each film uses romance as a metaphor for racial harmony and intercultural understanding. Although the romantic relationships seem doomed because of the British colonial establishment's racist condemnation of Asian-Caucasian intermarriages, love transcends all social taboos and misunderstandings. Needless to say, these fantasies are extremely contradictory. Love may triumph over social stigma, but each narrative upholds that stigma by exacting a price for criticizing accepted social practices.

In each film, in fact, the romantic relationship is carefully held in check by a narrative that consistently refuses to unquestioningly champion a racially tolerant society. The fate of each couple is linked to or contrasted with images of disease, death, corruption, destruction, and decay. Although *Love Is a Many-Splendored Thing* ends tragically with the hero's death and *The World of Suzie Wong* ends somewhat happily with the couple reunited at its conclusion, neither film allows love to conquer all.

The dearest price for romance, in fact, is paid by the films' female protagonists. Each narrative favors a reading that makes William Holden (who plays the male lead in both films) the vehicle of his lover's salvation and the institution of heterosexual marriage the ultimate hope for womankind. Even though each film calls for racial tolerance, neither questions gender inequality or the right of their heroes to tear the heroines away from their own cultures and independent life-styles.

Based on the semiautobiographical novel by Han Suyin, *Love Is a Many-Splendored Thing* opens in 1949. Dr. Han (Jennifer Jones) is a young, Eurasian physician at a Hong Kong hospital overwhelmed by refugees from mainland China. A colleague takes the overworked Dr. Han, a widow, to a party given by one of the members of the hospital's board of directors.

There, she meets unhappily married Mark Elliott (William Holden), a journalist. Despite warnings that a relationship with Elliott might lead to gossip and damage her reputation, Han Suyin lets Mark pursue her. She describes her attraction to this American to herself and to others as a struggle between her European and Chinese "halves." The European "side" favors it, while the Chinese "side" is appalled by it. Eventually, Han Suyin gives in to Mark.

However, Mark is unable to get his estranged wife's permission to divorce, and the scandal ruins Dr. Han's career. Fired from her job, she moves out of the hospital dormitory with one of the orphaned children she has cured and goes to live with some well-to-do Chinese friends. There, she learns that Mark has been killed while on assignment in Korea. The film ends with Dr. Han's return to the couple's favorite trysting spot behind her hospital where she has a final rendez-

Figure 12. Han Suyin (Jennifer Jones) and Mark Elliot (William Holden) embrace at their favorite trysting spot high above the urban sprawl of Hong Kong in Love Is a Many-Splendored Thing *(1955). Still courtesy of Jerry Ohlinger's Movie Material Store.*

vous with Mark's spirit (personified by a voice-over and hazy glimpse of his image).

In *The World of Suzie Wong* (based on Richard Mason's semiauto-biographical novel about his life in Hong Kong during the Korean War), Robert Lomax (William Holden) goes to Hong Kong to pursue his dream of becoming an artist. At his seedy hotel, he befriends a young prostitute, Suzie Wong (Nancy Kwan), who becomes his muse, posing for him on a daily basis. Gradually, Robert discovers how truly pitiable Suzie is—illiterate, orphaned, sexually abused as a child, brutalized regularly as a prostitute. After Suzie is dumped by an upper-crust British alcoholic with marital problems, Robert's heart finally melts, and he and Suzie become lovers.

Even the discovery that Suzie has an illegitimate baby does not interfere with their romance. However, money does. Robert's paintings fail to sell, and he cannot afford the financial burden Suzie poses. Rather than let Robert lose face, Suzie disappears. Ironically, his paintings begin to sell at the same time, and Robert's former girlfriend, Kay (Sylvia Sims), her eye now on a successful artist rather than a bohemian bum, urges Robert to forget about Suzie.

During a severe rainstorm, Suzie turns up in front of the hotel. She begs Robert to help her rescue her baby from the flood threatening to wipe out the hilltop slum. Despite their efforts, the baby dies. At the infant's funeral, Suzie and Robert reconcile and walk off together as a couple.

The plot lines of *Love Is a Many-Splendored Thing* and *The World of Suzie Wong* reveal a profound similarity in Hollywood's formulaic treatment of interracial romances between Caucasian men and non-white women. Both films broach, dramatically play out, and narratively resolve the same ideological issues by invoking some of Hollywood's favorite myths: the myth of the white knight, the myth of femininity, and the myth of the Orient. Through these myths, Hollywood takes up issues of race, ethnicity, and sexual identity, explores narratively the ideological contradictions they imply, and masks those contradictions by using cinematic conventions.

The White Knight

In *Femininity: The Politics of the Personal*, Barbara Sichtermann observes,

> As girls growing up, nearly all their dreams to do with love and sexuality and their emotional and physical future contain a *knight in shining*

armour. Instead of "knight" I could have written hero, or Prince Charming for that matter. At some point a shining figure is supposed to burst into the girl's world and transform everything.[2]

Stepping out of medieval romantic quest tales and into the present day, the heroic knight promises salvation from any number of woes ranging from simple lack of self-esteem, boredom, and sexual frustration to poverty, oppression, or the stifling confines of the family. As Sichtermann points out, the heroine is absolved by her passivity of any guilt related to the sexual nature of the fantasy. The knight spies her, finds her worthy, and scoops her up. She need not lift a finger.

The myth of the *white* knight circulates within a Western culture that has continuously defined itself against what it has identified as the nonwhite other from the Moor or the Jew of the medieval imagination to the black, Asian, or Hispanic of today. Thus, the myth operates to perpetuate not only gender inequalities but racism as well. Clearly, the knight's "whiteness" signifies his moral purity, his unquestionable natural right to carry the heroine away without being accused of abducting her.

He has legitimized white rule by saving womankind in general from what the myth characterizes as the *dark* aspects of sexuality, associated in the racist imagination with the nonwhite male antagonist. Chivalry, which developed as the European nations found it increasingly necessary to define themselves as superior to African and Middle Eastern cultures, has always acted as a way of assuring Western moral righteousness by pointing to its own enlightened treatment of the "weaker sex." The white knight's gender and racial superiority and concomitant moral imperative to rule are thus simultaneously affirmed.

In *Love Is a Many-Splendored Thing* and *The World of Suzie Wong*, both Mark Elliott and Robert Lomax function as white knights. (The William Holden star persona may, as a consequence, be forever linked to this modern-day romantic hero traipsing about righting wrongs in the Third World. In another film made around the same time, *Satan Never Sleeps* (1962), Holden plays a white knight priest in China saving the locals from the perils of communism.) Both Suzie Wong and Han Suyin must be saved. Although the nature of their distress varies, both clearly need the saving grace of the white hero's love.

In both films, Holden represents a very modern white knight, a peculiarly American, almost antiheroic version of the stock type. Elliott and Lomax are expatriates, who, like Rick Blaine in *Casablanca* to cite another well-known Hollywood example,[3] live abroad both to escape from and find themselves, to flee and search for their identity as Americans. In both films, the heroes, through their interracial love affairs, come to grips with their American dreams of melting-pot equality. In *The World of Suzie Wong*, for example, Robert physically battles a brutal, working-class British sailor and verbally attacks Kay's, her father's, and his alcoholic friend Ben's (Michael Wilding) attitudes toward Asians. In *Love Is a Many-Splendored Thing*, too, Mark has ample opportunity to show himself superior to his British contemporaries because of his liberal attitudes toward race. Because of this, when the real ideological workings of these films kick into full gear and they begin to shore up attitudes supporting white supremacy, that racism can always be softened by this comparison between American and British attitudes.

Moreover, the moral right of America to take over from the British in Asia becomes imaginatively rationalized through Holden's characters' growing sense of themselves as American. In *Love Is a Many-Splendored Thing*, Mark, even though he is only a journalist, dies on the battlefield as the predominantly U.S.-supported UN troops fight the invading North Korean Communist forces. In *The World of Suzie Wong*, a fortune-teller's prediction that Suzie will grow old in America seems to suggest that the couple walking away from the camera at the film's conclusion is also walking away from Asia toward an American future.

In addition to this crisis in national identity, both films also present their heroes with another identity crisis that must be resolved, that is, a crisis in their identities as men. In *Love Is a Many-Splendored Thing*, Mark is plagued by the off-screen presence of an estranged wife living in Singapore who refuses to give him a divorce. In addition, Suyin's commitment to her career as a doctor always threatens the relationship with the possibility that she will give up her love affair with Mark to pursue her vocation in China. In *The World of Suzie Wong*, Robert finds his male ego challenged by Kay O'Neill, whose active pursuit and attempts to control both his love life and career could mean a symbolic castration at every turn. Also, Suzie's success as a prostitute haunts Lomax, who cannot make a living as an artist, and threatens his self-definition as a "real" man able to provide for his woman.

However, in each film, the Caucasian woman remains independent and potentially dangerous, while both Suzie and Suyin give up their independence in the name of love. In playing the Caucasian women off against the Asian women, Hollywood can affirm male identity against the threat of the Western "new" woman, perhaps influenced by an emerging feminism or the memory of certain gender barriers relaxed while the men were away during World War II. The films present these characters as calculating, suffocating, and thoroughly undesirable enemies of "love." In fact, part of what both Suzie Wong and Han Suyin are saved from in each film is the threat that they may become like their Western sisters. Thus, the films can uphold both the gender and racial status quo by depicting Asian women as more truly "feminine," content at being passive, subservient, dependent, domestic, and slaves to "love." The films implicitly warn both white women and women of color to take the Western imagination's creation of the passive Asian beauty as the feminine ideal if they want to attract and keep a man.

In both *Love Is a Many-Splendored Thing* and *The World of Suzie Wong*, the heroines' love affairs save them from the potentially defeminizing threat of economic independence. Although prostitution may be a dubious career at best, Suzie Wong must give it up as her only means of support in order to keep Robert. In Han Suyin's case, the effect of her love affair with Mark has consequences far more deadening to the emerging independence of the postwar woman in America or abroad. As S. N. Ko points out in his essay, "Under Western Eyes," Mark Elliott's main function in the film is to woo Suyin and to "'save' her from a life dedicated to saving others."[4]

Throughout the course of the film, Suyin moves from the operating room, where she is first introduced, to her friend's guest room, where she sets up housekeeping as the adoptive mother of a little orphan girl. In the final scene of the film, she is shown at the lovers' trysting spot on a hill, governed by a single phallic tree set against an empty, mountainous horizon, where the modern Hong Kong skyline cannot be viewed. The ending visually returns Suyin to her rightful place within the domestic realm and nature, where women are women and men are men.

Moreover, Han Suyin has been saved from another threat to her femininity (and, therefore, to Mark's masculinity). That is, she has been saved from China, from the threat of communism, and from any gender leveling the new political order may advocate. Suyin wavers throughout most of the film between her devotion to Mark and her desire to return to mainland China to work as a doctor. By the film's conclusion, however, Suyin has definitely chosen America over China in the cold war as well as romance, "saving" her from the possibility of a Communist future.[5] Despite Mark's death at the end of the film, Suyin never is seen wavering from her decision to stay away from mainland China and remain with her adopted refugee daughter in Hong Kong.

Suzie's salvation in *The World of Suzie Wong* is even more literal, clearly affirming Western liberalism's claim to be able to criticize itself and press on for the good of "humanity." In the climactic scene in which a flood causes a landslide in the slum where Suzie's baby lives, Suzie seeks out Robert's help. Both struggle in vain to save the baby, and, through this lost battle, Robert, in fact, manages to save Suzie from the last emotional link she had with the slums of Hong Kong. At the baby's funeral, Robert and Suzie reaffirm their love, and she is effectively "saved" from returning to the world of prostitution, which led to this initial, tragic, failed domesticity. She is "free" to begin again under the protection of her white knight. Robert has a moral right to fulfill this role. As the "enlightened" American artist, he is positioned above the hypocrisy of the British (i.e., the sailors and Ben, who either brutalize or exploit Suzie) and the cruelty of the Asian male (the baby's unseen, but villainous father). Patriarchal, white, and American moral prerogatives, therefore, all neatly come together as the couple walk off into the distance at the film's end.

These fantasies of salvation are ideologically really more complicated, however, then they at first may appear. Although the assertion of American and male prerogatives is apparent in both Mark Elliott's conquest of Han Suyin and Robert Lomax's winning of Suzie Wong, Hollywood also casts these tales in the mold of the "woman's film" genre. They are stories about the vicissitudes of male desire, female sacrifice, the sexual double standard, the pain of social stigma for women, and a number of other themes associated with Hollywood films designed to appeal to female viewers. The white knight fantasy is a female fantasy. It represents a desire to be swept away from a sexless, quotidian existence, to have all one's problems solved by a stronger will, to escape from poverty and despair through the agency of a male hero.

In *Pocahontas's Daughters: Gender and Ethnicity in American Culture*, Mary V. Dearborn notes that interracial and interethnic unions between Caucasian men and nonwhite women form an important theme in American fiction written by women of color.[6] Although this union is often used to explore the dual oppression they feel because of their race and their gender in a white, American, patriarchal society, these writers have also fantasized about these unions as idealized "melting-pot" romances. In these cases, the relationship with the white male protagonist promises freedom of choice, material prosperity, and a Cinderella-like transformation of the ethnic female protagonist into an "American" herself, an accepted part of the larger society who has found her American Dream through romantic love.

That this aspect of the fantasy worlds of *Love Is a Many-Splendored Thing* and *The World of Suzie Wong* may appeal to female viewers, particularly to those marginalized by their class, race, ethnicity, or nationality, seems likely. The promise of the white knight erases the pain of racial and class differences, while affirming the promise that the man will provide materially and give his bride the benefit of his superior social standing.

Han Suyin and Suzie Wong act as points of identification for the female viewer to be drawn into this fairy-tale domain of the white knight cloaked in the trappings of the modern world. In both films, these female protagonists are stripped of their independence in the name of love and find themselves dominated by white men in a gesture of romantic expression that ostensibly flies in the face of bigotry. Through this contradictory play of gender and race, Hollywood manages to draw in viewers otherwise marginalized by the film.

Creating the "Orient": The Female
Body as a Site of Cultural Struggle

In *Orientalism*, Edward W. Said notes that although it would be wrong to look at the Orient as an idea without any material foundation, Europeans' ideas about Asia have more to do with Europe's definition of itself than with any genuine attempt to understand any other culture. Said states, "European culture gained in strength and identity by setting itself off against the Orient as a sort of surrogate or even underground self."[7] Logically, Said's argument can be extended to include America, which has also used the "Orient" as a convenient gauge for a contested and divided self-identity.

In *Love Is a Many-Splendored Thing* and *The World of Suzie Wong*, the heroes' own questionable national and gender identities, eventually buttressed by their romances with Asian women, are paralleled by the heroines' divided identities. Part of the narrative thrust of each film, in fact, revolves around the hero's attempts to define the heroine's "true nature." Through this role, each constructs his vision of the Orient in the person of his ideal lover and, in so doing, defines his own racial, gender, and national role.

The profession of each male protagonist allows each film to hide its ideological vision of the Orient under the guise of "artistic realism" or "objective reportage." As a journalist, Mark Elliott takes a supposedly professional, dispassionate view of the world around him. Thus, when Suyin decides not to leave Hong Kong for Communist China, it grows out of both her love for Mark as a man and a tacit acceptance of the American political position he represents. Her choice seems rational because of Mark's own willingness to give up his life reporting on the actions of the UN troops in Korea, dying in a struggle against Asian communism. He has created through his journalistic pseudo-objectivity but actual partisanship an Orient that Suyin accepts as authentic. Her acquiescence to Mark's political vision rationalizes the film's own cold war position for the viewer.

Similarly, as an artist, Robert Lomax creates the Orient through his paintings, while hiding behind the ideological ploy of simply "recording" Hong Kong life on canvas. Through his art, in fact, he creates an idealized vision of a maternal, "authentic" Suzie, hidden under her street-wise exterior. That only a Western artist could see beneath the surface of the Hong Kong slums is taken for granted. It is America's prerogative to come to Asia to reveal but actually create the Orient.

In both films, the Orient, which Mark and Robert create, is represented by their lovers, whom they force to conform to a Western patriarchal vision of both Asia and femininity. This Pygmalion fantasy of creating a woman as an idealized "other" has long been a favorite Euroamerican tradition, and it surfaces in both films as part of the mission of the white knight not only to save but to transform his beloved. Several similar scenes in *Love Is a Many-Splendored Thing* and *The World of Suzie Wong* underscore the dramatic force behind Mark's and Robert's insistence on defining the "essence" of the Orient by trying to manipulate their lovers' appearances.

When Mark picks up Han Suyin for their first date, she appears wearing a Western cocktail dress and evening wrap. He voices his disappointment and asks Suyin to change. She refuses and offers to make a present to Mark of the Chinese frock she had worn when they first met. This flippant but mild affront to Mark's masculinity marks Suyin's ability to stand up for herself, to wear whatever clothes she likes, to brazenly question her suitor's masculinity when he appears overly interested in her attire. However, this "Western," assertive side of Suyin quickly disappears later in the evening. The couple's celebration of the Moon Festival on a floating restaurant in Aberdeen brings out Suyin's "Chinese" side in her insistence on following Chinese superstitions.

Not surprisingly, Suyin appears in Western dress (a swimming suit) on only one other occasion in the film—the scene on the beach in which Mark makes love to her for the first time. Putting the issue of ethnic identity momentarily aside, the exposure of Mark's bare chest and Suyin's body contours lays to rest any question of Mark's masculinity or Suyin's femininity. Suyin's seduction at the beach silences the issue of proper gender roles completely, and in subsequent scenes questions of ethnic and racial identity dominate.

During the couple's rendezvous in Macao toward the end of the film, when the issue of Suyin's ethnic appearance resurfaces for a last time, Suyin is attired in a Chinese evening dress. Mark remarks, "I want all my friends to say, 'Who is that beautiful Chinese girl Mark Elliott is with?'" Although Suyin tries to assert her own identity, correcting him by saying "Eurasian," her choice of dress and acceptance

Figure 13.   Han Suyin and Mark Elliot in swimsuits leave no doubts about their "true" gender identities in Love Is a Many-Splendored Thing. *Still courtesy of Jerry Ohlinger.*

of her role as Mark's mistress attest to his ability to define both her gender and her race. In so doing, he has also safely guarded against any sexual or cultural blurring that may have threatened his dominant position. The film leaves no question about his right to define and maintain Western conceptions of difference.

The issue of dress and appearance also surfaces in *The World of Suzie Wong*. Like Mark, Robert is upset when his lover appears in Western attire. Although Suzie dresses in very revealing, tight, Chinese-cut dresses (cheong sam) throughout most of the film, Robert says nothing and simply accepts Suzie's attire, even though it clearly marks her as a prostitute.

In fact, the film makes it quite obvious that Suzie's sexual displays encourage Robert's muse. Before Robert paints Suzie for the first time, for example, he watches her dance with a sailor in the hotel bar. The camera centers on her in midframe, with her legs clearly on display. She provocatively plays with her hair and the sailor's hat as Robert looks on. The next shot shows Robert at his easel. He calls for Suzie—not for sex, as she thinks at first, but to pose for him. The spectacle of her sexuality, which could potentially give Suzie a castrating power over Robert, is transformed into Robert's project to paint the exotic. Thus, it does not threaten his identity either as a man or as a Westerner.

However, when Suzie arrives at Robert's, later in the film, in a European frock purchased by her British lover, Robert becomes enraged. Once again, the camera displays Suzie's body as visual spectacle by tilting slowly from her blue high-heeled shoes, up her legs, past her flower-patterned bag and dress, to her small, veiled hat. She smiles off-screen, looking for Robert's approval. He disappoints her by angrily snapping, "You look like a cheap European streetwalker." Robert then takes Suzie to his bed, strips her down to her black lingerie, and throws her European frock out the window. Grabbing the little hat, he continues, "You haven't the faintest idea what real beauty is!"

Clearly, Suzie's desire to define her own identity, to move up in the world by assimilating into Western society, horrifies Robert. Whereas her sexuality can be contained within her Chinese exoticism, it threatens when it takes on Western trappings and a potential independence. Suzie steps outside her bounds as a woman and as an Asian, and Robert violently, passionately, puts her back in her place. Robert insists on his prerogative to define "beauty," that is, to define Suzie's dress and identity. The film's commitment to the myth of the romantic artist as above petty social strictures, as a genius who can reveal the "truth," as a passionate defender of the Western right to create the Orient, places Suzie's own futile attempts at male approval, assimilation, and self-definition at a clear disadvantage.

Beneath all this high art posturing, moreover, is the simple male pleasure of the striptease. Any threat Suzie's sexuality may pose is stripped away with her clothes. Her exposed body can titillate the viewer without guilt, since she was disrobed as a "punishment." The film allows the viewer the pleasure of lascivious interests coupled with an ostensible claim to moral superiority.

Later, Suzie accepts Robert's right to define her identity when she agrees to be painted in a traditional Chinese costume. Dressed in the white (ironically, the color associated with death and mourning in China) finery that Robert has purchased for her, she kneels to him and takes on the attitude of a traditional Confucian bride, kowtowing to her master. Robert has defined "beauty," "femininity," and the "Orient" as a Western patriarchal fantasy of white male domination. His artistic license has revealed the virginal Chinese bride beneath the Westernized prostitute. The line between the Orient and the Occident, China and America, spectacle and observer, creator and creation, female and male, is made natural under the cloak of romantic love and sealed with a kiss. Their sexual union does not blur but, rather, shores

Figure 14.   Robert Lomax (William Holden) creates the "Orient" in his ideal-ized portrait of the prostitute Suzie Wong (Nancy Kwan) in The World of Suzie Wong *(1960). Still courtesy of the Museum of Modern Art/Film Stills Archive.*

up differences that might otherwise threaten Western patriarchal power.

In both *Love Is a Many-Splendored Thing* and *The World of Suzie Wong*, the heroes' ability to define their lovers' identities is rational-ized by the initial presentation of the heroines as confused, divided personalities in need of this sort of romantic relationship to sort out their lives. Indeed, Han Suyin's Eurasian identity perhaps disturbs the ethnic and racial status quo more than Suzie's simple desire for Robert's approval and acceptance. Suyin's divided identity can never totally be subsumed by Mark's desire to make her his "Chinese" mis-tress.

Another character in a position similar to Suyin's provides a moral foil for the heroine. Suzanne (Jorja Curtright), like Suyin, is Eurasian. However, unlike Suyin, who prefers to pass for Chinese and live as a respectable widow, Suzanne dyes her hair blond, passes for English, and has a series of love affairs with well-to-do married Englishmen. Like Suyin, she challenges British bourgeois morality by upsetting the prohibitions against both adultery and miscegenation. However, unlike

Suyin, Suzanne plays the game by trying to pass for European and by keeping her love affairs secret. Interestingly, Suyin's love affair ends tragically, while Suzanne, presented ambiguously as both a welcomed friend of the heroine and as a hypocrite and opportunist, does not suffer for her transgressions. Thick-skinned, Suzanne has fit into the system, while Suyin remains an outsider. Mark's and Suyin's contempt for British colonial social conventions serves to place their love affair within a different order. They symbolize a new, idealistic liberalism, while Suzanne represents an older colonial hypocrisy, underscored by her own unexplained parentage. Thus Hong Kong colonialism is presented as morally bankrupt and decadent, whereas American liberalism emerges as a "natural" way of fixing and displaying difference, of affirming an old racial and sexual hierarchy under a new veneer of free expression.

Suzie Wong is similarly introduced as a confused soul in need of a more fixed identity. Whereas the question of Suyin's identity revolves around gender roles and race, Suzie's identity crisis is primarily rooted in issues of sexuality and class. She first meets Robert riding on the Star Ferry, which connects the Kowloon Peninsula to Hong Kong Island. Her claims to be "rich" and a "virgin" seem suspect, belied by her body movements, speech, and overall behavior. Soon, Robert realizes that the Mei-ling he encountered on the ferry is simply a persona created by the troubled and exploited prostitute Suzie. Suzie, then, is first presented as a child-woman, playing games to escape her brutalized existence.

Through his portraits of her as well as through his paternal and romantic interest, Robert reconciles the "virgin" Mei-ling with the "whore" Suzie. In Robert's paintings, Suzie becomes a Madonna holding her infant, a traditional beauty dressed in virginal white. Robert portrays her as an idealized Asian face severed from its environment in paintings that isolate Suzie visually from the Hong Kong slums. Just as Mark "saves" Suyin by creating a persona of the devoted, submissive, exotic, and erotic "Chinese" girl, Robert lifts Suzie from the gutter by creating an image of pure, maternal, dependent "Oriental" femininity.

If the "Orient" is seen reflected in these heroines, then it, too, metaphorically is presented as divided, contradictory, self-deceiving, childlike, and in need of the strong, paternal hand embodied by these American heroes. Both *Love Is a Many-Splendored Thing* and *The World of Suzie Wong*, then, define not simply the identity of individual women but the essence of an entire continent.

Neither *Love Is a Many-Splendored Thing* nor *The World of Suzie Wong* can be looked at as a clear, uncomplicated presentation of a particular or fixed ideology. Although both favor readings that ultimately uphold a dominant white, male, bourgeois ideology, enough gaps remain to draw in marginalized viewers. Hollywood's white knights do have their appeal to female and non-Western viewers, since they represent social advancement, assimilation, and the promise of the American Dream.

To recognize both the pull of these fantasies as well as their ability to subordinate many of the viewers drawn in by them, neither race, gender, ethnicity, nor class can be taken as isolated categories for analysis. If, on the one hand, issues of race and assimilation were taken in isolation, for example, both *Love Is a Many-Splendored Thing* and *The World of Suzie Wong* might be celebrated as liberal calls for racial harmony and tolerance. On the other hand, if gender issues were paramount, Han Suyin might be held up as a model of the emerging "new" professional woman of the postwar era and Suzie simply condemned as another incarnation of the Hollywood child-woman or "whore with the heart of gold" favored on American screens since the silent era. If, however, the films were treated only as cold war parables, the insistent, patriarchal discourses that shore up American identity as well as male privilege would be lost to the analysis. The figure of the white knight endures because of these narratives' ability to flexibly take into account a variety of ideological positions for a heterogeneous audience.

7

Tragic and Transcendent Love

Sayonara and *The Crimson Kimono*

Within the body of Western literature depicting romantic love, parallel pairs of lovers with opposed fates play a key role—for example, Emily Bronte's *Wuthering Heights* and Sir Walter Scott's *Ivanhoe*. In *Wuthering Heights*, for instance, unresolvable ideological issues brought up by Cathy's relationship with the dark, brooding foundling Heathcliff (e.g., issues concerning class, race, incest, and the excessive qualities of women's sexual passion) are displaced onto a younger generation where they find a certain equilibrium and sense of closure. If the excessive passions of the first tragic couple promise the transcendence of social taboos in death, then the second, younger couple allows for the possibility of a more earthly transcendence of cultural norms through their romance.

Thus, these narratives offer a dual perspective on the sexual taboos with which they deal. Death allows the first tragic couple to criticize society without changing it. This provides a sense of the inexorable workings of fate rather than a genuine plea for reform. The second couple, however, absorbs the social criticism of the first, weakens it, and allows for its accommodation within a slightly modified social order.

Hollywood has often used the device of parallel love stories to achieve similar ends. In the case of the interracial romance, the two couples provide the tragic "punishment" for those who cross racial barriers as well as the liberal "happy ending" for those who can be assimilated into the American mainstream. The tragic couple acts ambivalently as both the voice of social critique and as confirmation of the racial status quo. The couple that transcends the social taboo against miscegenation usually provides a weaker indictment of racism, since their union, at the conclusion of the film, confirms that American society is the tolerant melting pot it claims to be.

Moreover, the differences between the couples tend to mollify their usefulness as romantic critiques of a rigidly racist culture. For example, the tragic couple may not only break racial taboos but also challenge other cultural norms involving class divisions, gender roles, the patriarchal organization of the family, or heterosexuality. Race may be only the most obvious element in their inevitably doomed relationship. Similarly, the couple that transcends racial taboos may otherwise be the model of the American, bourgeois, patriarchal, heterosexual norm. Thus, these parallel couples tend to soften any genuine social criticism either the pathos of the tragic end or the relief of the happy union may otherwise provide.

Sayonara (Joshua Logan, 1957) and *The Crimson Kimono* (Samuel Fuller, 1959) provide two examples of Hollywood's use in the 1950s of the parallel love story to treat the issue of interracial sexuality. Although *Sayonara* is a large-budget, Academy Award-winning star vehicle and *The Crimson Kimono* a grade B exploitation film, closer examination reveals the profound structural similarities between these two films as well as the similar ways in which each orchestrates ideological contradictions arising from race, class, and gender representations.

Love and Death in *Sayonara*

Sayonara (based on a novel by James A. Michener) deals with a love affair between Major Lloyd Gruver (Marlon Brando), a pilot serving in the Korean War, and Hana Ogi (Miiko Tara), a star of Matsubayashi, an all-female musical company. Other interracial relationships parallel this principal one, including those between Gruver's Anglo-American fiancée, Eileen Webster (Patricia Owens), and a Kabuki performer, Nakamura (Ricardo Montalban), and between an enlisted man serving under Gruver, Joe Kelly (Red Buttons), and his Japanese wife, Katsumi (Miyoshi Umeki).[1]

Sayonara ostensibly makes a statement against racial intolerance within the context of postwar U.S.–Japanese relations. As in many Hollywood films, romance is used as a metaphor for interracial and intercultural understanding. As such, *Sayonara* is another entry in a long Hollywood tradition of social problem films that use melodrama and romance to make concrete (but also personalize, individualize, and often trivialize) broader social or political concerns.

Figure 15. Hollywood sells interracial romance and the exoticism of Japan in this poster for Sayonara *(1957). Still courtesy of Jerry Ohlinger.*

In fact, *Sayonara*'s message seems quite clear and its sympathetic treatment of interracial romance a move toward increased liberalization on the part of a film industry whose production code had strictly outlawed representations of miscegenation just a few years before. However, when looked at more closely, the film presents the viewer with a far more contradictory picture of race, culture, and sex than might first appear to be the case. In fact, *Sayonara* can be looked at as structured by a series of narrative transpositions that serve to obscure a good deal of the film's apparent social criticism. Through these narrative twists, the film manages to voice and then ignore ideological contradictions by transforming them into more distant but related problems. According to Roland Barthes's analysis of classical realist narratives in *S/Z*,[2] plots are usually driven forward by a series of such transpositions that create narrative interest, obscure ideological contradictions, and lead to an eventual narrative closure that promises to resolve both narrative and, symbolically, ideological conflicts in one movement.

Sayonara begins this narrative process with war, which stands in this film as the extreme form of cultural, national, and racial intolerance. A title reads "Korea 1951," setting the tale during the Korean War. In 1945, Korea, which had been under Japanese rule, was divided at the thirty-eighth parallel. In 1950, after the withdrawal of American troops in the south following the removal of Soviet troops in the north, North Korea, supported by the newly established People's Republic of China, crossed the dividing line in an attempt to reunify the country. UN troops, predominantly American, came to the aid of the Republic of Korea in the south. President Truman was able to manage UN involvement because the Soviets were boycotting Security Council meetings at the time. The cold war mind-set that surfaced after World War II now found expression on the battlefield. Eventually, a truce was reached under Eisenhower, and the country remains divided along the thirty-eighth parallel to this day. Controversy surrounding the war came from various sources: some thought it was illegal because no formal declaration of war ever existed; others condemned any U.S. involvement in foreign civil wars; still others thought it unwise to support the notoriously corrupt South Korean government, believing unification under the Communists to be inevitable. The U.S. Left, assailed by the House Un-American Activities Committee (HUAC) hearings and all the concurrent problems associated with the cold war domestically, was, however, unable to organize any clear opposition to the war.[3]

Although *Sayonara* seems to ask to be read as an antiwar film, the reality of the Korean War and the controversy it generated are quickly placed on the back burner. Early in the film, Gruver, apparently disillusioned with American involvement in Korea, mumbles that one of the pilots he shot down that day had a "face." This is the film's only real reference to the actual morality of war, and rather than take the Korean War as a historical event in its own right, the film instead chooses to quietly question war in general by allowing Gruver to comment on the humanity of his enemy.

Sayonara very quickly places the Korean War at an even greater distance in the following scene. During a medical examination a doctor announces that Gruver will be transferred to Kobe, in occupied Japan, at the request of his future father-in-law, General Webster. Leaving Korea behind, narrative interest moves to Japan, to a *post*war setting, where issues involving war, morality, and the nature of the enemy have an even greater temporal and emotional distance. Simultaneously, the dialogue shifts from a discussion of "downing" enemy planes to romance. The doctor asks, "Wouldn't you like to tango with one of those Japanese dolls?" Instead of questioning the morality of the Korean War or exposing the conflict between conscience and duty within the military, the narrative shifts from war to romance, obscuring the issue of war in the process but still making the romantic relationships understandable only through a reference to war and racial otherness.

Later, when Gruver ruminates on the meaning of his life and career choice, the fact that he may have had a disturbed conscience on his last mission in Korea fades even further into the background. At this point, that Korean "face" comes to symbolize a very personal dissatisfaction with Gruver's agreeing to conform to his own father's expectations. (The casting of Marlon Brando as Gruver distances the issue of the morality of the Korean War even further, since Brando is often associated with young, rebellious male characters who simply cannot conform to social expectations—for example, *On the Waterfront* [1954] and *The Wild One* [1954]) Even the vaguest questioning of the morality of the Korean War becomes here simply the expression of an Oedipal dilemma, thereby personalizing antiwar sentiments as rebellions against the father more than the military establishment he represents. Attitudes toward the war become more a question of individual psychological makeup than broader moral or political concerns.

However, the Korean War is not the only "structuring absence"[4] that kicks *Sayonara*'s plot into operation. To understand the impact the film had in 1957, it seems necessary to view the film's ideology against the backdrop of American history and the pressing social issues of the day.

By 1957, films dealing with the occupation of Japan and the aftermath of World War II already existed in fairly significant numbers. In fact, *Sayonara* must be seen as one of many films, like *Teahouse of the August Moon* (1956, which coincidentally features Brando as a comic Okinawan), *Cry for Happy* (1960), and *Japanese War Bride* (1952, discussed in the following chapter), which called for a new evaluation of America's view of Japan as an enemy nation within the framework of a story about interracial romance.

Sayonara, for example, argues that both sides suffered during the war. Pearl Harbor, Japan's expansion into Asia and the Pacific, and the massive horrors of the war fade away. However, as in its treatment of Korea, the film puts politics aside and focuses instead on the personal, for instance, on Hana Ogi's loss of her father to an American bomb. By taking its statement about peace and the horrors of war away from Korea, moreover, *Sayonara* removes one element of controversy that may have made the film less commercial. By removing some of the blame for World War II from Japan, the film can also symbolically remove some of the blame America might feel for Korea. Making war in general more problematic, the film makes Korea seem less of a fiasco.

In a similar fashion, *Sayonara* can be looked at as a veiled reminder of HUAC and its impact on Hollywood. Like *High Noon* (1952) and *Invasion of the Body Snatchers* (1956), *Sayonara* deals with the paranoia faced by insiders who suddenly find themselves on the outside. In this case, Gruver, the model officer and son of a model general, finds himself branded as a "rebel" and "troublemaker" because of his love for a Japanese woman. The thaw after Joseph McCarthy's downfall meant that this suppressed, socially critical side of Hollywood could again surface, and *Sayonara* must also be placed within this body of films.

However, although *Sayonara* begins as a statement on war, peace, and American militarism, it very rapidly shifts to the issue of race and sexuality. More than either Korea or World War II, civil rights is the issue closest to the emotional heart of *Sayonara* and, certainly, more recently on the minds of its 1957 audience. In "*The Searchers*: An American Dilemma,"[5] Brian Henderson notes that, although John Ford's *The Searchers* deals with relations between Native Americans and white settlers, the power of the film and the problems it treats relate more to the controversy surrounding blacks and civil rights in the mid-1950s than to Native Americans and the threat of interracial sexuality in the post-Civil War era. Like *The Searchers*, *Sayonara* deals with race and sexuality at a safe remove. Like Ethan Edwards, the protagonist of *The Searchers*, Lloyd Gruver is a Southerner, a military man who represents conservative Southern values. Supposedly, both characters stand for a South in transition. However, the power of

Brown v. *the Board of Education of Topeka*, which marked an end to legal school segregation, and the increasingly visible black civil rights movement are kept out of the picture.

This preoccupation with issues of racial separation and sexuality, though perhaps oblique, actually blurs *Sayonara*'s antiwar message. By dealing with race and war simultaneously, the film sidesteps any direct confrontation of either issue. Instead, it teeter-totters between both issues. War drifts even further out of the picture in a scene in which Joe Kelly and Gruver compare photographs of their fiancées. As Gruver tries to talk Kelly out of his planned marriage to a Japanese woman, race and the threat of miscegenation become the pivotal concerns.

Gruver describes his fiancée Eileen as an "American girl, with fine character, good background, good education, good family, good blood." Gruver links "blood," quality, and acceptability in his discourse, and his Southern drawl underscores the fact that race is the key element of the equation. Kelly then produces a photo of Katsumi, and even Gruver admits she is attractive. Kelly complains about racism in the military and produces several pamphlets, including "Things You Are Required to Know Before Marrying Orientals," and "But Will Your Family Accept Her?"

Certainly, a call for racial tolerance remains a central concern throughout the film; however, *Sayonara* complicates even this issue. After being chastised for threatening to give up his American citizenship to marry Katsumi, Kelly challenges Gruver's love for Eileen: "Perhaps you don't feel as strongly about your girl as I do about mine." At this point, the film twists away from the theme of racial tolerance to a questioning of gender identity and heterosexual romance. If *Sayonara* is about racial tolerance and understanding, it is also about keeping women in their "place" as wives and mothers. Rather than adhering to its initial interest in war, race, and national identity, the film takes a decidedly different turn and offers a very traditional view of femininity, masculinity, and romance as a bulwark against the other fundamental social and ideological changes alluded to within the film. Here, the conservative treatment of gender stands as a corrective to the film's more liberal treatment of race.

Romeo and Juliet in Japan: Transcendent Love and the Ideology of Romance

Any critique *Sayonara* may make of war, racism, or militarism is very firmly held in check by the film's very conservative treatment of romance. Within Western thought, from stories of courtly love during the Middle Ages to nineteenth-century bourgeois romantic notions of love as the key to personal salvation,[6] there has been an important link between social criticism and the dually forbidden and transcendent nature of romantic love. Standing outside laws and conventions that forbid it, romantic love acts as a corrective to social norms that are seen as restrictive, irrational, inhumane, intolerant, or hypocritical. However, even though the notion is linked to social criticism, it also quiets that criticism by placing it in the realm of individual eccentricity. Rather than calling for sweeping social change, romantic love only calls for a bit of tolerance. Further, since romantic love is so often linked to death and tragic ends of various sorts, that social critique is usually viewed as a hopeless cause even before the tale begins.

Moreover, romantic love also has its profoundly conservative side— a side keenly felt in *Sayonara*. Linked to emotion, the "natural" expression of deeply held feelings, romantic love makes a case for heterosexual coupling, and usually marriage, as the fulfillment of all desires and needs. Even more than national or racial boundaries, patriarchal ideology presents gender lines as beyond culture, "natural," "genuine," ahistorical, and immutable. If *Sayonara* questions national and racial boundaries on one level, it also affirms and solidifies very conservative notions of gender identity and sexuality on another.

In fact, perhaps more than anything else, *Sayonara* deals with the definition of heterosexual love and contrasts it indirectly but clearly to homosexuality, which the film presents as alluring but ultimately "unnatural" and "perverse." *Sayonara* expresses the threat homosexuality poses to traditional, patriarchal definitions of gender in three ways: (1) through the expression of female sexuality outside the realm of male control; (2) through the questioning of the definition of masculinity and its link to war and the military; and (3) through the challenge the Japanese theatrical convention of cross-dressing poses to gender boundaries.

By introducing Gruver as a man in moral turmoil because of a barely voiced suspicion that the Korean War is unjust, *Sayonara* implicitly places Gruver's identity as a man in crisis. Until he meets Hana Ogi, Gruver is presented as drained of power, of masculine potency. For example, the doctor finds him run-down; Kelly questions his love for Eileen; Eileen questions his lack of interest in sex; he himself questions his dedication to the military.

However, instead of openly saying that this identity crisis is linked to Gruver's male identity and war, *Sayonara* puts the blame on women—namely, on Gruver's fiancée Eileen. The film introduces Eileen in two photographs—one in which she is seated with her mother and the other showing her scantily clad in a bathing suit. In both, she represents potential threats to Gruver's sense of identity. In the first, as the "girl next door," the proper daughter of a general, she embodies all those values that Gruver has begun to question through his own realization that the Korean War may be wrong, that is, that the enemy has a face. In the second, as the smiling bathing beauty, Eileen represents female sensuality, a sexuality that may be beyond Gruver's power to control.

Kelly's fiancée Katsumi, by contrast, sits passively in her photograph, wrapped demurely in a traditional kimono, smiling up at the photographer. If Eileen has the force of military tradition and the threat of female sexuality behind her, Katsumi simply represents a meek agreeability.

The differences between Katsumi and Eileen become even more striking when the two appear on screen. Eileen dresses flamboyantly in clothes that accentuate her figure. When alone with Gruver, she confronts him directly about his future plans and asks him why he is not

Figure 16. Major Lloyd Gruver (Marlon Brando) attends the wedding of enlisted man Joe Kelly (Red Buttons) to Katsumi (Miyoshi Umeki) in Sayonara. *Still courtesy of Jerry Ohlinger.*

more passionate about their relationship: "Haven't you ever felt like grabbing me and hauling me off to a shack somewhere?" She also complains about Gruver's father's cool treatment of his mother, that she is kept at home, at a distance from his father's work and public life. Clearly threatened by Eileen's questions, Gruver defends traditional marriages, the military, and sexual restraint.

The scene that immediately follows features Kelly and Katsumi's wedding, with Gruver in attendance as the best man. Unable to speak English, quiet and still, Katsumi stands in marked opposition to Eileen. Gruver speaks to Katsumi quietly and slowly, as one might to a child, and, at the conclusion of the ceremony, he kisses her lightly on the mouth. Katsumi smiles and blushes. Unlike Eileen, Katsumi is not openly sexual but passive, dependent, and childlike. Gruver clearly envies Kelly his bride.

The film holds Katsumi up as a paragon of female virtue. Later, she is shown performing her domestic tasks, cooking, serving guests, bathing her husband, cheerfully and quietly. Her devotion to Kelly is all-consuming and unquestioning. At one point, Katsumi even contemplates self-mutilation, in the form of a questionable eye operation, to please her husband by "fooling" the authorities into thinking she is white. Kelly beats her for this stupid idea, exercising his control over her body and her identity. Gruver steps between them and quiets Katsumi paternalistically by telling her "not to do it again." Once again, he clearly envies Kelly his devoted wife.

If *Sayonara* calls for tolerance on the part of the viewer to accept this interracial marriage, the text also seems to be warning American women to take a lesson from Katsumi's passivity and devotion. After all, Katsumi keeps her man, while Eileen loses hers. Moreover, although *Sayonara* attempts to criticize racism, the film, as it shores up traditional gender definitions, also sticks to accepted stereotypes about Asians, particularly Asian women, as passive, childlike, and servile. Moreover, the passive Katsumi seems to act as a metaphor for the defeated Japan by reworking earlier racist stereotypes. In *War Without Mercy: Race and Power in the Pacific War*,[7] John W. Dover notes that the postwar pro-Japanese representations of Japan really differed little from wartime stereotypes. Rather, the same stereotypes were simply placed in a new context. For example, if Japanese childishness was seen as "irrational" and "unthinking" during the war, the same childishness meant "good little ally," "faithful imitator," and "dependent trading partner" in the postwar era.

In this case, Katsumi's passivity and dependence represent an idealized femininity. In the American popular imagination, women of color often function stereotypically as "natural" earth mothers, the embodiment of a belief in a "genuine," exotic femininity beyond cultural control, something her more modern Western sisters supposedly lost by their grumblings about emancipation.

This ideologically absolute notion of femininity informs Gruver's desires and adds another complicating factor to the film. *Sayonara* may call for peace and tolerance, but it also demands the strengthening of male dominance over women. Moreover, by making the men Anglo-American and the women Japanese, the film supports America's own paternalistic attitude toward Japan. *Sayonara* seems to be saying that just as it is natural for men to love and dominate passive women, it is natural for America to take a similarly dominant posture toward Japan. Although mildly broached at the film's outset, questions surrounding both male and military prerogatives are eventually put to rest, and white, male, American hegemony is ultimately upheld.

The clearest working out of this ideological crisis of male, national, and racial boundaries comes in the narrative complication and resolution of Gruver's love affair with Hana Ogi. Structurally, the film places Hana Ogi between the active Eileen and the passive Katsumi. As the narrative unfolds, however, Hana Ogi moves away from the independence and sexual expression represented by Eileen to the more traditional, servile, domestic role represented by Katsumi. The film presents Gruver as "saving" Hana Ogi from the excesses of her own culture, which permits women in certain circumstances to live apart from and independently of men. Gruver puts her in touch with her "true" nature, that is, her desire for a "normal" domestic life and children.

Although Katsumi does represent the "ideal" woman, there is another side to *Sayonara*'s vision of Japanese gender relations. If Katsumi stands for the everyday domestic aspect of Japanese sexual conventions, then Hana Ogi represents the larger-than-life theatrical world of Matsubayashi, where ordinary gender definitions do not apply in the same way, a world that is coded as "perverse." Likely based on the Takarazuka Young Girls Opera Company,[8] Matsubayashi is a musical theater in which all the roles are played by women. Part entertainment venture, girls' school, and nunnery, the Matsubayashi parallels the U.S. military in its propensity for rule making, hierarchical relations, and a sex-segregated environment.

Hana Ogi is the star of Matsubayashi, famous for her portrayal of male roles. When Gruver first sees her, she is on her way to the theater, dressed in boyish drag, wearing knickers, a turtleneck sweater, and a felt hat with a long pheasant plume. She dramatically stands out from the other women, who are dressed in kimonolike uniforms of various colors. Her association with a transgressive but beautiful

Figure 17.   Gruver with Hana Ogi (Miiko Tara) in drag surrounded by other performers in the all-female musical company Matsubayashi. Still from Sayonara *courtesy of the Museum of Modern Art/Film Stills Archive.*

androgyny is further accentuated when she is given a white cock by a fan. Gruver is mesmerized. Hana Ogi embodies the ultimate personification of forbidden love; not only is she a member of an enemy nation, a different race, and part of a theatrical troupe that absolutely forbids its members to marry or even date but she is also in drag, a male impersonator who conjures up an even more forbidden homoeroticism.

If Korea and Eileen put Gruver's masculinity in doubt, then certainly Hana Ogi adds another dimension to the depth of his rebellion against tradition and the film's own play with yet another taboo form of love. Needless to say, after putting this last possible transgression into play, *Sayonara* reverses itself. As Gruver wins Hana Ogi over from Matsubayashi, he symbolically makes her into a "woman," and she gradually puts aside her mannish attire to dress in traditional kimonos.

However, before becoming involved with Gruver, Hana Ogi represents a dream of androgyny, since she has the ability to change gender from one musical number to the next. In the first performance Gruver sees at Matsubayashi, for example, Hana Ogi appears in Western tie and tails, a Western evening dress, traditional Japanese kimonos, and male attire from various historical periods. Within the musical spectacles, she visually transcends nation, race, and gender.

A good deal of the contradictory play of *Sayonara*'s narrative revolves around the power of Hana Ogi's provocative performance and the promise Japanese theatrical traditions seem to offer, that is, the promise of a world in which cultural, racial, and gender boundaries can be toyed with and aestheticized rather than fought over and upheld through war. However, if part of the force of Gruver's attraction to Hana Ogi (and, through identification with the protagonist, the viewer's) comes from a latent homosexual desire, a wish to live in a utopian world without socially constructed and constricting laws governing race, nation, or gender, then the film allows this titillating possibility to surface only briefly.

After a sequence in which Hana Ogi, always in drag, silently rejects Gruver's advances on a daily basis, she finally agrees to meet her persistent admirer at Kelly and Katsumi's. When Gruver enters the room where she is waiting, he is dumbfounded. Kneeling at a low table, eyes downcast, dressed in a woman's kimono, Hana Ogi's gender has visibly changed. No longer coded as "male," as an androgyne, she has become a woman, and it is not surprising that this scene should mark the beginning of Gruver and Hana Ogi's love affair. Hana Ogi apologizes both for her rude behavior and for hating Americans. Here, gender change and submission to American authority coincide. Just as the woman apologizes for stepping outside her gender and snubbing the advances of a man, the nation also symbolically apologizes for what the film supposedly seeks to condemn in American society—racism and intolerance. By projecting bigotry back onto the object of prejudice, the film's critical bite softens yet again.

Conveniently, Gruver's love affair with Hana Ogi restores three important power hierarchies that the film had placed in crisis—those between the East and the West, nonwhites and whites, and women and men. It is somewhat ironic that Gruver learns racial tolerance through the sexual subjugation of a woman, who sacrifices her independence for his enlightenment. The didactic point of the narrative blurs, and the viewer may begin to wonder if by putting Hana Ogi back into her proper "place" as a woman, Gruver is not also symbolically putting the racial and national other into its "place" as subordinate to white America.

Hana Ogi performs her last musical number in the film dressed as a Japanese bride mounted on a white horse. Visually, even before Gruver appears to talk her into marriage, he has won her, "saved" her from the "perverse" celibacy and androgyny of the Matsubayashi stage. In the climactic scene that follows, Gruver tells Hana Ogi that they have an obligation to have children, and, when, at the film's conclusion, Hana Ogi makes a statement to some reporters about her future, she reiterates this.

If at one point in *Sayonara*, the choice for Gruver seemed to be between a career and love, that choice is no longer much of an issue by the film's conclusion. General Webster has already informed Gruver of the military's plan to become more lenient toward interracial marriages. Although stigmatized by the relationship, Gruver loses less and actually regains the virility and masculinity the film had implied were in crisis at its outset. Hana Ogi, by contrast, sacrifices her career, her independence, and the free play of gender roles she represented.

Through the conservative treatment of gender, the film also silences its antiwar and antimilitary messages. The liberal promise of new laws to rectify racism and the excesses of the military is fulfilled, and the social crisis referred to at the film's beginning has been fixed without overturning the status quo. Gruver has again become a "real" man because he has saved Hana Ogi from the supposedly perverse excesses of a life without men by making her a "real" woman—a future bride and mother. The U.S. military has cleaned its house and remains intact.

The issue of the Korean War never resurfaces. The survival of Hana Ogi and Gruver's romance brings all narrative and, symbolically, social conflicts and contradictions back into balance. Narrative closure reaffirms gender, racial, and cultural norms with little variation.

Loose Ends: Subplots and Unsolved Social Conflicts

Although the social criticism promised by *Sayonara* really fizzles out in the resolution of the main plot line, the film's two principal subplots involving interracial romances remain more problematic. Kelly and Katsumi's constant harassment by racists within the military and their eventual double suicide point to a possibly more biting denunciation of American racism, military injustice, and class bias. Similarly, Eileen's relationship with Kabuki performer Nakamura indicates that the gender questioning squelched by Gruver's pursuit and conquest of Hana Ogi may not have been completely obliterated through the operation of patriarchal ideology.

The two relationships represent unanswered narrative questions. The first revolves around why Kelly and Katsumi commit suicide, while for Hana Ogi and Gruver death never comes up as a possible solution to their dilemma. The other narrative question involves whether or not Nakamura's relationship with Eileen is platonic. Through these two unresolved dilemmas, the narrative opens up a certain space for a possible ideological interrogation of class and gender shut off by the main plot.

Throughout *Sayonara*, Kelly is coded as "working class"—an Irish ethnic and an enlisted man under Gruver's command. In contrast to Kelly's working-class roots, Gruver represents the aristocratic old South, West Point, military privilege, and power. Kelly openly questions the military hierarchy and vocally criticizes its institutionalized racism. However, his criticisms are never actually articulated as "antimilitary" or "antiwar." He remains personally loyal to Gruver, his immediate superior, even after Gruver rather viciously opposes Kelly's marriage, calling his fiancée a "slant-eyed runt."

As Gruver changes from a virulent bigot to a supporter of interracial romance, the military, too, symbolically cleans its house. Particularly after the tragedy of Kelly and Katsumi's deaths and an anti-American riot by Japanese who oppose Gruver's relationship with Hana Ogi, the military decides it is time to use the propaganda power of Gruver to its own advantage. It seems appropriate that Gruver and Hana Ogi's reconciliation should be celebrated in front of the Japanese and American military press outside Matsubayashi's Tokyo theater. Here, both for the stage-door fans in the fiction as well as for the spectators in the movie theater, Gruver and Hana Ogi's relationship becomes legitimate as a "news story," a spectacle that seemingly publicizes the dream of American "democracy in action" in the realm of social change.

Flamboyant and theatrical, Gruver and Hana Ogi are placed at a considerable distance from the more mundane problems facing the working-class couple, Kelly and Katsumi. Clearly, Gruver, despite his relationship with a Japanese woman, still has certain privileges that Kelly does not have—namely, money. Although never expressed as such, it is implied that Kelly and Katsumi are doomed because they simply do not have the financial resources to go against the system and live out their lives as a reproach to bigotry and racism. Gruver and Hana Ogi do have this privilege. For example, although Kelly had threatened to give up his U.S. citizenship to be with Katsumi, when the order comes for him to go back to the States, he chooses suicide rather than going AWOL or the more mundane possibility of serving out his stint in the military and returning to his wife in Japan.

The absurdity of the suicide is never voiced. Rather, in keeping with the traditions of the Western melodrama, it is simply presented as "tragic," reified as "fate." In fact, the film aestheticizes the double suicide by first introducing the idea in a Bunraku puppet performance featuring two doomed medieval lovers, the Japanese equivalents of Shakespeare's Romeo and Juliet. Katsumi and Kelly, as well as Gruver and Hana Ogi, are in attendance. When the star-crossed lovers in the puppet drama prepare to die, Katsumi and Hana Ogi are framed in a two shot. This visually underscores the possibility that either's forbidden romance may lead to a similar end.

However, it is Katsumi who dies, not Hana Ogi. Conveniently, *Sayonara*, conservatively articulating the truism that forbidden interracial love leads to tragedy, allows the working-class couple to sacrifice themselves to make the drama of the upper-class couple more poignant. Narratively, then, the double suicide, like the Bunraku play, makes aesthetic, if not logical, sense. It also keeps in play an ideologically conservative element within a fantasy that purportedly condemns racism.

The film opens up at least two possible readings of the suicide. One favors a bourgeois, romantic interpretation that Kelly and Katsumi could not continue to live in a cold world insensitive to their love. The other reading—somewhat against the grain of a film that aestheticizes death and romance—involves looking at class differences and military injustice as the principal motive force behind the double suicide. This opens up the possibility of a more critical stance against racism and the military.

Interestingly, Katsumi's suicide also suggests a reading against the ideological grain on the question of gender roles. Although coded as "feminine" and a "good woman," Katsumi is also presented as weak and dependent in an implicitly negative way. Hana Ogi, by contrast, has been "saved" from the gender questioning her male impersonations promised, yet she is still praised for her strength, clarity of thought, and ability to survive. Whereas Katsumi has nothing without Kelly, Hana Ogi always has Matsubayashi and the power and independence of money, prestige, and a secure job. In fact, it is, ironically, because of her independence that she can survive to become Gruver's wife. Once again *Sayonara* seems to ideologically hedge its bets by explicitly condemning professional women while implicitly praising their accomplishments.

Similarly, although Eileen loses her "man" because she is not as "feminine" as Japanese women, her relationship with Nakamura opens up some potentially subversive possibilities for reading gender as something other than eternally fixed and for looking at interracial sexuality in a different light. In and of itself, any relationship between a man of color and an Anglo-Saxon woman is more threatening to the status quo than the obverse relationship. Within American popular thought, the Anglo-American female represents hearth and home, the continuation of white-defined and dominated culture. If stolen or seduced away from white men, she represents a challenge to white

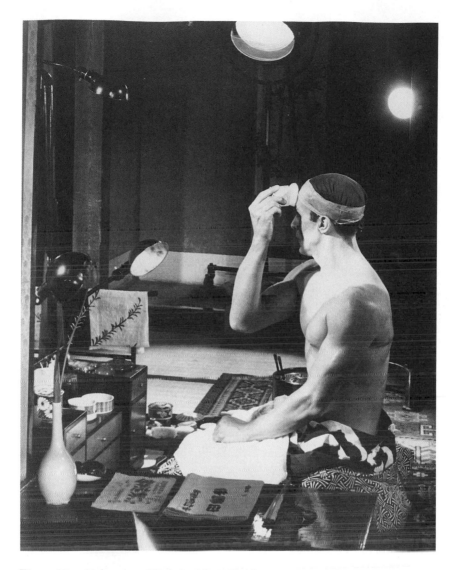

Figure 18. *Nakamura (Ricardo Montalban) prepares to defy gender classifications as he applies his Kabuki makeup in* Sayonara. *Still courtesy of the Museum of Modern Art/Film Stills Archive.*

male identity and authority. Not only does she question the truism that white American culture is superior to all others, she also challenges male authority by asserting herself as a woman who chooses to look outside the confines of her own culture for sexual expression. Thus, this relationship makes problematic both the racial and gender hierarchy within American culture.

Sayonara indicates that Eileen is fascinated by Nakamura because he is a Kabuki performer, a "male actress," able to play both female and male roles. Just as Hana Ogi magically transcends gender boundaries in Matsubayashi, Nakamura performs with the "grace of a woman and the power of a man." He can transform himself from an elegant lady into a fierce lion spirit within a few seconds on stage. For a woman like Eileen, who is openly critical of the traditional wifely role (although she is critical of it for being "unromantic," and she states that she wants to live "body and soul" with and for her man), this free play of gender roles has a very special appeal.

However, *Sayonara* keeps this couple at a distance from one another as well as the viewer. Although clearly enamored of Nakamura, Eileen takes every opportunity to proclaim her love for Gruver. Moreover, in the only scene in which Eileen and Nakamura are actually alone together, the series of close-ups used to present their dialogue visually keeps them separated. The possible increased intimacy of a two shot is avoided. Both Nakamura and Eileen look off-screen away from one another as Nakamura, in a contradictory gesture, discusses Eileen's beauty while claiming "not necessarily" to be making love to her. Eileen abstractly replies that she needs to learn much more about Japan and everything else. Whether this implies that Nakamura will teach her about sex as well as Kabuki and cherry blossoms is left to the viewer's imagination. Since this scene is the last in which the two actually appear together, the nature of their relationship remains obscure. Certainly, too, the fact that Nakamura's part is played by a Latin (Ricardo Montalban), rather than an Asian, actor further removes the threatening racial aspect of the fantasy, while keeping a certain exoticism at its core.

Despite this, the fact that a romance between Nakamura and Eileen is even hinted at opens up the possibility of another reading of the strictly conservative rendering of gender roles that the film features in its main plot. By choosing a relationship with a man of another race and an "enemy" nation, Eileen asserts her autonomy in a way that Gruver could never accept. Moreover, the free gender movement and sensuality that the Kabuki theater promises also allow for the potentially disruptive expression of female desire. All these possibilities, however, are only hinted at and then dropped, while *Sayonara* remains quite conservative in its treatment of both gender and class differences.

In fact, romance makes *Sayonara* a profoundly conservative film despite its seemingly genuine plea for peace and racial tolerance. Moving from war to race and subsuming both within the sexist ideology of romantic love weds a call for change to the reaffirmation of male—and, by implication, American—domination of the racially, ethnically, and sexually other.

Although ostensibly a critique of racism sugarcoated by a Romeo and Juliet love story, *Sayonara*, more profoundly perhaps, exists as a historical document that illustrates how the dominant ideology deals with social and cultural change by both acknowledging and squelching it. Although the film implies that Gruver and Hana Ogi ultimately live happily ever after as husband and wife, the rumblings of class and gender inequalities heard within the film's subplots do not seem to be wrapped up as neatly.

In fact, the rambling, contradictory sweep of such melodramas as *Sayonara* helps to explain the staying power of this particular genre. There is something for everyone. Gender play and female autonomy exist for women who had recently tasted other roles during World War II, only to have those alternatives taken away after the war by the reassertion of male privilege and the ideology of heterosexual romance. Racial tolerance and the promise of America's peaceful intentions vis-à-vis the rest of the world are there for the nonwhite and non-American viewer. Working-class issues are also voiced for the majority of viewers who may not identify completely with the film's principal bourgeois couple. All these possibilities, however, are checked by *Sayonara*'s ultimate rationalization of white, male, bourgeois privilege and power.

The "B" Version: Interracial Sexuality and Cold War Politics In *The Crimson Kimono*

The B-movie has traditionally filled a number of social and economic functions in the American cinema. Reaching their peak during the Depression when low-budget short features or serial dramas served as the second feature of a longer program, B-movies were designed as an added value to draw in financially strapped viewers. One type of B-movie, the "exploitation film," survived the decline of the double bill after World War II, when serials and other B-movie fare began to die out. Because of limited budgets and lowered aesthetic expectations, exploitation films have always been somewhat freer to explore issues that might shock a general audience and reduce revenues. Drug addiction, prostitution, transvestism, physical deformities, bigamy, and juvenile delinquency all promise to give the exploitation-film audience a voyeuristic pleasure in seeing the forbidden as well as a sense of moral, intellectual, or physical superiority.

Many of these low-budget films, using the hurried nature of their production to best advantage, are able to be topical in a way more carefully planned and laboriously produced films cannot. Also, as studio costs increased and the exploitation films moved out onto actual locations, the hand-held cameras, grainy film stock, and spontaneous feel began to give these films an additional gritty, journalistic edge. In many, a tension can be felt between this almost documentary-like topicality and the exaggerated histrionics of acting styles and melodramatic flourishes.

Marginalized by the preponderance of large-budget productions in Hollywood, the topics of racism and race relations always provided the exploitation market with appropriately provocative subject matter. Particularly in the post-World War II era, when the decay of the studio system and the death of the production code meant that even "prestige" pictures needed to test new ground to compete with television, the exploitation film had to become more excessive to turn a profit. Many big-budget features like *Sayonara, Love Is a Many-Splendored Thing, The Searchers*, and *Imitation of Life* had already tested the taboos against miscegenation by the end of the 1950s, challenging the exploitation film to go a step further.

Samuel Fuller, for example, became famous for his low-budget meditations on race and racism in America. *The Crimson Kimono* (1959) represents only one of Fuller's B-movie treatments of this issue. (Fuller's *China Gate*, analyzed in chapter 5, provides another example of his treatment of racism in American culture.) Virulently anti-Communist, Fuller was able to use the exploitation film to picture America as a society striving for equality within its own ranks as it also waged a cold war against the Eastern Bloc and its allies. Since he wrote, directed, and produced many of his own films (including, in this case, *The Crimson Kimono*), Fuller had the freedom to return time and again to issues of international politics and domestic civil rights as long as his films turned a profit.

Within his oeuvre, Fuller employed several different narrative strategies to attempt to reconcile the contradiction between American domestic racism and the United States' moral right to wage war in Germany to vanquish fascism and in Korea and Indochina to eliminate communism. Although the fellowship of the all-male military group provided one way for him to explore this issue dramatically, Fuller also used romance to depict the interpersonal dynamics of racism.

In *The Crimson Kimono*, for example, two Korean War veterans turned homicide detectives, Joe Kojaku (James Shigeta) and Charlie

Bancroft (Glenn Corbett), fall in love with the same woman, Chris Downes (Victoria Shaw). All three are thrown together during a murder investigation. Although attracted to Charlie at first, Chris soon discovers she is in love with Joe. Loyal to his friend Charlie, Joe tries to repress his feelings, but eventually they explode violently. As he confesses his love for Chris, Joe claims to detect a racist look on Charlie's face, which sparks an identity crisis for Joe that drives him away from Chris. Eventually, Joe admits that his charges of racism were unfounded, and although he only partially reconciles with Charlie, he is able to freely embrace Chris and kiss her at the film's conclusion.

Although not as provocative as a kiss would likely have been between a black actor and a white leading lady in 1959, this kiss between an Asian male character (actually played by a Japanese-American actor) and a Caucasian woman still tested the boundaries of what could or could not be depicted within the commercial cinema. The film plays with character types and viewer expectations springing from a history of Hollywood's villainous mandarins and "yellow peril" barbarians. However, although this kiss challenged racist attitudes to a degree, it did so at the expense of silencing any genuine interrogation of racism by making racial barriers a question of Joe's paranoid delusions.

Like most Hollywood narratives, *The Crimson Kimono* is a highly contradictory discourse that offers viewers a number of interpretive positions. The film attempts to balance an image of America as a melting pot, morally and culturally equipped to defend freedom abroad, with a view of America as an unequal society divided within. This uneasy balance is achieved through a narrative that upholds gender inequality by killing off, jailing, or domesticating virtually all signs of female independence, by denying that racism exists anywhere except in the deluded minds of its victims, and by holding the American military up as an exemplary champion of human rights. Thus, like *Sayonara*, it uses its parallel love stories to broach and then eliminate the ideological challenges interracial love affairs pose to the racial status quo.

High Art, Low Art, and the Domestication of the Exotic

Part of the way in which *The Crimson Kimono* keeps this ideological play in operation is by linking issues of race, exclusionism, and assimilation to questions of exoticism, sexuality, and aesthetics. Battles are played out between the sexes, between high art and low art, and between the superficial, decorative differences associated with ethnic otherness and actual cultural distinctions. In fact, the issue of racial difference surfaces rather late in the film, almost as an afterthought.

As the credits roll, the painting of the kimono of the film's title gradually emerges from a pencil sketch to its completed form. Although the painting itself is representational, it is shown on an easel, with brushes and paints next to it, with more abstract, Cubist-influenced paintings in the background. A brush appears in frame and signs the painting "Chris."

The scene changes from this decidedly "high" art world of academic painting to the "low" art milieu of a Los Angeles burlesque theater, where the striptease artist Sugar Torch (Gloria Pall) is performing. After her act, she goes backstage and is shot by an unidentified figure dressed in a fedora and trench coat. She runs out onto the boulevard and collapses dead in the middle of the street.

In these two opening scenes, *The Crimson Kimono* sets into operation its major narrative questions: Who is Chris? Who killed Sugar Torch? What is the relationship between the two? Or, put another way, what is the relationship between high art and striptease, between the B-movie world of the crime thriller and the art academy? How are all these questions related to the convergence of the Japanese exoticism of the kimono and the vulgar eroticism of Sugar Torch's blond wig and stripper's spangles? What is the relationship between the painter's voyeurism in the service of art, the spectator's enjoyment of the striptease, and the mystery of death and sexual allure? The mysteries associated in the Western patriarchal imagination with Asia, the female body, the nature of artistic genius, and the ultimate inscrutability of death all merge in these two opening scenes to set the stage for the complex unraveling of what, on the level of pure plot, is a very formulaic *policier*.

The close-up of Detective Joe Kojaku's face at the beginning of the film's third scene seems to offer some hope for the resolution of the contradictory images of demure kimono-clad beauty and brazen stripper. When it becomes clear that the figure in the portrait is none other than Sugar Torch, the question is immediately raised, Did she have a Japanese boyfriend?—offering an interracial love affair gone sour as the solution to the murder and the mystery of a blond geisha.

However, it soon becomes apparent that Sugar Torch transgressed aesthetic rather than racial divisions. Her search for a new striptease act rather than for romance—interracial or otherwise—led to death. Ironically, it is the Japanese policeman who is drawn into an interracial love affair rather than the dead woman whom he suspects is involved in one. A dressing room filled with sketches of Japanese martial arts and traditional Japanese gowns and coiffures point to a desire on Sugar Torch's part to use the aesthetic qualities of Japanese culture to transcend the "low" art world of burlesque, that is, to rise above herself in terms of taste and class. It is this transgression that proves fatal.

Figure 19.   The working-class cop Charlie Bancroft (Glenn Corbett) meets the polished artist Chris Downes (Victoria Shaw) in The Crimson Kimono *(1959). Still courtesy of Jerry Ohlinger.*

Given the markedly "low" art qualities of the B-movie category to which *The Crimson Kimono* belongs, it is interesting that this low art/high art tension should be so important to the narrative. With really only one exception, all the major characters in the film fit into one category or another, with the B-movie viewer placed squarely in the low-art camp. High-art highbrows (including the interracial lovers, Joe and Chris) remain outside their ken, speaking in a language that the film seems to maintain is beyond their innate ability to comprehend.

The jilted Charlie functions as the principal lowbrow point of identification. Whereas Joe plays piano, appreciates painting, speaks Japanese, and understands both Western and Japanese aesthetics, Charlie is more interested in Chris's face and figure than in her artwork and, admittedly, knows little about art beyond martial artistry. When duty calls, Joe finds his investigations leading him to convents and Buddhist shrines, while Charlie's sleuthing always seems to return him to skid row bars, cheap hotels, and the company of sleazy informants.

In fact, Charlie goes to skid row to seek the help of the one character who has the ability to mediate the high-art and low-art domains carved out in the film. To solve the first mystery of the identity of the artist Chris, Charlie turns to Mac (Anna Lee), an alcoholic skid row muralist. In fact, if Charlie stands in as the average B-movie viewer, more at home in a bar than in an art gallery, then a case can be made that Mac occupies a special position in the narrative since she can navigate between the high-art world of opera and painting and the low-art world of strippers and B-movies. Nicholas Garnham, in his study of Fuller's films, makes the following observation about Mac:

> Her art is equated with Fuller's. They both share the same setting and the same concerns. Mac . . . is an informer. She reveals truths. This she can only do because she is fully involved with the seamy side of life. She rightly diagnoses the weakness of Chris's art as due to lack of experience.[9]

A drunken eccentric who may be either a genius or a bum, Mac poses no threat to the B-moviegoers' taste and sensibility. As such, she can mediate between Charlie's inability to understand why Chris loves Joe and the film's demand that the interracial romance be looked at as proper, natural, and genuine. By simply accepting Chris's statement, "I love Joe Kojaku," without questioning the attraction, Mac allows the viewer to read the relationship as the meeting of like-minded peo-

Figure 20.   Mac (Anna Lee) bridges the gap between high and low art. Here she lectures Joe. Still from The Crimson Kimono *courtesy of Jerry Ohlinger.*

ple, artistic eccentrics who could only be understood by "one of their own"—someone like Mac. In this way, Mac allows the film to mask the issue of race by using a discourse involving aesthetics.

In order for the film to maintain an ideological equilibrium that will neither allow for an expressed racism nor a radical call for complete desegregation, this displacement of racial onto aesthetic concerns becomes crucial. When looked at in terms of race, Chris's choice of a Japanese lover could radically disturb the status quo. If, on the one hand, Chris must turn to a Japanese man for romance, the implication is that Caucasian men are somehow inadequate. If, on the other hand, Chris turns to Joe because of his artistic sensitivity, because he represents a high-art aesthetic sensibility, this may not upset the B-movie viewers who likely place both Joe and Chris at a distance from themselves. After all, Joe and Chris are "highbrows"—eccentric, incomprehensible, elitist, and outside the quotidian rules that govern the rest of society.

The dialogue in the scene in which Joe and Chris first discover their love for each other helps to underscore this reading of their relationship. After playing the piano (with a bust of Beethoven prominent-

Figure 21.   Romance and high art aesthetics come together in front of a bust of Beethoven as Chris and Joe Kojaku (James Shigeta) discover their mutual attraction. Still from The Crimson Kimono *courtesy of the Museum of Modern Art/Film Stills Archive.*

ly displayed to assure Joe's high-art qualifications) and a discussion of Joe's artistic father, both Joe and Chris end up sitting close together on the sofa. While fondling a small Japanese martial arts statue, Joe begins to discuss Chris's art with enigmatic phrases like "It's unfinished," "It's as if you were sitting on the edge of a volcano," "It's as if you were hunting for something." After Chris calls Joe a "sensitive critic," the conversation switches to love. The couple gets up from the sofa. Joe moves behind Chris, touches her, but then moves off to sit at the piano. The scene ends with Joe playing moodily; his face darkened and obscured by the webbed music stand on the piano which acts as a frame within the frame. Both aesthetics and sexual attraction across racial lines remain incomprehensible, available only to the "sensitive," to the initiated, to the realm of high art beyond the average viewer's ken.

This call to look at Joe's and Chris's relationship as a romance between two kindred souls rather than as a romance between a Japanese man and an Anglo-American woman also brings to the surface further challenges to the American social order that must somehow be dealt with or suppressed. Chris's choice of Joe over Charlie unleashes the possibility of female self-determination, a female independence that the film struggles on several levels to contain.

In fact, in *The Crimson Kimono*, the potential threats posed by sexual and racial differences to a vision of America as the melting pot, as free, equal, and just for all its citizens, are linked together and dealt with through domestication and denial. The exoticism and sexual allure of the painting of Sugar Torch in a Japanese kimono threaten the image the rest of the film tries to maintain of Los Angeles' Little Tokyo and its inhabitants as completely assimilated, patriotic, and content with an American identity. *The Crimson Kimono* both recognizes a certain voyeuristic fascination with this Japanese otherness and tries to deny that fascination by literally domesticating the Japanese.

Joe and Charlie's apartment bears witness to this domestication. Iconographically, it is a meeting ground of East and West with a bust of Beethoven on the piano and Japanese lacquers and prints on the walls. Any threat racial or cultural differences may pose is symbolically miniaturized in the collection of Japanese dolls on display behind the sofa. Joe, too, has been domesticated. No tension exists in his relationship with Charlie. At the beginning of the film, he and Charlie live together in absolute harmony. Joe is apparently completely assimilated—complaining of his inability to communicate with girls raised in Japan, speaking unaccented English, unquestioningly working for a police force that monitors his community. He represents the charm of Little Tokyo, where chopsticks are used in the local diner and little girls dressed in kimonos march to American brass bands.

Even Joe's relationship with Charlie fits into a long tradition of close friendships between Anglo-American and nonwhite men. He is like the Lone Ranger's Tonto or the Green Hornet's Kato, an unthreatening, domesticated, emasculated, and completely loyal companion. However, Joe's relationship with Chris threatens this domestic harmony. In a complex way, the love affair threatens on two fronts. First, it unleashes the demon of racial difference, which is violently played out during a *kendo* (Japanese sword) match when Joe throws out all the rules and beats Charlie unconscious. If Japanese culture appeared as generally unthreatening before this scene, the violence and potential destructive power of this alien culture erupt as Charlie is literally beaten senseless at a Japanese game he assumed he played well. That he has no clue about what may be going on in his best friend's head shows that the American melting pot can boil over unexpectedly.

Second, Joe's and Chris's love affair represents a strong challenge to 1950s American manhood. Assailed by the emergence of women during World War II as significant members of the labor force, American masculine identity was shored up by all sorts of undisguised propaganda glorifying housework and idealizing the suburban home as the pinnacle of female bliss. That Chris should prefer the "sensitive" and exotic Joe to the down-to-earth, blue-collar Charlie raises the issue of what type of masculinity could emerge out of this postwar identity crisis. Suffice it to say that it is crucial that someone should end up at the conclusion of *The Crimson Kimono* embracing Chris. She must be domesticated to remove the threat of the independent career woman and to silence any possibility that the homoerotic bond between the roommates Joe and Charlie could prove stronger than the Hollywood ideal of heterosexual romance.

In fact, any gender transgression the sensitive Japanese male may represent is displaced onto the female characters in the film. The women in *The Crimson Kimono* are not only undomesticated but they are literally dangerous and certainly a threat to men as well as to other women. If Joe represents an unvoiced homoeroticism and Chris a potentially castrating independence, then the solution to the murder mystery and the reunion of Chris and Joe as a heterosexual couple at the end of the film quells sexual tensions.

In many ways, in fact, gender difference is presented in *The Crimson Kimono* as a greater threat to the social order than racial or ethnic differences. However, while race and racism are openly addressed as issues, gender and sexism remain unvoiced but insistent topics throughout the film. Virtually all the women in *The Crimson Kimono* transgress gender boundaries and engage in behavior considered unacceptable within a male-defined and male-dominated society. Parallel love triangles provide the film with its narrative structure, and, in each triangular relationship, a woman is positioned as a source of danger, mystery, and narrative disequilibrium.

The first love triangle is the fiction-within-the-fiction of Sugar Torch's Japanese-inspired striptease. Sugar plays a geisha who arouses a karate expert (*karateka*). When the geisha's boyfriend, a samurai swordsman, arrives, the karateka and he duel. The karateka defeats the swordsman and kills the geisha, as she weeps over her lover's dead body. The cynical theater manager who tells the story to Joe and Charlie adds that the dead lovers provide a "Romeo and Juliet touch."

In *Underworld USA*, Colin McArthur observes that *The Crimson Kimono* has an "almost Shakespearean symmetry."[10] The two other principal love triangles in the film echo Sugar Torch's proposed kimono act. While Joe and Charlie battle over Chris, the murder investigation reveals another love triangle involving Sugar Torch, the chief suspect, Hansel (Neyle Morrow), and his girlfriend, Roma Wilson (Jaclynne Greene). Hansel, a librarian specializing in Asia, whose real name is Paul Sand, and Roma, a Caucasian woman who makes Japanese wigs, seem an unlikely duo to be involved in the murder of a stripper. As in Sugar Torch's act, female sexuality and jealousy lead to murder when Roma mistakes the relationship between her boyfriend and the stripper as a love affair rather than a business deal.

Roma's misunderstanding of Hansel's relationship with Sugar Torch parallels Joe's misinterpretation of Charlie's questioning of his proposed marriage to Chris as racism. Because of this suspicion of racism, Joe not only moves out on Charlie but also breaks his engagement with Chris, resigns from the police force, and goes to Little Tokyo to sulk. Only when Roma, shot in the back by Joe and bleeding in his arms, confesses that she had let her jealous imagination run away with her when she murdered Sugar Torch, does Joe admit his mistake. He apologizes to Charlie. Finally, Joe is brought back into mainstream white society when he kisses Chris. Ironically, this happy ending is accomplished by his identification with a murderess whom he has shot and arrested. Even if his relationship with Charlie remains somewhat unresolved, any question of his gender identity is quieted when he uses his male police prerogative to shoot Roma and his simple prerogative as a man to kiss Chris. If either Roma's or Chris's sexuality or fascination with Japanese culture or transgression of any other racial or gender boundaries proved threatening in any way, that threat is obliterated by the working out of the film's denouement. Not only is Joe redomesticated by his acceptance of mainstream American society but he is also firmly placed within the patriarchal domestic order with his woman in his arms.

Joe's reintegration into the melting pot is not the only domestication that takes place, however. Women are also controlled and brought back to patriarchal society. Roma is brought into police custody, and Chris is wrapped in the protective arms of her fiancé. Their independence and dangerous sexual expression (even Chris is associated with the power to destroy intimate bonds and provoke violence) has been curtailed. Sugar Torch's transgression of gender, cultural, and class boundaries in her pursuit of a high-art dream of a "tasteful" Japanese striptease has been shattered, and her death has been explained away, soon to be forgotten.

Even Mac, who figures in a love triangle hinted at but suppressed in the film, which involves Chris, Charlie, and herself, ends up in a two shot with Charlie at the end of the film. Throughout *The Crimson Kimono*, Mac and Charlie, despite the differences in their ages, which would belie any romantic involvement, engage in all sorts of suggestive bits of business (Mac drunkenly falls into Charlie's arms) and exchanges of dialogue (Mac, drunkenly, and Charlie, sleepily, both say, "I love you," supposedly joking). If Chris and Joe's kiss represents racial harmony, the triumph of romantic love, the celebration of heterosexuality, then Mac and Charlie's two shot and comic exchange symbolically reconcile low-art taste with high-art pretensions. An element of cynicism or irony is added. Identifying perhaps more with Mac and Charlie, as a comic couple, than with the seriously romantic Joe and Chris, viewers can appreciate Joe and Chris at a distance, as part of the spectacle of Little Tokyo, which may or may not have any bearing on relationships in the quotidian world of the B-moviegoer.

"You Only See What You Want to See": Race, National Identity, and the Suppression of History

The Crimson Kimono's happy ending rings somewhat false with viewers who know for a fact that racism is more than the paranoid delusions of nonwhites. To better understand ideological operations involved in this denial of racism, a closer examination of those things left out of the narrative or put at the margins within the film as ancillary moments of pure spectacle may prove useful.

At one point in *The Crimson Kimono*, Joe must meet with one of his informants at a cemetery. Before this meeting takes place, however, the plot comes to a halt. The camera lingers over several shots of a memorial to Nisei soldiers, who died in Europe during World War II, including shots of statements of commendation by Generals Dwight D. Eisenhower and Mark W. Clark. Eventually, the camera pulls back to reveal Joe's informant tending the grave of his son, who died in the Korean War in 1950.

These memorials to World War II and the Korean War dead from the Japanese community, as well as Joe's military service during the Korean War, stand as unquestioned and unquestionable symbols of America's ability to assimilate the racially and ethnically different in wartime. The film also justifies American foreign campaigns because of this internal championing of democracy and justice. Nowhere is any mention made of the internment of Japanese Americans during World War II. *The Crimson Kimono* remains silent about the fact that the federal government, because of a racist paranoia about the Japanese community during the war, imprisoned not only naturalized citizens but also second-generation Nisei born in the United States and all others of Japanese ancestry in the western United States. This internment, which did not affect Americans of German or Italian origin, virtually wiped out the Japanese community in California. Even after the war, with homes, farms, and businesses confiscated, the Japanese community in Los Angeles could never be the same. Both the bustling world of *The Crimson Kimono*'s Little Tokyo and the inclusion of this memorial to the Nisei who fought in Europe hide the real American racism that sent Japanese Americans to concentration camps.[11]

If Japanese Americans were willing, if unable (the government forbade the stationing of Nisei troops in the Pacific), to fight the Japanese during World War II, then Korea becomes particularly significant as a symbol of Japanese Americans' loyalty to a white-defined American identity. No mention is made of the fact that the Korean War saw the first integrated American troops ever in U.S. history. Rather, Joe's informant's pride springs from having had his son die in Korea. This pride is underscored by the inclusion of a narratively unmotivated but ideologically charged scene in which the workings of the plot halt and the informant attends a Buddhist ceremony, conducted in Japanese, to commemorate his son's death. Joe waits impatiently outside the temple while this takes place. Only when it is over and the point is emphatically made that Asian Americans are as patriotic as anyone else can the plot again move into gear.

The Crimson Kimono's use of a racially integrated American military force in Korea to prove that racism is a dead issue in American society again surfaces in another scene that makes little narrative sense. The murder investigation leads Charlie and Joe to the karate expert Sugar Torch wanted for her show, a Korean man named Shuto (Fuji), who has recently moved to Little Tokyo. When Joe tries to question him, he runs off. Later, Joe finds Shuto in a pool hall and calls in Charlie to help him subdue the gigantic karateka. Using both

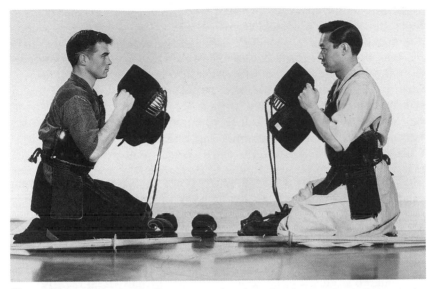

Figure 22.   Joe and Charlie prepare for their kendo match. Still from The Crimson Kimono *courtesy of the Museum of Modern Art/Film Stills Archive.*

karate and Western boxing techniques, Joe and Charlie manage to take in Shuto. For the detectives, who met "in a foxhole" in Korea, this scene, which does little to further the narrative, serves as a replay of their military experience. Joe and Charlie, the Nisei and the Anglo-American, fight together to subdue the Asian antagonist, proving Joe's loyalty to America over Asia and confirming America's moral right to fight any perceived Asian threat. The multicultural blend of fighting techniques ideologically affirms the power of American culture to assimilate the foreign and, thereby, strengthen itself.

In a similar way, Joe's kendo match with Charlie momentarily halts the narrative. This enables the ritual display of the kendo competitors' march into the Little Tokyo gymnasium and the exoticism of their preparations for the match to be savored visually. Only the cold exchange of glances between Joe and Charlie before they mask themselves for the duel sets the narrative back in motion, presaging the explosion of Joe's unchecked anger.

This kendo match marks a particularly contradictory moment in the film. In this scene, Joe, the winner in the love triangle, vents his supposedly unjustified anger on the innocent Charlie. It is a moment when Joe, excused by the eruption of his emotions, displays his superior swordsmanship, even if it is by breaking the rules. Up to this point, Joe has been the model cop and ideal best friend, even trying to set aside his love for Chris for Charlie's sake; however, as Joe beats Charlie to the ground, a potentially racist fear of the Japanese as vicious and incomprehensible surfaces. Although this reading is held in check by the inclusion of several close-ups of Japanese spectators condemning Joe's behavior, thereby separating him from the community, reading the battle as a struggle between a Nisei and an Anglo-American is certainly possible.

Thus, although Joe's accusation of Charlie's racism comes after the fight, it seems to have been simmering under the surface long before. Charlie, hearing that Joe loves Chris, asks, "You mean you want to marry her?" Without any thought, Joe labels the remark as racist: "You wouldn't have said it that way if I were white." A new narrative theme, overshadowing both the murder mystery and the romance, arises: Is Charlie a racist or simply an angry, spurned lover? Is Joe a victim of racism or paranoid?

Having already established Joe as a bit off during the kendo match, the film uses every means at its disposal to guide the viewer to interpret Charlie's remark as personal anger rather than racial bigotry. Joe, in effect, becomes the "bad guy" in need of a moral education.

Later, Joe explains to Chris his interpretation of Charlie's look and remark as racist:

> I saw that look, Chris. It's a look I've never seen before in his face or anybody else's. I'm no wet nose. Nothing like that should hit me below the belt. . . . Take a good look, Chris. Do I look different today than I did yesterday? Did my face change? I never felt this way in the army, in the police. . . . Maybe it's five thousand years of blood behind me bursting to the front. For the first time, I feel different. I taste it right through every bone inside of me. For the first time, I catch myself trying to figure out who I am. I was born here. I'm American. I feel it, live it, and love it. But, down deep, who am I? Japanese American? American Japanese? Nisei? What label do I live under, Chris? You tell me.

That a Japanese American man, in his twenties or early thirties, who must have grown up during World War II, with virulently racist anti-Japanese sentiments common throughout the United States, should be given a speech in which he claims to have never experienced racism before seems ludicrous. That a Nisei involved in an interracial love affair should have a genuine identity crisis and feelings of apprehension because of a personal history of racism (likely including internment) makes quite a bit of sense. This possibility is completely suppressed, however. The film musters all the representatives of reason and rationality it can, including Charlie, Chris, and Mac, to highlight the interpretation that Charlie's look came from "normal, healthy, jealous hate," as he claims. Isolated and presented as crazy, Joe finally comes to his senses when Roma confesses in his arms, but nagging doubts remain. If racism is all in Joe's imagination, why does Charlie accuse Chris of saying "something" that upset Joe when he first notices a change in Joe's behavior? If the possibility that Chris could make a racist remark comes to his mind, why should Joe be presented as paranoid when he interprets Charlie's look and remark as racist?

Despite Joe's acceptance of and reintegration into American society, which is sealed with a kiss, *The Crimson Kimono*'s denial of racism must perplex some viewers as much as the interracial kiss would provoke others. Narrative closure cannot give the final word on the social contradictions the film voices and denies. *The Crimson Kimono* really cannot be taken seriously as the daring antiracist statement promised by that kiss, since it also so vehemently demands that the racism it combats is all an illusion. In typical B-movie fashion, *The Crimson Kimono* promises transgression but delivers merely titillation and exploitation.

8

Japanese War Brides

Domesticity and Assimilation
in *Japanese War Bride* and *Bridge*
to the Sun

Hollywood embraced with a passion narratives involving Japanese American love affairs in the 1950s and early 1960s—for example, *The Gentle Wolfhound* (1955), *Three Stripes in the Sun* (1955), *Teahouse of the August Moon* (1956), *Sayonara* (1957), *The Barbarian and the Geisha* (1958), *The Crimson Kimono* (1959), *Cry for Happy* (1961), and *A Majority of One* (1961). With these dramas, Hollywood took advantage of exotic locales afforded by the occupation of Japan, capitalized on the topicality of U.S.-Asian relations in the aftermath of the Korean War, sensationalized domestic racial tensions by transposing them onto the less threatening sphere of white-Asian rather than white-African American relations, and showed itself to be a champion of American "freedom" in the wake of HUAC. Moreover, these dramas used the myth of the subservient Japanese woman to shore up a threatened masculinity in light of American women's growing independence during World War II.

Few of these wartime romances or semitragic love stories deal with marriage and domestic relations, and most remain based in Asia, avoiding any discussion of the depth of American racism at home. Other potentially more challenging topics are thus avoided—miscegenation laws, prejudice against Amerasian children, racism within the family, and spouse abuse. Although the interracial romance has traditionally been a staple of Hollywood fiction, the interracial domestic melodrama has not enjoyed the same popularity. This does not mean that interracial marriages do not appear. Though lovers often marry in Hollywood interracial romances, they usually do so at the conclusion of the film (as in *Sayonara*), or the marriage is relegated to subplot status (as in *Three Stripes in the Sun*), or is depicted as completely dysfunctional or "false" from the beginning (as in *Madame Butterfly*). Seldom does Hollywood give serious attention to domestic issues in these films, such as housework, the rearing of children, relations among in-laws, or the quotidian relationship between husband and wife.

Japanese War Bride (1952, King Vidor) and *Bridge to the Sun* (1961, Étienne Perier),[1] however, do provide two examples of films that paint a detailed picture of interracial domestic relations involving Japanese American marriages. *Japanese War Bride* depicts a marriage between a U.S. serviceman involved in the Korean War and a Japanese Red Cross worker. *Bridge to the Sun* deals with a marriage between a Japanese diplomat and a naive Southern belle who meet in Washington, D.C., in the 1930s and later spend the war years in Japan.

Although made nearly a decade apart under quite different circumstances, *Japanese War Bride* and *Bridge to the Sun* share some markedly similar narrative and thematic elements. Both take domestic relations seriously and focus dramatic attention on housework, children, and the extended family. Like most domestic dramas, they take up social tensions arising from the hierarchical organization of the bourgeois patriarchal family. Thus, both films deal with the threat sexuality (particularly female sexuality) poses to the familial status quo, questions of legitimacy and property relations, generational tensions, and divisions between and within the public and domestic spheres as well as the relationship between the nuclear family and larger historical, cultural, and economic forces. Moreover, like most Hollywood melodramas, both films present a contradictory picture of the nuclear family, recognizing domestic tensions while working to contain them within the ideological workings of the narrative.

This examination of *Japanese War Bride* and *Bridge to the Sun* focuses on how these two films further complicate the tensions found in the Hollywood domestic drama by the addition of racial differences, national animosities, and intercultural misunderstandings. After looking at the historical backdrop for each narrative and how these melodramas both voice and deny the subversive ramifications of their stories, the study moves to the question of how each film addresses the challenge an interracial marriage poses to the Hollywood depiction of domesticity, sexuality, and gender relations within the patriarchal family.

History, the Hollywood
Melodrama, and Postwar Japan

The Hollywood melodrama, given its diverse manifestations as the "woman's film," the wartime melodrama, the social problem film, the domestic melodrama, the costume or period melodrama, the maternal melodrama, and the "love story," to name a few, has been difficult to pin down as a coherent genre. Some melodramas avoid dealing directly with any topic outside the immediate realm of the nuclear family, while others take up issues as diverse as alcoholism, drug addiction, juvenile delinquency, child abuse, racial prejudice, and the problems of returning war veterans. Moreover, whereas some melodramas seem to exist in an ahistorical, nondifferentiated, suburban, middle-class milieu that functions as the "norm," others go out of their way to specify a place or a time removed from what otherwise passes for the "typical" American household. Although the melodrama may present the domestic realm over the public sphere, these narratives still depict domesticity as constantly threatened by the public world of the military, the government, the educational system, the legal system, industry, or other social institutions.[2]

In those melodramas that focus on topical issues or historical themes, there exists an uneasy relationship between the bourgeois myth of the patriarchal family as a stable, unchanging haven and a recognition of the forces of social change. Often this tension between the exterior forces of social change and the idealized, mythic constancy of the family takes on a particular significance. These dramas work to reconcile the impossible contradiction between the vicissitudes of history and the absolute ideological certainty of an enduring bourgeois patriarchal domesticity. Any threat social change may pose, then, is devoured by the Hollywood absolutes of heterosexual romantic love, the sanctity of motherhood, and the middle-class, male-dominated domicile.

Japanese War Bride and *Bridge to the Sun* provide examples of two domestic melodramas that betray a tension between the supposedly closed, unchanging world of the bourgeois family and the tremendous changes in the public sphere brought to bear by both the civil rights movement and American wars in Asia. On the one hand, both films are tales of national reconciliation, liberal calls for tolerance and understanding. On the other hand, each film seeks to contain any challenges that position may pose ideologically by containing these social forces within the safe haven of domesticity. Racial intolerance becomes a clash of intrafamilial personalities; World War II and the Korean War dissolve into domestic, generational conflicts. Historical change tends to lose its potency, constrained by the unraveling of formulaic plots.

In the case of *Japanese War Bride*, for example, history enters the melodrama quite directly with references to a topic that had become part of the popular literature on World War II, the occupation, and the Korean War—the Asian war bride. In "Strain and Harmony in American-Japanese War-Bride Marriages," Anselm L. Strauss quotes J. B. Pilcher, the American consul general: "Between June 22, 1947, and December 31, 1952, 10,517 American citizens, principally Armed Service Personnel, married Japanese women. Over 75 percent of the total Americans are Caucasian."[3] In July 1947, the U.S. government briefly allowed soldiers in Japan to legally marry Japanese women. After August 1950, Japanese war-bride marriages again became legal. In addition to James Michener's *Sayonara* serialized in *McCall's*, other popular periodicals picked up on the war-bride theme. For example, J. E. Smith and W. L. Worden's "They're Bringing Home Japanese Wives" appeared in the January 1952 issue of the *Saturday Evening Post*.[4]

In light of the media attention devoted to the topic, it is not surprising that Hollywood should have also picked up on the Japanese war-bride phenomenon. It seems appropriate, moreover, that King Vidor should be attracted to this topic, since he was already associated in Hollywood with social problem melodramas—*The Big Parade* (1925), *The Crowd* (1928), *Hallelujah!* (1929), *Bird of Paradise* (1932, which involves an interracial love affair), *Our Daily Bread* (1934), *Stella Dallas* (1937), and *Duel in the Sun* (1946), which also includes an interracial romance).

In *Japanese War Bride*, Vidor uses a familiar strategy of dramatizing social conflicts within the domestic sphere to address racism in postwar America. While stationed in Korea with the American forces, Lieutenant Jim Sterling (Don Taylor) is wounded and sent to recover in Japan. There, he meets Japanese Red Cross nurse Tae Shimizu (Shirley Yamaguchi), and they fall in love. Despite her grandfather's initial objections, they marry and return to the Sterling farm in Salinas, California.

When they arrive to live with the extended family, problems arise. Jim's brother Art (Cameron Mitchell) has married one of Jim's old flames, Fran (Marie Windsor), who still has designs on her former beau. Another of Jim's former girlfriends, Emily Shafer (Sybil Merritt), has lost a brother in the war. Although Emily tries to renew ties with both Jim and Tae, her mother cannot accept Jim's marriage to a Japanese woman. Jim's parents attempt to accept Tae, but they also find it difficult. The closest neighbors to the Sterling farm, the Hasa-gawa family, struggle with the consequences of their internment during the war. For the most part, Tae tries to make the best of her hostile environment, while Jim lashes out verbally and physically.

When Tae learns that she is pregnant, Jim begins to build a house for her. However, familial tensions come to a head when Tae delivers a baby with Asian features. An anonymous note to Jim's father ac-cuses Tae of adultery with her neighbor, Shiro Hasagawa (Lane Na-kano), and threatens him with expulsion from the financially important farmers' association. Disgraced, Tae goes to the Hasagawas, with her baby, for help. In Tae's absence, Jim forces Fran to admit she wrote the "anonymous" note out of envy. Art slaps his wife, and the rest of the family apologizes to Jim. At the film's conclusion, Jim is reunited with Tae.

In *Japanese War Bride*, Tae represents the intrusion of the Pacific war, racial tensions, and economic uncertainties into the domestic order of the American home. She symbolizes a potentially uncontrol-lable force for change within the supposedly unassailable bastion of the patriarchal family. Only through the cleansing properties of hetero-sexual love can she be salvaged as an acceptable part of the domestic and moral order. As Tae and Jim embrace at the end of the film against the natural backdrop of the Pacific Ocean, history comes to a stand-still and Hollywood's romantic mythos replaces any genuine social ten-sion the narrative may have conjured up. The legality and morality of the internment of Japanese Americans during the war, miscegenation laws, and the economic basis for racial tensions in California agricul-ture fall by the wayside as the heterosexual couple is elevated above the tempestuous sea below, standing alone from society and, as a consequence, from any moral imperative to help change it. The main-tenance of the family takes precedence over social change, and toler-ance takes the place of protest. The events of history become simply another part of a drama that can be dismissed as the peculiarities of an atypical family that finds its way into the mainstream by maintain-ing the basic strictures of patriarchal rule.

Bridge to the Sun has an even more direct relationship to actual his-torical events than does *Japanese War Bride*, since it is based on the autobiography of the same name by Gwen Terasaki.[5] The voice-over narration of Gwen Harold-Terasaki, which comes up periodically to clarify events or bridge temporal or spatial distances, also serves to narrow the gap between the memoir and the fictional narrative of the film.

Unlike *Japanese War Bride*, which attempts to depict a social phe-nomenon through fiction, *Bridge to the Sun* tries to use its unusual and very specific story of a diplomatic marriage to draw a more general moral lesson about national reconciliation and racial tolerance. In fact, in its broad outlines, *Bridge to the Sun* reproduces the general tone and dramatizes many of the events described in Gwen Terasaki's book. However, in transforming *Bridge to the Sun* into a Hollywood melodrama, the emphasis shifts from the broader sweep of the book, which includes more detailed descriptions of the political events of the 1930s and 1940s as well as the couple's postings in China, Cuba, Washington, D.C., and Japan, and their remarkable voyage from the United States to Japan after Pearl Harbor. As these places and political events vanish from the film, domestic details, discussions of personal feelings, and interpersonal relations replace the history of the war.

On a visit to her aunt in Washington, D.C., Gwen Harold (Carroll Baker), a young woman from Johnson City, Tennessee, meets Terry Terasaki (James Shigeta), a midlevel Japanese diplomat, at a party at the Japanese embassy. Despite objections from Gwen's family and Terry's bosses, the couple decides to marry.

They sail to Japan. Although Terry has no immediate family, his extended family has difficulty accepting the outspoken American Gwen, and she has trouble fulfilling her role of proper wife. Terry's longtime friend, Giro, has particular difficulty with Terry's new bride. A conservative militarist, Giro provokes Gwen into voicing her political views, which precipitates a public argument between Terry and his wife. However, Terry and Gwen reconcile, and the news that Gwen is pregnant helps to solidify their renewed bond.

After their daughter, Mako, is born, Terry again finds himself posted to Washington, D.C. Although Terry becomes involved in a plan to appeal directly to the emperor to stop the Pacific war, Pearl Harbor dashes his hopes for peace. Gwen decides to return with Terry and Mako to Japan. When conditions in Tokyo (bombings, street demonstrations, and political intrigues) make life impossible, Terry moves his family to the countryside. However, he leaves them almost immediately to continue his vaguely described peace efforts.

Pursued by the authorities, Terry returns and unsuccessfully tries to hide with Gwen and Mako. On the eve of the Japanese surrender, Terry finally stumbles back home. His health ruined, he takes Gwen on a last trip to Kyoto and insists that she immediately take Mako back to the United States. When Gwen realizes Terry does not want his wife and daughter to see him die, she reluctantly acquiesces. Gwen bids farewell to Terry as she sails away with Mako on a steamer.

In many ways, the plot lines of *Japanese War Bride* and *Bridge to the Sun* mirror one another. In *Japanese War Bride*, a Japanese woman leaves her family to marry an American; in *Bridge to the Sun*, an

American marries a Japanese man. Even though Gwen Terasaki, unlike Tae Sterling, is not a "war bride" in the strictest sense, Gwen does go to Japan as a bride during the war, and both films explore the contradictions of a woman choosing to marry not only outside her race but also within an "enemy" culture. Both films depict the difficulties these brides have fitting into their new environment and establishing their place within a multiracial and multicultural household. Moreover, both films ostensibly favor racial tolerance and national reconciliation. Characters voicing other perspectives are sorely chastised by the protagonists in each narrative.

However, in many ways each film's apparent plea for racial tolerance plays a secondary role within a melodramatic narrative that favors an exploration of domestic rather than social relations. As David N. Rodowick points out in his essay, "Madness, Authority and Ideology: The Domestic Melodrama of the 1950s," the melodrama concerns itself with the interior dilemmas of the family, on the one hand, while using that family as a microcosm for the entire social fabric, on the other:

> The domestic melodrama is attentive only to problems which concern the family's internal security and economy, and therefore considers its authority to be restricted to issues of private power and patriarchal right. . . . Institutional and familial authority are condensed in the figuration of patriarchal power as an overdetermined instance in the representation of social power *per se*. As the linchpin on which narrative conflict must turn, the problem of familial authority and stability therefore establishes a frame of reference against which the logic and order of the representations of social relations are measured.[6]

Thus, the centrality of patriarchal authority within the melodrama helps to explain the translation of other sociohistorical issues and events into questions of patriarchal legitimacy.

In *Japanese War Bride*, for example, legitimacy plays a role that involves both questions of race and gender roles. The question of Jim and Tae's son's legitimacy becomes crucial not only to the continuation of their marriage but to the economic survival of their entire extended family; that is, if the family cannot be accepted by the community agricultural association, it will lose a significant part of its income.

In *Bridge to the Sun*, legitimacy does not surface directly. However, Gwen's threat to Terry's male potency seems clear. Terry does not emerge as a triumphant hero of a new, nonhierarchical family but rather fades from view and eventually disappears as an ineffectual invalid doomed to extinction.

Moreover, Gwen suffers for her involvement with Terry. *Bridge to the Sun* thus remains amenable to the conservative reading that a Caucasian woman's love for a nonwhite male must somehow end in death. Like *Broken Blossoms* and *The Bitter Tea of General Yen*, *Bridge to the Sun* may allow its heroine to assert her autonomy and find love outside the boundaries of her race, but a price must be paid. The film may even allow its heroine to "save" her lover from the violent or "deviant" excesses of his own pagan world. However, any threats to eliminate racial boundaries or to allow women to achieve a certain degree of autonomy within a more egalitarian marriage are ruthlessly denied by the death of the hero.

The history that surfaces most insistently in both *Bridge to the Sun* and *Japanese War Bride* is not the history of World War II, racial intolerance, or national postwar reconciliation. Rather, both films seem to acknowledge and then contain the threats posed in the postwar era to the patriarchal household by the war bride. By seeping into the domestic sphere, history transforms itself into the myth of heterosexual romance and the ideal of the patriarchal home.

Domestic Spaces

The Hollywood melodrama makes concrete the familial tensions it deals with through the mise-en-scène. The visual depiction of the domestic sphere—the living room, the kitchen, the bedroom, and even the bathroom—becomes a key way in which contradictions involving class, gender, and race surface in these narratives. However, the home also stands as a visual icon of an unchanging patriarchy that symbolizes a stability that can absorb the most violent public upheaval. In "Tales of Sound and Fury: Observations on the Family Melodrama," Thomas Elsaesser notes,

> The setting of the family melodrama almost by definition is the middle-class home. . . . [It] brings out the characteristic attempt of the bourgeois household to make time stand still, immobilise life and fix forever domestic property relations as the model of social life and a bulwark against the more disturbing sides in human nature.[7]

When history knocks on the door of this domestic citadel, race, sexuality, war, or the economy disturb this myth of the unassailable patriarchal home. Quite often these tensions, resolved through dialogue or the working out of the plot, remain more problematic within the mise-en-scène.

The domestic space becomes inextricably bound up with issues of identity in the melodrama. Very often, the home provides the arena in which characters must resolve their own identity problems to assure the reproduction of bourgeois patriarchal relations. As Geoffrey Nowell-Smith notes, "What is at stake . . . is the survival of the family unit and the possibility for individuals of acquiring an identity which is also a place within the system, a place in which they can both be 'themselves' and 'at home'."[8]

For Tae and Gwen, as well as for Jim and Terry, being "themselves" poses a threat to the racial and ethnic homogeneity and stability of the household. As a result, both *Japanese War Bride* and *Bridge to the Sun* devote a good part of their narratives to the exploration of this dialectic between individual and familial identity. They search for a reconciliation of the contradiction between the regulating power of bourgeois patriarchy and the threat that female sexuality and racial differences pose to its smooth functioning. Much of this dramatic tension is visualized through the mise-en-scène. The characters try to be "themselves" and "at home" by literally reconstructing domestic space. As in many Hollywood melodramas of the same era, interior design and interior identity function as two sides of the same coin.[9]

In *Japanese War Bride*, the first domestic space represented is Tae's family home. A palatial exterior, numerous servants, the luxury of several totally empty tatami rooms in an overcrowded country, and a carefully cultivated garden visible in depth through the doorway of one of the barren parlors, all give the impression of understated wealth and power. However, the austerity of these empty spaces also connotes rigidity, sterility, and loss.

Tae's grandfather, Eitaro Shimizu (Philip Anh), lame, elderly, lacking in physical vigor, heads the household, which also includes Tae and her mother. When Mr. Shimizu greets his perspective grandson-in-law, the women remain silent and attend to the tea ceremony, quietly acquiescing to the old man's authority. They say nothing when Mr. Shimizu threatens to slay two monkeys as a sacrifice to celebrate the occasion, causing Jim to flee the house in disgust. Although Tae does run after Jim to explain her grandfather's ploy to test his sincerity, a disturbing image of Japanese domesticity has already been represented and offered as a contrast to the American home. This image of violence, sterility, repression, and decadence may be false, but it resonates throughout the film as the concrete reason Tae leaves her Japanese domicile to be "at home" in America.

When Jim and Tae arrive in Salinas, the Sterling family home stands at the opposite extreme as a visual icon of the vigor of the American patriarchal home. Whereas the Shimizu estate represents the decaying

Figure 23.   Jim Sterling (Don Taylor) visits Tae Shimizu (Shirley Yamaguchi) at her family's estate with her grandfather (Philip Anh) in attendance. Still from Japanese War Bride *(1952) courtesy of the Museum of Modern Art/Film Stills Archive.*

wealth of a defeated nation, the Sterling family farm stands as an idealized representation of the self-sufficient hardiness of the agrarian capitalist. This is not the haute bourgeois home of Sirk's *Written on the Wind* (1956) or the professional petit-bourgeois home of Ray's *Rebel Without a Cause* (1955); rather, *Japanese War Bride* features an almost nostalgic image of the rural family homestead (on the decline in the United States well before the Depression, which essentially marked its demise on any notable scale).

By focusing on a war bride in the countryside, *Japanese War Bride* re-creates a type of household not generally favored in the Hollywood melodramas of the 1950s, that is, what Eli Zaretsky describes as the "early" bourgeois family, "the family as a self-contained productive unit."[10] In contrast to the Japanese aristocratic household, this rural American family embodies those traditional values the film lionizes as the best of the American Dream: economic self-sufficiency; male potency and dominance; the conflation of the worlds of production and reproduction; and no separation of the roles of boss, laborer, husband, father, or citizen. Certainly, these ideals had been threatened for many decades before this film was produced and were clearly under siege in the postwar era, challenged by the growth of corporate capitalism and the attendant emasculation of the company man as a cog in a larger economic machine further threatened by the emergence of women in the work force.

The household depicted in *Japanese War Bride*, however, is free from all the economic and psychic stresses of advanced capitalism. Indeed, it represents a model view of Zaretsky's early bourgeois home:

> At its head was the *paterfamilias* who worked alongside his wife, children, employees, and wards. He was solely responsible for the economic and spiritual welfare of his family and represented in his person the supposed unity and independence of the family. The domestic relations of the household were an explicit part of the production relations of early capitalism.[11]

As Tae happily moves from her Japanese family to this American family farm, she symbolically empowers Jim and this particular vision of America as a land of small private enterprises run by strong patriarchs. By having Tae marry into this farm family, the film argues for its continuing viability at a time when it appeared to be doomed to extinction. The war bride represents a false threat, mystifying the real economic and social changes that make this type of bourgeois, patriarchal, rural household anachronistic even in 1952.

Indeed, a sense of nostalgia adheres to the farm's representation throughout the film. Perhaps this is most clearly felt in the scene in which Jim and Tae first come to the farm as husband and wife. For the veteran Jim, it represents a homecoming. When the family car drives up near the white picket fence of the family house, Mrs. Sterling, dressed maternally in a print dress and pearls, rushes to embrace her son. Tae stands awkwardly at the gate to receive a reluctant kiss on the forehead from her new mother-in-law. The picket fence and gate (a stock Hollywood icon of the enclosed protection of the bourgeois home) act as membranes, filtering out what can and cannot be absorbed into the family unit. As Tae enters, exits, and reenters through that gate, she accedes to her assimilation. However, the picket fence does not protect Tae or her in-laws from the internal tensions of the bourgeois home. The fence may nostalgically conjure up images of a safe haven from the perils of the external world, but it ironically also symbolizes the suffocatingly claustrophobic qualities of the home that offers Tae little hope of escape.

Because the Sterling farm functions as a miniature of society, as a regulator of patrilineal descent, production, morality, and social authority, it represents the bourgeois norm as an ideal under threat from interior and exterior forces. If Jim had saved Tae from the decadence and sterility of her aristocratic upbringing to become part of the bourgeois American norm, then a further decline in class standing represents a threat to that vision of the status quo. Tae, thus, must be protected from a fall into the working classes to maintain her efficacy as a symbol of the moral legitimacy of white, male, bourgeois rule embodied by Jim.

The threat of using Tae as an icon of the legitimacy of white patriarchal rule comes from her possible assimilation into the Asian American community. Indeed, the Hasagawa family serves as an example of a failed, nonwhite patriarchal order. Assimilation into the American bourgeois mainstream remains outside their grasp because of old Mr. Hasagawa's failure to forget his internment. Like Tae's grandfather, old Mr. Hasagawa represents a declining Japanese patriarchy that gives way to the ascent of the American patriarch who shores up his own masculinity, proves his moral superiority, and emasculates his former enemy by the single act of marrying a Japanese woman. The decline of the family remains rooted in its patriarch's stubborn refusal to accept the decline of Japan and the appropriateness of his internment, which his children seem to see as at least somewhat justified. Unable to provide the coveted domestic sanctuary the film holds up as the cornerstone of American society, the family can pose no serious threat to Jim's total possession of Tae, who dreams only of being a good American housewife.

When Jim goes to the Hasagawa family to search for his wife and finds that she has taken refuge with an even less well-to-do family of Japanese fishermen, Jim seems to be reclaiming Tae not only to shore up his threatened right to patriarchal rule but also to prove his rural bourgeois home as the proper domicile for his wife and baby. If the Shimizu household is too rich and the Hasagawa clan is too poor, then the Sterling home, and the American bourgeois mainstream it symbolizes, must be just right.

Interestingly, the Sterling home remains an impossible ideal for Tae and Jim. To assert his patriarchal prerogatives fully, Jim must move out of the family home and show he can build and head his own version of the Sterling homestead. He must physically reproduce the bourgeois home. In terms of the mise-en-scène, this becomes particularly clear when Tae's doll collection arrives from Japan. There is no room in the couple's little bedroom for their permanent display. Like her dolls, Tae cannot be "herself" (that is, ethnically different) and "at home" on the Sterling farm, and, when Jim plans to build his own home, shelves for the dolls become a key part of the floor plan. In fact, the announcement of Tae's pregnancy and her labor pains accompany Jim's plans for the dolls, and the baby's Japanese features become associated with the dolls, which simply cannot fit into place in the mainstream American home.

Although Tae and Jim are reunited at the end of *Japanese War Bride*, their new domestic space never materializes. Despite narrative closure and the apparent ideological expulsion of the threats of racism as well as female emancipation from the film fantasy, this place where Tae, Jim, and their son can be both "themselves" and "at home," a bourgeois haven from the outside world in which the patriarch, Jim, can fully protect his multiracial family, never becomes a concrete part of the mise-en-scène. Rather, it remains an unrealized dream, which, coupled with the nostalgia that adheres to the Sterling farm's apparent stability and actual economic fragility, belies the film's ostensibly happy ending.

If *Japanese War Bride* offers a nostalgic view of the American, rural, patriarchal household as both a social norm and an impossible ideal for its interracial couple, *Bridge to the Sun* provides no similarly stable domestic space in which its interracial couple may even hope to reside. Rather, *Bridge to the Sun*'s constant shift from one temporary home to another continuously puts in doubt Terry's and Gwen's ability to be "at home" anywhere.

Like Tae, Gwen struggles to be a good "housewife" without a house. Throughout the course of the film, the dramatic force of Gwen's defiant marriage to an inappropriate, that is, Japanese, man and her later struggles against the sexist rigidity of the Japanese patriarchy fade as she battles to provide a traditional home for her nuclear family. The narrative quells any notion that supports a woman who defies both American and Asian patriarchal authority to assert her own desires—that is, to be a supportive wife and nurturing mother without an identity separate from her husband or child.

Although the mise-en-scène seems to echo the film's principal thematic concern for creating a cultural bridge between two nations and races in its depiction of both Japanese interiors with Western elements and American interiors with Asian motifs, another agenda surfaces through the costume design in the film. *Bridge to the Sun* makes little attempt to produce even the vaguest impression that the film takes place in the 1930s and 1940s rather than in the early 1960s. Throughout most of the film, Carroll Baker wears billowy A-line skirts, tight at the waist, often cut low at the bodice, characteristic of women's fashions of the late 1950s and early 1960s. James Shigeta also sports a hair style and casual, open-collared shirts out of keeping with the 1930s and 1940s ambience.

Figure 24.   Gwen Harold-Terasaki (Carroll Baker) with her husband Terry Terasaki (James Shigeta) in Bridge to the Sun *(1961). Still courtesy of the Museum of Modern Art/Film Stills Archive.*

The point here is not to condemn *Bridge to the Sun* as inaccurate or poorly crafted. Rather, the anachronisms in the mise-en-scène reveal the film's interest in making its story a *contemporary* tale of the education of a woman in the domestic virtues. Thus, *Bridge to the Sun* must be taken as a 1960s rendering of the threat of the independent woman to traditional notions of gender roles and domesticity more than as an evocation of recent history and a call for postwar reconciliation. While the latter may be favored in the dramatic events depicted, the former appears to be of principal interest within the film's mise-en-scène.

As a feisty, young, American woman, Gwen begins her domestic education in the first scene of the film, when her ability to function independently is assaulted by her ignorance of Japanese customs and manners. Gwen drops her lipstick into a tray of hot hors d'oeuvres at the Japanese embassy and cannot retrieve it with her chopsticks. Terry comes to her rescue and deftly recovers the lipstick and puts it on his own plate, without mentioning it to the already embarrassed Gwen. Although the sexual significance of the fallen lipstick would likely not be lost on an audience familiar with the popular Freudianism of the day, Gwen's inability to handle food, to play the proper feminine role, betrays her need for an education in domesticity. When Gwen declares her love for Terry later in the film, she states, "I feel so small, and I know so little."

No stable domestic environment is pictured during Terry and Gwen's courtship, however, to provide a model household for this domestic instruction. Rather, Terry's embassy and Gwen's Washington, D.C., hotel room provide a sketchy picture of any current or future household. Since Gwen elopes with Terry before she can return to her family in Tennessee, the bourgeois American home never becomes a concrete representation of the norm in *Bridge to the Sun* as it does in *Japanese War Bride*.

Rather, Gwen's domestic education takes place in Japan and takes the form of the search for an ideological equilibrium between the extremes of the "new," independent, uncontrollable, American woman and the traditionally rigid Japanese patriarchy. After their marriage, the couple stays with Terry's uncle and aunt at their Tokyo home, where Gwen has difficulty assimilating. The customs of the Japanese home elude her: she can barely feed herself with chopsticks; she moves to get into cars before the men of the household; she questions Terry's aunt when the older woman instructs her niece-in-law to retire so that the men can speak among themselves after supper; she complains about sitting on the floor; she becomes embarrassed when introduced to a family friend in a public bath; she cannot get used to wearing a kimono and wig in the summer heat when entertaining; and, of course, Gwen has difficulty holding her tongue during political discussions.

Her expansive gestures look awkward in the traditional Japanese home, and the paper screens and doors that divide the household space seem to close in on Gwen, restricting her movements while providing no sanctuary for her obvious differences. Terry habitually knocks before entering his wife's bedroom, accentuating her separation from her surroundings, where doors even form a barrier within the expected intimacy of her marriage. Gwen expresses her inability to be "herself" and "at home" with Terry in Japan: "I want to make a good wife for you, Terry. I want to fit in. It's just that everything seems so strange. You seemed like a different person sitting there tonight in your kimono. It was as if you were in one world, and I was in another." Although Terry assures her they are in the "same world," he continues to knock before entering the bedroom.

Just as the traditional, Japanese court dolls stood as icons of Tae's disruptive racial difference in *Japanese War Bride*, Gwen's thorny, little cactus plant acts, in a similar fashion, as a visual emblem of her alien presence in *Bridge to the Sun*. During an argument precipitated by Gwen's criticism of some of Terry's guests' militaristic political opinions, the camera follows Gwen into a corner of the bedroom where she lashes out like a caged animal at her husband: "I'm sick of a place where people can't show their real emotions, where women are treated like pieces of furniture, and it's a quaint old custom for fathers to sell their baby daughters." Pinned in her corner, caged by the ribbing of the traditional paper walls and doorways, Gwen's use of the "furniture" metaphor to describe women's social role in Japan seems particularly apropos. She refuses to become a "piece of furniture" and, therefore, can never fit into the Japanese home.

At this point, the enraged Terry upsets Gwen's little cactus and throws the uprooted plant outside the door into the darkness of the garden. He then storms out himself. However, when he returns to reconcile with Gwen later in the evening, he first gingerly salvages the little cactus as a sign of his acceptance of Gwen's difference. He knocks, enters the bedroom, puts the cactus on a little table, and says, "I was cruel and stupid. I do not want a Japanese wife, I want you." Terry's acceptance of his wife as different carries with it a wealth of contradictory interpretations. On one level, it can be looked at as an acceptance of Gwen's apparently feminist stance that refuses to bow to traditional patriarchal values. In another sense, however, it can also be viewed as an affirmation of America over Japan, of the supposed superiority of American paternalistic regard for the sanctified purity of women or of the superiority of American values of individualism. In yet another way, Terry's gesture can be looked at as a sign of his emasculation, of the inevitable decline of Japan and its patriarchal legitimacy, as the first step on the road to Terry's complete loss of potency.

However, the revelation later in the scene that Gwen is pregnant makes another interpretation possible. When the baby girl takes the place of the thorny cactus as the pivotal object in compositions depicting Gwen and Terry's more intimate moments, Terry, too, appears to have been "converted" to a more liberal, "Americanized," protective, paternal stance. Gently covering his infant daughter and grasping Gwen's hand, Terry confesses, "I have a terrible secret. All my life I've wanted a daughter. Very un-Japanese, but true." If motherhood tames Gwen, fatherhood does not necessarily shore up Terry's threatened masculinity. Rather, it puts his patriarchal prerogatives in further doubt as he expresses his preference for a daughter. Thus, the baby can be viewed as an idealized bridge across the Pacific, which forever links husband and wife, Japan and America, or as an icon of a dual domestication of the threat of independent femininity and a potent Asian masculinity.

The next domestic setting in which the family is placed seems to confirm that Gwen and Terry represent a racial and national equilibrium within the bourgeois, patriarchal, American household. The camera dollies past a radio, stuffed toys, and a Japanese doll and pulls back to reveal a standard American living room with sofa and chairs and a small dining room with the table set for Thanksgiving dinner. Bound books and European scalloped drapes indicate class standing. It appears to be a typical Hollywood representation of the bourgeois domicile, both lived-in and formal, elegant and simple. Any hints of racial difference are domesticated through the inclusion of "Japaneseness" as an innocuous doll. Moreover, any threat Gwen may have posed to the sexual status quo has been completely subsumed by depicting her as totally at home as hostess and mother. She no longer uncomfortably plays the role of Japanese wife and disgruntled hostess, trapped within the boxlike enclosures of her in-laws' Tokyo home.

However, this image of the American bourgeois home proves deceptive. Rather than the self-contained idealized domestic sanctuary, this home is assailed by a hostile external world, represented by a radio broadcast of Franklin Delano Roosevelt's 1941 Thanksgiving address, ominous telephone conversations, and discussions of the impending Pacific war. Moreover, this home exists within the provisional space of an apartment hotel. Unlike the domestic security assured by the picket fence as a barrier against the outer world in *Japanese War Bride*, this impermanent space is easily penetrated by spies, who can listen through the thin walls of the flat to the most intimate conversations. On the surface, *Bridge to the Sun*'s interracial couple appears to have achieved the American ideal of domesticity; however, that supposed sanctuary cannot be defended and easily collapses. After the attack on Pearl Harbor, an FBI agent appears to evict the family.

Back in Japan, Gwen and Terry again find it impossible to be "themselves" and "at home." At risk in their Tokyo home, they move to the countryside and set up housekeeping on a small Japanese farm. Once again, the fragility of their domestic space becomes evident as American planes fly over and the Japanese military police appear unexpectedly at their cramped, dark, traditionally bare little home. Even their clothing signifies their provisional domestic status. The family dresses in tattered combinations of Western raincoats, knitted sweaters, kimonos, and peasant pajamas.

Gradually, Terry fades as a presence in the home. On the lam from the authorities, Terry is replaced by a waiting ritual that Gwen and her daughter perform. Each night, they put a dish of food out for Terry, hoping for his return. Dissolves from close-up to close-up of the dishes create both a sense of the passing of time and a fading of Terry as a patriarchal force. Moreover, the domestication of Gwen reaches its ultimate extreme in this series of shots. No longer the independent, outspoken, active, "new" woman, she has become a passive victim, unable to act to help her husband or herself. As Elsaesser has noted,

> The more the setting fills with objects to which the plot gives symbolic significance, the more the characters are enclosed in seemingly ineluctable situations. Pressure is generated by things crowding in on them and life becomes increasingly complicated because [it has become] cluttered with obstacles and objects that invade their personalities, take them over, stand for them, become more real than the human relations or emotions they were intended to symbolize.[12]

Even though the partially filled bowls give way to Terry's return near the end of the war, the Terasaki home never seems to recover from its association with these pitiful icons of Terry's absence.

Although the possibility of a bourgeois home is nearly realized in their Washington apartment, the film never allows its interracial couple to attain this sanctified banality. Instead, even though Gwen does receive her domestic education through motherhood and Terry becomes the emblem of Japanese capitulation to the moral and cultural superiority of America, *Bridge to the Sun* allows no concrete representation of a new domestic order that could accommodate its interracial couple. Like *Japanese War Bride*, *Bridge to the Sun* calls for racial tolerance but insists on it only within the boundaries of traditional patriarchal relations and remains vague about the viability of any multiracial domestic relationship. Although heterosexual romantic love may guarantee transcendence in Hollywood, it does not necessarily allow for a happy interracial domesticity.

Thus, like most Hollywood melodramas, *Japanese War Bride* and *Bridge to the Sun* offer contradictory fantasies about the desirability and continuing viability of the traditional, American, bourgeois, patriarchal home. Like the domestic dramas of the eighteenth century, both films seem to instruct the viewer about the proper moral position that should be taken and, specifically, the social role women should fulfill within the home. However, neither film allows that idealized home to be represented. Although racism is condemned and women are instructed to be good wives and mothers by staying in the home, neither heroine realizes her dream. Instead, Gwen's and Tae's pains and sacrifices, rather than their idealized positions as housewives, may make a stronger impression on many women in the audience who are similarly frustrated in their quest for the "typical" American home.

9

The Return of the Butterfly

The Geisha Masquerade in *My Geisha* and "An American Geisha"

Throughout its history, Hollywood has had a romantic fascination with the geisha. These traditional Japanese female entertainers have appeared as both principal and supporting characters in many comic and dramatic films. One peculiar variation on these stories features Caucasian women who travel to Japan and masquerade as geisha. Whether as a lark, to trap a man, or for "scientific" investigations of anthropological significance, these American geisha tales tend to highlight representations of both racial and sexual otherness.

Although Hollywood has always allowed for the convention of "yellow face" (the portrayal of Asian roles by Caucasians), these American geisha stories provide some of the very few instances in which yellow face becomes part of the narrative and the issue of Asian otherness becomes an explicit part of the plot. As Frantz Fanon has demonstrated in his classic study *Black Skin, White Masks*,[1] race, more than a biological marker of difference, is a social construction deeply rooted in the psychological formation of self-identity. These geisha masquerades make the potentially subversive notion that racial differences are not "natural" but culturally constructed and subject to historical change quite clear. As a consequence, these films implicitly critique the racial hierarchy of mainstream American culture, since they feature the conscious and deliberate impersonation of another race, putting aside a supposedly racial superiority so as to become part of a supposedly inferior culture.

Although part of the pleasure of these stories may revolve around the mastery of an alien culture and its customs, female spectators might also enjoy an imagined freedom from the perplexing contradictions of Western femininity. On the one hand, women can indulge a sense of liberation and adventure in stories that feature remarkably accomplished women who can pull off their impersonations. On the other hand, these narratives allow women to indulge in the appeal of the de rigueur sexual allure and male approval that comes with the geisha role.

For male viewers, these stories promote a fantasy in which a desire for the exoticism of a nonwhite beauty can be rationalized by the fact that the beauty is really Caucasian. Moreover, the desire on the part of these white women to become passive, doll-like man pleasers also affirms the myth of women's basic masochistic drive to subordinate themselves to men. Perhaps, at bottom, however, these tales, like all geisha stories, allow for the indulgence of the pleasure of watching female bodies set in a beautiful locale, where Western conceptions of morality do not take precedence over sexual desire.

These narratives, then, tend to be ideologically complex, offering conservative affirmations of Western heterosexual marriage and the separation of the races, while also acknowledging the intellectual and artistic accomplishments of their clever female protagonists. They are fantasies of liberation as well as of glamorous bondage for women. For men, they offer sexual titillation as well as a core of moral certainty that will not abandon the ideal of the same-race, heterosexual marriage bond as the acceptable outlet for the male libido. Situated somewhere between women's romance fictions that feature naive young girls cast adrift in a foreign world of dark strangers and more rugged travel adventures of Americans staking their claims to alien cultural secrets and treasures, these female-centered narratives can appeal in different ways to different viewers.

My Geisha (Jack Cardiff, 1962) and "An American Geisha" (Lee Philips, 1986) highlight the ideological complexities and narrative pleasures of these American geisha fantasies. Although made over twenty years apart, they share striking similarities in their treatment of interracial romance, female sexuality, and gender roles. Thus, they provide excellent points of departure for an examination of the way in which Hollywood plays with the sometimes perplexing allure of the white geisha.

Geisha-Happy in Hollywood

The Hollywood geisha functions somewhat differently in the Japanese arts than she does in American popular culture. In Japan, the geisha, originally male, first appeared during the Tokugawa shogunate (also known as the Edo period, 1600–1867) as entertainers associated with licensed prostitution. Eventually, female geisha began to appear, and they became popular as singers, dancers, musicians, and hostesses in the licensed quarters like the Yoshiwara in Edo (later known as Tokyo). Because they were not prostitutes themselves (in fact, they were forbidden by law to interfere with prostitutes' customers in any way), they, unlike the sequestered prostitutes, were free to move in and out of the licensed districts at will. As a result, they gained a reputation for being worldly and modern, gifted conversationalists, innovative performers, and trendsetters. They were valued as fitting companions for businessmen and politicians, who never socialized with their wives outside the home, and who required something more in their sojourns in the pleasure districts than a prostitute could offer.

This is likely the origin of the Western confusion of the geisha trade with prostitution. Although the geisha often became the mistresses of their clients or would occasionally acquiesce to their sexual advances for other reasons, they could not take business directly away from prostitutes under penalty of law. Western fiction also occasionally mistook the fact that geisha were not prostitutes for an elevated moral sense or prudery that could not be further from the truth, since the geisha drink, engage in sexual repartee, and flirt as part of their occupation. Moreover, since they were often gifted artists, politically active, or astute businesswomen, the passive geisha of Hollywood differ considerably from the outgoing Japanese image found in *ukiyo-e* (prints dealing with the "floating world" of entertainment and prostitution in traditional Japan) as well as in films like Kenji Mizoguchi's *Sisters of the Gion* (1936) and *A Geisha* (1953).

After World War II, the geisha image did change. Bar girls in Western dress began to replace the geisha as party companions, and the geisha became living symbols of the traditional arts and culture. Her services became the acquired taste of connoisseurs rather than the relaxed good time she represented in an earlier period. This image of the geisha as a nostalgic tribute to Japan's past accomplishments does surface in Hollywood. However, it remains linked to a notion that the geisha continues to embody the very idea of "sexiness" to the Japanese man, which she has not done at least since World War II.[2]

As the geisha was losing popularity in Japan, she began to gain interest in Hollywood. After the American occupation of Japan (1945–1952), in fact, films involving geisha reached their peak. These postwar geisha tales included *Teahouse of the August Moon* (1956), *The Barbarian and the Geisha* (1958), *Cry for Happy* (1961), and *My Geisha* in 1962, among others. For a time, in fact, it appeared as if the geisha was Hollywood's chief emblem of postwar reconciliation. Although on the surface she might appear cool, distant, mysterious, or morally suspect, underneath she was seen as docile, eager to please, malleable, child-like, and vulnerable. Metaphorically, a bellicose Japan, through the figure of the geisha, became a yielding and dependent nation.

Moreover, as part of a general reaction to the emergence of women as an economic and social force during the wartime absence of men on the home front, these geisha tales could also very conveniently serve as postwar moral fables for independently minded American women. The point being made is quite clear: white American women should put aside their own interests to return to the prewar male-dominated order that their geisha sisters gladly accept as the "natural" way of the world.

In the 1950s and early 1960s, Japan and the geisha also provided Hollywood with the opportunity to exploit new technology to its best advantage. Exotic and picturesque, Japan provided the perfect location for the new wide-screen technicolor spectacles that appeared in the 1950s in response to inroads made by television. Bronze Buddhas, cherry trees, sumo wrestlers, Kabuki performers, and, of course, geisha helped to give these films a larger-than-life quality, a sense of Asian sumptuousness and extravagance, and a feeling of an all-encompassing experience of something out of the ordinary that the small, flickering, black-and-white television picture could not rival.

My Geisha goes beyond being a simple bedroom farce to include a certain self-aware commentary on its own exploitation of wide-screen processes and advanced color techniques. As such, the film falls within another minor, but significant, Hollywood genre—the "movie about the movies."[3] In the late 1950s and early 1960s, several of these films attained a degree of popularity: *Man of a Thousand Faces* (1957), *Will Success Spoil Rock Hunter?* (1957), *Too Much, Too Soon* (1958), *The Errand Boy* (1962), *Sweet Bird of Youth* (1962), *The Patsy* (1964), and *Inside Daisy Clover* (1965). Like these other films, *My Geisha* offers a behind-the-scenes look at the movie industry. In fact, it combines two plot lines (one dealing with the making of a film version of Puccini's *Madame Butterfly* and the other involving a farcical case of mistaken identity) to create a variety of possible viewing pleasures.

In *My Geisha*, Lucy Dell (Shirley MacLaine), a popular Hollywood comedic actress, becomes concerned when her film-director husband and collaborator, Paul Robaix (Yves Montand), decides to go to Japan to film *Madame Butterfly*. (This aspect of *My Geisha*'s plot may have been inspired by the 1958 Japanese-Italian coproduction of *Madame Butterfly*, from Toho, Rizzoli Films, and Gallone Productions, which also attempted a more authentic rendering of the opera by making use of Japanese locations and Japanese actors and actresses.)[4] Despite the protests of his producer, Sam Lewis (Edward G. Robinson), Paul takes

Figure 25. *In* My Geisha *(1962), Lucy Dell (Shirley MacLaine) tricks her husband Paul Robaix (Yves Montand) into thinking she is the geisha Yoko Mori to win the role of Madame Butterfly in Paul's film. Still courtesy of the Museum of Modern Art/Film Stills Archive.*

along Lucy's usual leading man, Bob Moore (Robert Cummings), to play Lieutenant Pinkerton and sets off without her.

Unbeknown to Paul and Bob, Lucy decides to go to Japan to surprise her husband. Upon her arrival, Lucy discovers Paul and Bob at a teahouse with geisha. She dresses in geisha clothing on a bet with Sam and, indeed, easily fools her husband. When Paul decides to cast a real geisha as Cho-Cho San, Lucy and Sam conspire to make Paul unwittingly choose Lucy's geisha alter ego, Yoko Mori, for the role. They plan to reveal Yoko Mori's true identity as a publicity stunt, making the film a star vehicle rather than a minor foray into highbrow subject matter for a hack comedy director.

Everything goes as planned until Bob and then Paul begin to take a romantic interest in Yoko Mori. Lucy begins to feel she may lose her husband to her geisha alter ego. Paul then discovers Lucy's deception through a freak problem with the filmmaking process, which forces him to watch a color negative of Yoko Mori with Lucy's red hair and blue eyes. His ego damaged, Paul, not revealing that he knows the truth about her identity, makes a pass at Yoko. Realizing the threat her deception has meant to her husband's ego, Lucy decides to forgo the possibility of an Oscar and, instead, allows Paul all the approbation for masterfully directing an unknown geisha in an "authentic" rendition of *Madame Butterfly*. By not revealing her identity to the public, Lucy saves her marriage at the expense of her career.

On an obvious, rhetorical level, *My Geisha* advocates monogamous, heterosexual, uniracial marriage, the conservation of Japanese tradition, and the glories of the cinema. It pokes fun, in a disapproving way, at multiple marriages and divorces, the Americanization of Japan, the loss of conservative values, and the possible decline of the cinema as the dominant mode of entertainment and spectacle internationally. All these ideas interweave and support one another in *My Geisha*.

"Color" and "realism" are touted in discussions in *My Geisha* of film aesthetics and the *Madame Butterfly* project. When he first mentions his intention to film *Madame Butterfly*, for example, Paul exclaims, "It was made for *color* film." He goes on to explain, "I'm going to use a *real* Japanese girl. That's the kind of picture it's going to be—real. Not just an opera but real . . . Lucy in the part of Madame Butterfly would be offensive."[5] Interestingly, Paul refuses to cast Lucy in the role, not because a Caucasian playing an Asian role would cast doubt on the film's claimed authenticity but because Paul finds his wife limited as an actress. It would be "outside your range," he tells Lucy.

Thus, although much is made of the aesthetics of color cinematography and the authentic and exotic photographic potential of Japan and the Japanese, little is made of racial difference, notions of equality, or the ethics of allowing other races or nations their own voices and identities in the cinema. While "color" can connote racial difference and "realism" can be looked at as a conception of the "real" that legitimizes social hierarchies based on nation, race, and gender, through the illusion that the cinema can capture the authentic "essence" of a culture, the film deals directly with neither. Rather, both become insistent "absences" that structure the narrative.[6]

It is appropriate that Paul should come to realize that Lucy has tricked him during a viewing of a color negative. At this point, he suddenly discovers the artifice behind his belief in realism. His faith in the innocence of his wife, his own masculine ego, and his belief in the natural essence of Japanese culture all come into question through this self-referential cinematic trope. Suffice it to say, through the working out of *My Geisha*'s denouement, all these profound contradictions involving artifice and authenticity, nature and culture, Caucasian and Japanese, male and female, find their resolution in the reunion of the married couple.

My Geisha is not unique in its use of color cinematography to highlight social differences of various sorts. Color cinematography and films dealing with questions of race have sometimes gone hand-in-hand in film history.[7] In 1912, *The Durbar at Delhi*, a Kinemacolor process documentary on George V's visit to India in celebration of his coronation, used color to celebrate the continuation of the British Raj.[8] The first two-color technicolor film was *Toll of the Sea* (1923), a *Madame Butterfly* story set in China starring Anna May Wong. In this tragic interracial romance, color cinematography accentuates the difference in skin tones between the Anna May Wong character and her Caucasian husband, his wife and her Caucasian-looking son.

My Geisha, however, is careful to relegate any discussion of race or miscegenation to a minor role. Any discomfort created by the treatment of interracial sexuality is, at its most basic level, alleviated by the fact that the viewer knows from the outset that both Paul and Bob are attracted to a Caucasian woman. Moreover, the film goes out of its way to avoid issues of racism and sexuality. At one point, for example, Paul insists that his objection to Bob's plans to marry Yoko has nothing to do with racial prejudice. The subject is then quickly dropped.

Later, a New York-based executive producer carefully makes any casting decision a question of money rather than race. Addressing himself to Lucy, who has been trying to use her box-office clout to help her husband, the executive reasons, "Look, I like *Madame Butterfly*. I'll even pay my two dollars and go to see it. What I won't do is pay two million dollars to have Robert Moore kissing a Japanese girl. The film public wants to see Robert Moore kissing you, and your artistic husband should know that."

Paul's conception of "truth," "authenticity," and "realism" as the genuine artistry of the film medium is also called into question by the fact that his film is very much an illusion. Paul's *Madame Butterfly* celebrates the great power of film to "lie," that is, the fact that a Caucasian plays the leading role is kept from the fictional public. It could be argued that *My Geisha* makes suspect its own ideological claims to knowing the genuine "nature" of gender and racial difference by this plot development.

If anything, *My Geisha*'s representation of the off-screen machinations that go into the making of *Madame Butterfly* actually enhances its very conservative treatment of race and gender. As both Dana Polan[9] and Barbara Klinger[10] have pointed out, not all instances of irony or self-reference in Hollywood films can be taken as an indication of either a latent or a manifest progressive political orientation. In fact, in the case of *My Geisha*, the opposite seems to be true; the film's own self-consciousness tends to solidify its conservatism.

As a made-for-television movie drama of the mid-1980s, "An American Geisha" belongs to a wholly different genre, medium, and era. With its drama sandwiched between the requisite commercial interruptions, "An American Geisha" entices the viewer to return to the fiction through its spectacular display of the "forbidden" sexual underworld of Japanese life. Indeed, "An American Geisha" brings with it much of the seriousness of its source, Liza Dalby's *Geisha*, which was based on the doctoral dissertation she completed at Stanford University in 1978.[11]

Although drawing on this anthropological research, "An American Geisha" does not present itself to the viewer as a documentary exposé of the geisha world. Rather, this made-for-television movie really takes on most of the attributes that Molly Haskell describes as characteristic of the "woman's film," which reached its apogee in the 1930s and 1940s.[12] Although meant to sell the American woman on the norms of bourgeois, male-dominated, consumer-oriented family life, the woman's film genre also tends to recognize the trials and tribulations women must endure to maintain this norm. Hollywood completes this particular generic version of bittersweet female life by coating it with a piquant layer of heterosexual romance—happy, tragic, pathetic, transient, transcendent, all-consuming, and always fulfilling.

By applying this formula, television transforms Dalby's *Geisha* into a fairly typical woman's film. Like many similar fictions, it features an extraordinary heroine, Gillian Burke (Pam Dawber), a Harvard scholar, fluent in Japanese, who must face several of the problems Haskell identifies as typical of this type of narrative—competition, choice, and sacrifice. Before the movie itself begins, a male announcer introduces the fiction over a preview montage: "Driven by a spiritual passion, an American woman breaks an ancient tradition and enters a world forbidden to outsiders. But, passion for geisha life abruptly collides with

passion for a man she cannot have . . . torn between loyalty and love."
This precredit introduction sets up the main tensions of the text succinctly: spiritual versus carnal passion; American versus Japanese; outsider versus geisha insider; love for a man versus geisha sisterhood;
duty versus romantic love. This initial overview shapes the telefilm
from the outset. In a sense, this controlling male voice haunts the film
and vies with Gillian's voice-over commentary for authority, just as the
drama plays with the divided interests of its heroine.

After the credits, a title superimposed over a traveling long shot of
the Boston skyline appears: "The following story is based upon the
actual experiences of the only American woman to ever enter the
world of the Geisha." It, too, lends a distanced air of authority to the
narrative, keeping Gillian's own subjective commentary in perspective.
The narrative itself begins with Gillian's decision to go to Japan to research geisha life, despite her Caucasian boyfriend's desire for her to
accompany him on his own research trip to New Guinea.

In Tokyo, Gillian meets Konguro (Richard Narita), a Kabuki performer, who pursues her relentlessly. Instead of pursuing her romantic
adventures in Tokyo, however, Gillian moves on to the old capital of
Kyoto, where a friendly *okasan*, the "mother" of a geisha house, agrees
to take her in as a favor to her former patron and lover, Mr. Hashimoto (Robert Ito). In Kyoto, Gillian also meets up with a friend from
an earlier trip, Ann (Dorothy McGuire), who had been married to a
Zen master and has lived in Japan for many years.

Impressed by Gillian's sincerity, the *okasan* of her house agrees to
let her train as a geisha. With the help of her geisha sister Kohana,
"Little Flower," Gillian eventually makes her debut as Korin, "Little
Bell," the American geisha. She is an immediate success, which provokes a certain jealousy from her sister geisha. Putting her loyalty to
her fellow geisha above her own success, she purposely makes a faux
pas by appearing in Western dress (pants no less) when Mr. Tanaka
(Kenji Kamei), the customer Kohana has a crush on, invites her on an
outing to impress some American business associates. Although Mr.
Tanaka and Kohana do become a couple, their happiness comes to
an abrupt end when Kohana, after confirming her sisterly bond with
Gillian in a traditional geisha ceremony, dies in a fire.

Konguro reappears in Gillian's life and proposes marriage. However, after meeting with his parents and discovering that he has been
betrothed for years to a Japanese woman of similar standing, Gillian
decides to have one last fling with her lover and leave him and Japan
behind.

A final voice-over commentary by Gillian, paralleling the earlier
voice-of-God introduction, summarizes her experiences as she walks

through the airport on her way to catch an airplane back to the United States: "The geisha opened the gates of the teahouse garden and I went through. I learned to love a man and live the moment, and I learned the meaning of sisterhood. Now, I must let go." A title superimposed over a slightly slow-motion image of her actually going through the entrance gate to board the airplane adds a further note of closure: "Today, Gillian Burke lives in Berkeley, California, with her husband and two children. She received her doctorate in anthropology and still remains in contact with the Geisha community in Kyoto." Her reentry into the American domestic mainstream is emphasized; her academic career and further involvement with geisha remain vague and take on a secondary significance.

Aside from the general plot line of an American training as a geisha with the help of a friendly *okasan*, a few incidents like the actual death of Liza Dalby's geisha "big sister" in a fire, and some voice-over commentary quoted directly from *Geisha*, "An American Geisha" owes little to the book on which it is based. Rather, as Gillian unwittingly competes with her geisha sister for the attention of customers, as she must make choices between her conception of duty, her career and her romantic desires, and as she must sacrifice her own happiness for the perceived greater good of Konguro's career, this fiction owes a far greater debt to the woman's film than to any anthropological examination of geisha.

In fact, in many ways, "An American Geisha" is typical of recent films and television dramas that offer an updated version of the woman's film to contemporary female viewers. As Charlotte Brundson, Julia Lesage, B. Ruby Rich, among other feminist film scholars,[13] have pointed out, these revised woman's films, such as *An Unmarried Woman* (1978), *The Turning Point* (1978), and *Girlfriends* (1978), feature "independent" heroines and rhetoric taken directly from the women's movement. However, these women's independent lives are inevitably contained by narratives that paradoxically offer salvation through heterosexual romance and marriage. In "An American Geisha," for example, Gillian, the cultural anthropologist, is involved in "women's liberation" and her career before being confined to her eventual role as wife and mother.

As in these other revised women's films, the women's movement is offered as a topical draw while simultaneously delivering the comforts of an essentially conservative depiction of women's social roles. Although based on a "true" story, "An American Geisha," as a fiction paying only minimal attention to its source, has freely buried beneath its surface ideological issues and concerns that might otherwise interfere with viewing pleasure.

Both *My Geisha* and "An American Geisha," moreover, share a tendency to relegate issues of race and miscegenation to the background, while emphasizing the problem of gender difference and the threat a Western liberated woman poses to traditional notions of masculinity. By donning geisha attire, both Lucy and Gillian learn to adjust their desires to fit the dominant order, ending up as proper wives to their husbands. Japan serves as a metaphor for traditional patriarchal sexual relations, and these films seem to argue that, beneath an exotic veneer of Kabuki and geisha artifice, men are men and women are women.

However, Japan and the geisha function slightly differently in each film as metaphors for traditional gender divisions and a happy acceptance of female subordination to men. In post-Occupation films like *My Geisha*, the geisha helps to cast Japan as the conquered enemy, the submissive servant to the conqueror America. In "An American Geisha," a different relationship between the United States and Japan provides a backdrop to the fantasy. The growth of Japan as an industrial and mercantile power finds expression in Mr. Hashimoto's prosperous international business and Mr. Tanaka's lucrative robotics firm. The geisha may still represent a xenophobic desire to look at Japan metaphorically as a subservient woman, but "An American Geisha" seems to recognize, too, that this era has passed.

"An American Geisha" emphasizes the closed nature of the geisha world. With Gillian's submission to the Japanese custom of parents' choosing marriage partners for their children, "An American Geisha" uses romance and marriage as a way of legitimizing its preference for this view of Japan as an isolated island nation, posing no real threat to American international expansionism either economically or militarily. Given that the only interracial marriage represented is Ann's childless marriage to a Zen master, none of the Japanese, nor the business interests they symbolize, decides to promote a public internationalism by allowing for a marriage with a non-Japanese. By making this a part of both its main narrative line as well as its various subplots, "An American Geisha" projects a xenophobic fear of interracial marriage and internationalism. Gillian, the naive American liberal, simply acquiesces to what is depicted as a Japanese abhorrence of interracial contact.

In this sense, "An American Geisha" can be looked at as another entry into an increasingly paranoid American public discourse that looks at Japanese economic and industrial expansion as a more serious threat than its pre-1945 militarism. By choosing to see Japan metaphorically as a cloistered teahouse, as the secluded world of the geisha quarters, the telefilm affirms a conservative American belief that the Japanese really prefer their isolation.

A desire for an ancient, nonthreatening, passive, and picturesque Japan links up with each film's nostalgia for a pre-women's liberation view of gender. Both *My Geisha* and "An American Geisha" try to use the geisha as a symbol for a desired female servility and passivity threatened by the women's movement as well as a plea for greater access for women to the public sphere. Each film transforms its initially self-possessed heroine into a subordinated creature who, by donning geisha attire, sacrifices her own desires for the greater good of the man in her life. Thus, *My Geisha* and "An American Geisha" manage to reconcile a recognition of women's growing independence with a conservative desire to keep them from threatening the power and prerogatives of men.

The Woman Traveler

In many Hollywood narratives, including the captivity stories discussed in chapter 3, a heroine leaves home, usually against the wishes of a father, husband, or boyfriend, and travels to a foreign country. This uncharacteristically independent action taken by a female character breaks with the social norm of female inactivity and dependence. The point of many of these Hollywood narratives becomes, then, to draw the heroine back into the patriarchal mainstream, after she has made a suitable sacrifice for her hubris.

In the geisha impersonation tale, the heroine ironically chooses, as her act of independence and defiance of male authority, a role that (in the Western imagination at least) glorifies female servility and acquiescence to male privilege. In both *My Geisha* and "An American Geisha," for example, the donning of geisha attire comes as a "natural" desire by the heroines to win back a husband, learn the true meaning of heterosexual romance, or in some other way find their "true" selves. At the beginning of each film, the heroine appears as confused, as somehow unhappy being a successful and liberated woman.

The tension between "natural" and "unnatural" gender roles appears at the start of each film. In *My Geisha*, Lucy Dell first appears crouching on a pool table, wearing tight slacks, with the camera placed so that her posterior is prominent in the shot, her face hidden, and an arm bent in the action of striking one of the pool balls with a cue. (Later in the film, Lucy's buttocks again become the focus of attention when she must awkwardly raise her rear in order to sit on a Japanese tatami mat.) Although played as comic, the fact that this image may conjure up a potentially disturbing homoeroticism becomes even clearer when Lucy descends from her pool table perch to reveal her close-cropped red hair, boyish physique and outfit, with only a strand of pearls and light eye makeup to mark her as "feminine" in accordance with Hollywood conventions.

As the scene continues in the living room with her husband dressed "effeminately" in a bathrobe, the film makes it clear that Lucy literally as well as figuratively wears the pants in the house. Indeed, Paul wants to make a film of *Madame Butterfly*, at least in part, to escape from his wife's overshadowing star presence and, thus, to assert his own masculine ego. Her unselfconscious tomboyish gestures, for example, casually placing her legs on the sofa, jauntily moving freely around the rather stuffy living room filled with white furniture and abstract modern art, indicate that she is completely unaware of any connection between her own boyishness, her success, and her husband's ambition. However, the bending of those cultural codes associated with female dress and demeanor visually asserts the ideological disequilibrium that initially moves the plot forward.

When Lucy does decide to don geisha dress, her action is presented as a lark, but, underlying its playfulness, the film hints at a darker, inappropriate side to the ruse in which a woman dares to trick her husband, manipulate him, delight in her own cleverness, and threaten his masculine ego. By continuing her charade, Lucy asserts her own ego as well as her ability to act in other than comic roles. Thus, she breaks with the patriarchal proscription against an independent female identity.

While Lucy travels to Japan on a whim and naively attires herself as a geisha, Gillian's trip to Japan and her geisha adventures are taken much more seriously and, as such, may be more threatening to the sexual status quo. In *My Geisha*, Lucy can be dismissed as a mischievous child on holiday; in "An American Geisha" Gillian is depicted as a serious Harvard graduate student, an anthropologist pursuing research. However, from the outset, the academic significance of this research is downplayed in favor of the more conventionally "feminine," personal, emotional reasons for Gillian's decision to travel to Japan.

From the precredit teaser, Gillian's journey is labeled a "spiritual quest." Having traveled with her parents to Kyoto as a child, Gillian expresses a desire to return to look for a sense of "belonging" and "family." The telefilm intimates that her modern relationship with her boyfriend in Cambridge does not fulfill her "spiritually," that is, as a woman, and her search becomes a nostalgic quest for the more traditional family of her childhood (with its more traditional roles for women).

This quest finds visual expression in the Japanese print she looks at longingly in her Cambridge apartment which shows a Japanese female entertainer with her *shamisen* (three-stringed, guitarlike instrument), a beautifully dressed child at her knee, holding an equally elaborately attired Japanese doll. Thus, from the outset, Gillian's spiritual longings are associated with the perceived notion that Japan still promises traditional domestic values and rewards. Although her boyfriend dismisses her research trip by saying, "Oh, come on, Gillian, spiritual quests went out in the seventies," the telefilm seems to allow the viewer to take Gillian's travels seriously.

Certainly, no "spiritual quests" appear in Dalby's *Geisha*, where a gift for the Japanese language and an exploitation of her gender allow the anthropologist access to a subject unavailable to her male colleagues. In *Geisha*, Dalby emphasizes the independence, commitment to the arts, business acumen, and freedom from the boring routine of domesticity the geisha often enjoy in Japan. If anything, a certain feminist interest in this rare community of women, both dependent on male patronage but free from many of the constraints imposed on traditional Japanese wives, motivates the inclusion of much of the information and many of the anecdotes found in Dalby's book. In "An American Geisha," however, no explanation is given for Gillian's search for spirituality in Tokyo's and Kyoto's pleasure quarters, rather than at a Buddhist monastery with a Zen master (like her friend Ann) or in any number of other, less worldly, pursuits. In voice-over self-examinations, Gillian mouths appropriately vague pronouncements: "I came to find myself" and "Somehow the strangeness of Japan makes me feel my strangeness has a place."

Quickly, however, this ill-defined "strangeness" becomes a less obscure problem of female sexuality, moral values, and the appropriate gender roles for women in the 1980s. Female intellectuals always seem to be represented as asexual in American popular culture, so Gillian's search for femininity seems logical in the context of the narrative. Very early in the telefilm, gender identity becomes an explicitly discussed topic. At supper with Konguro, after meeting him at a Kabuki rehearsal, their first lengthy discussion involves the *onnagata*, the female impersonators of the Kabuki theater. Prefiguring her own similar transformation from one race to another, this mention of the *onnagata* also serves as an entrée into the topic of gender divisions in Japanese culture. Konguro almost lectures: "My grandfather used to say, 'When a woman is feminine, it's not art, it's nature. But, when a man is feminine, when he creates the feminine on stage in its most perfect form, that's art. There is no conflict with the masculine self. I guess, in a way, both are true and both are false." Thus, if the search for the "essence" of an eternal, feminine identity in the geisha world of artifice should at first appear odd, this speech helps both to reaffirm a belief in a "natural" feminine identity and explain the role of artifice in the pursuit of its perfection. Later in the conversation, Konguro seems to summarize the discussion by saying, "It's established, then, I'm a man and you're a woman."

In fact, a great deal of the ideological work in both *My Geisha* and "An American Geisha" involves the construction of what must appear to be a natural, essential, passive, and submissive femininity. Part of the way in which this ideological work is cloaked in both films revolves around the claim of each to present the viewer with a supposedly authentic, almost scientific, insight into geisha life and Japanese culture. Although Hollywood seeks to entertain rather than instruct, part of the pleasure of narratives like these seems to include the illusion, at least, that the viewer can learn something about a foreign land from the story. However, the inclusion of this information goes beyond the instructional, since it acts to legitimize the racial, ethnic, and sexual status quo and makes xenophobic assumptions part of its "objective" observation.

For example, *My Geisha* includes statistical information on the weight and ritual practices of sumo wrestlers, commentary on the separation of the public and the domestic in Japan, with the geisha serving as "wife" to a businessman in his public role (quite separate from his actual wife who remains at home with the children), information on the apprenticeship of geisha who must endure practicing their musical instruments outside in the winter to discipline themselves, the complexity of the Japanese tea ceremony, and more. Since "An American Geisha" features an actual scholar as its protagonist, it goes even further in providing the illusion of real insight into geisha life. In addition to Konguro's lecture on the *onnagata*, Gillian's voice-over commentary provides information on Zen Buddhism, Kyoto history, the origins of the geisha trade with male entertainers in the 1660s, the meaning of *en* (spiritual affinity), the place of the *ukiyo* (the "floating world" of entertainers, geisha, Kabuki performers, and prostitutes) in Japanese society, an explanation of why *shamisen* warp, and a discussion of Bon (the Buddhist festival of lanterns and lights to honor the dead). All these extraneous bits of information, only very loosely motivated by the narrative, serve ideologically to justify each film's ability to present a "true" picture. Thus, the films claim to be accurate about cultural and historical details as well as about their conceptions of femininity and masculinity, racial divisions, and traditional marriages.

As the heroines digest this information and turn away from their false, "liberated" attitudes about the role of women in society, the viewer follows along, learning about the perils of stepping outside patriarchically defined gender boundaries. All these "objective" facts, from information on Buddhist philosophy, which calls for submission to fate (to be born a woman means to be destined to fulfill the subordinate role of the female) to the exaggerated masculinity of the sumo and femininity of the geisha, serve not simply to provide interesting information on a foreign culture but to instruct the viewer on supposedly universally accepted gender norms. As the woman traveler learns through her adventures, no matter where or how far she may go, she can never escape the inevitability of patriarchal strictures and limitations placed on her by her gender. The films serve to externalize the confused heroine's interior search for her "true" femininity, her genuine desire to put the women's movement behind her and suppress her own will for the sake of her man.

The Geisha Masquerade

If Lucy and Gillian disturb the smooth operation of the patriarchal gender system by becoming independent travelers, they also challenge the "natural" social order by adopting geisha dress. In fact, the contradiction between independent female self-determination and the exploitation of the geisha as a male erotic fantasy forms a key narrative paradox in each film. Not only is much made of the difficult training and hardships involved in becoming a geisha but the very act of the self-construction of a woman's identity seems to confirm both that gender roles are not natural but culturally constituted and that women have the power and skills necessary to transform themselves. Even though the geisha may symbolize servility and passivity for most men, this alluring exterior belies her ability to create this identity. On the one hand, she represents a beautiful polished image to be admired and desired; on the other hand, she embodies the potential threat of female self-creation and self-determination. The white geisha impersonator makes this doubly evident by crossing national and cultural borders to create an entirely new self-identity.

Although donning geisha dress may be Lucy's and Gillian's first step in their discovery of their "true" femininity, it cannot be taken as an unambiguous first step on the road to submission to the patriarchal order. The geisha must always leave an element of doubt about any ideological assumption that an essential or authentic femininity exists.

In her introduction to the anthology *Fabrications: Costume and the Female Body*, Jane Gaines notes that feminist film criticism has tended to look at the female body in one of two ways, either as a fetishistic or voyeuristic object of the male gaze or, metaphorically, as a masquerade.[14] Given the paradoxical nature of the Caucasian geisha, both these models shed a certain light on the appeal of these fantasies. However, even when taken together, they still fall short of a complete explanation of these pleasures for male as well as female viewers. Still, these theories do provide a starting point to explain this fascination with the American geisha.

The first model, based on Laura Mulvey's "Visual Pleasure and Narrative Cinema,"[15] is the better known of the two. In this widely quoted essay, Mulvey uses a psychoanalytic conception of the psyche to investigate the pleasure men take in looking at women on screen. Given that Freud observed that men tend to fear the possibility of castration by the female body, with its lack of a penis, unconscious mechanisms for containing this fear and guilty pleasure in looking must come into operation for men to enjoy women in the cinema. Mulvey divides these mechanisms into two types: fetishism, which obviates the threat of the castrated female figure by transforming her body through cinematic spectacle into a phallic substitute; and voyeurism, which involves the discovery and display of the perceived female threat and its containment through a sadistic fantasy of the women's punishment or elimination.

In *My Geisha* and "An American Geisha," both fetishism and voyeurism come into play in the way in which these fantasies deliver pleasure to the male viewer. In *My Geisha*, for example, voyeurism plays an explicit role early on in the narrative. Huge close-ups of Lucy's eye peering in on the geisha party Paul and Bob are attending immediately precede her decision to dress as a geisha. As Mulvey points out, viewers tend to identify with the gazes of both characters and the camera itself in the cinema. Here, Lucy's surreptitious look gives the viewer permission to look with her into the hidden world of a teahouse party. Since the male viewer gazes at the geisha through the point of view of a female character, any guilt associated with the eroticism of the gaze can be rationalized somewhat by Lucy's supposed lack of interest in the geisha as sex objects.

In the next scene, the camera follows Lucy into the dressing room, where another voyeuristic fantasy unfolds as the geisha help her disrobe and put on makeup. When she returns to the party to be scrutinized by Paul, the viewer again gets a certain symbolic permission to closely study Lucy's face and body along with Paul, the director, who, folding his hands to simulate the viewfinder of a motion picture camera, must take a close "professional" look at the "bone structure" of the Japanese face. Later, this same directorial gaze allows Paul to voyeuristically enjoy ordering Yoko to kiss Bob for a screen test. It also enables him to uncover the "truth" about Lucy's deception and suitably punish her with the threat of an imagined illicit affair before reclaiming her as his wife.

My Geisha gives its viewers permission to look at women erotically. The film places any threat women may pose at a distance by depicting them as fetishistic objects of visual contemplation. When Paul's imagined viewfinder becomes an actual camera lens in the film, the narrative, at various points, halts to allow for the spectacular display of the female body set against the exotic backdrop of the Japanese landscape. These moments of spectacle, then, usually involve Paul's making of *Madame Butterfly* and the professional license he gains to look at this fictional character allows him to take the male viewer along guiltlessly for a glimpse. At one point, Paul even exclaims, "What do I need out of this girl? A face." He thereby divides the woman into parts, objectifying her and fetishizing her body parts to replace the threatening whole.

"An American Geisha" uses similar tactics to deliver a guiltless visual eroticism for viewers. Gillian's voice-over invites a voyeuristic foray into the closed geisha world: "A house is like the geisha. High walls on the outside that shut out the world. Strangers are shown only the mask of femininity." Tantalizing the viewer with what might lie under this "mask," Gillian legitimizes voyeurism with her "scientific" interest as a cultural anthropologist in the personal life of the geisha—that is, their sexuality. However, the viewer accompanies Gillian not only on her investigations of the geisha community but also on her romantic adventures. "An American Geisha" does not avoid scenes that show Konguro and Gillian kissing and, later, making love in bed, a burning candle gradually consuming itself used as a coy metaphor for their physical passion.

"An American Geisha" also allows for a fetishistic delight in the dismantling, fragmentation, and objectification of Gillian's body as she becomes the geisha Korin. Preparations for Gillian's debut as a geisha are presented through a montage of quick takes, all in close-up: a jar of white makeup; a portion of her face; Kohana's hand coming into frame to paint Gillian's lips red; her elaborate black wig; a foot sliding into a *tabi* sock; her back displaying her ornate *obi* sash; a fan stuck into the *obi*. Finally, a full-figure shot of Gillian shows her striking a pose in her kimono as the completed object ready for erotic contemplation and male approval.

In Hollywood, where formulaic repetitions play such an important part, there seems to be an unwritten law that every film set in Japan must include at least one bath scene to satisfy voyeuristic interest. Both *My Geisha* and "An American Geisha" comply with this accepted practice. Using both actual Japanese custom and the "innocence" of simply taking a bath, these bath scenes allow for a titillating fantasy of exposure to surface when, in fact, little flesh is ever revealed. The bath scene in each film has a comic quality—broader in the case of *My Geisha*, slightly more subdued in "An American Geisha."

In *My Geisha*, Paul and Bob manipulate Lucy/Yoko and her geisha guide Katsume into agreeing to meet in the communal bath. Afraid of discovery, Lucy plots with Katsume to turn up the steam in the bath so that only silhouetted figures can be seen. Paul and Bob, embarrassed by bumping into total strangers in the bath, run out. Bob exclaims, "East is East and West is West, and it's not ever going to meet in this bathtub." After the men depart, the girls, dressed in towels, step out and giggle over the success of their ruse. Although a prurient peek at the women is denied to Paul and Bob, the viewer does receive a certain visual satisfaction at the end of the scene when the women appear clad only in towels.

In "An American Geisha," the bath scene enfolds in a somewhat different way. While Gillian bathes in an elegant sunken tub in the geisha house, several geisha—giggling, girlish, in Western dress—burst in without knocking to interrogate the American on her attitudes toward sex, marriage, Western literature, and movie stars. Yoshiko, the most serious, asks about D. H. Lawrence and the spiritual nature of sex. Abruptly, a bell rings in the distance, and they all leave without explanation.

In this case, the comedy of the scene grows out of the non sequiturs that pour from the young women's mouths and overwhelm the startled Gillian, made more humorously vulnerable by her nakedness. Unlike the bath scene in *My Geisha*, this scene presents a single gender encounter, which ostensibly highlights cultural differences involving privacy and tact rather than gender differences involving voyeurism and its comic, metaphorically castrating, frustration.

In many ways, this bath scene in "An American Geisha" can be taken as emblematic of a promise of voyeuristic entry into the exotic, and potentially erotic, world of the geisha, while masking that world under a more high-toned, pseudofeminist cloak that tries to emphasize the naiveté and schoolgirl-like sisterhood of the geisha. Giggling, ignorant geisha, who live remarkably puritanical lives, complement the prudery associated with Gillian, the woman scholar. All sorts of details add to this picture: Gillian's initial Tokyo residence in a convent; her relationship with the Zen devotee Ann; her initial resistance to Konguro's sexual advances; her constant disavowal of the Japanese perception that American women are sexually "liberated"; the emphasis placed on Kohana's innocence when she dreams of finding a first love in a man who will paint in the eyes of the dove on her hair ornament to show she has a male admirer.

Although this fictional journey into the Japanese bath and the closed world of the geisha can be looked at as visually pleasurable to men, perhaps this insistent innocence points to more than a simple strategy to alleviate the male guilt associated with forbidden visual pleasures. Although Mulvey has tried to expand her model to include the female viewer,[16] there still seems to be a certain "excess" of detail in the depiction of the female body in these two films that perhaps could be better explained by an alternate model of visual pleasure. Although less frequently cited than Mulvey's approach, many feminist film scholars have turned to the model of looking at visual pleasure for female spectators using the metaphor of "masquerade."[17]

Although the preponderance of this work on masquerade and female spectatorship has focused on films that feature women masquerading as men, many of the observations that have been made have a direct bearing on the racial masquerade in *My Geisha* and "An American Geisha." Given the ways in which these films emphasize issues of gender over race, the geisha masquerade can be looked at as a way of dealing with gender uncertainty quite similar to the way the same problem is dealt with in films like *Morocco* (1930), *Sylvia Scarlett* (1935), *Ann of the Indies* (1951), *Victor/Victoria* (1982), or any of the other Hollywood films that have prompted interest in the phenomenon of the feminine masquerade.

In "Femininity and the Masquerade: *Anne of the Indies*," Claire Johnston discusses the bisexual nature of the fantasy in the Jacques Tourneur film. Although the female protagonist masquerades as a man, Johnston refers to the work of the psychologist Joan Riviere, who discusses femininity, not masculinity, as the real mask behind which her lesbian patient hides. Johnston summarizes Riviere as follows:

> "Femininity" is assumed as a mask to hide the possession of "masculin-ity" in the female subject; it becomes a masquerade. Thus a homosexual woman asserts her masculine characteristics as a game, while retaining the heterosexual love object, the mask of femininity and all the visible attributes of "normal" womanhood.[18]

Johnston goes on to note that the mask of femininity often expresses itself through the enigmatic female characters found in many Hollywood films, who pose a vaguely defined threat to the hero who must get to the root of their mystery.

In "Film and the Masquerade: Theorizing the Female Spectator," Mary Ann Doane clarifies what remains somewhat ambiguous in the

Johnston essay, that is, that the female masquerade involves a mask of femininity and that fantasies of female transvestism operate differently from, and may be less threatening in many respects to, patriarchal relations, since men can clearly see why a woman might prefer to be a man even though nature has denied her that possibility. Returning to Joan Riviere's essay for her inspiration, Doane states, "The masquerade, in flaunting femininity, holds it at a distance. Womanliness is a mask which can be worn or removed."[19] Doane goes on to use the concept of the masquerade as a possible explanation for female viewing pleasure. She argues that it allows the female viewer a distance from her cultural role as a woman and frees her to enjoy a pleasure in her own awareness that gender roles are not absolute. A part of the pleasure of the artifice of the geisha role, then, could be looked at as a recognition of this gender fluidity.

Doane, however, also recognizes a masochistic pleasure for women in the loss of identity afforded by the masquerade. Unable to escape from the roles offered by the patriarchy, female masochism can represent a desire to disappear, to escape, or to lose oneself completely by submitting to the patriarchal definition of the female role. In both *My Geisha* and "An American Geisha," some of the masochistic desire to lose one's own identity behind the mask of another culture's conception of femininity surfaces. Both films provide appealing fantasies of escape from a disturbingly ambiguous gender identity in an unsympathetic male-dominated world. The loss of the self under the mask of the geisha offers the possibility of a respite for the heroines from their romantic conundrums in the West.

In "Masochism, Masquerade, and the Erotic Metamorphoses of Marlene Dietrich,"[20] Gaylyn Studlar draws on Gilles Deleuze's analysis of the pre-Oedipal masochism found in Leopold von Sacher-Masoch to discuss the visual pleasures offered by images of potent, eroticized, maternal figures like Dietrich. For Studlar, both masquerades of "excessive femininity" and female transvestism offer similar pleasures arising from the rebellious defiance of the strictures imposed by the patriarchal reification of gender roles as natural.

Since both fantasies of extreme femininity and transvestism seem to play an important role in many lesbian subcultures, it comes as no surprise that many lesbian viewers have remarked on either their identification with Dietrich as a star or their erotic interest in her as a specular object. Although Studlar recognizes this, she limits her examination of any lesbian desires that the Dietrich masquerade may conjure up in self-identified lesbian spectators, dismissing any notion that self-identified heterosexual viewers may enjoy the hints of homoeroticism in these films.[21]

Given the "masculine" coding of Lucy as a tomboy in *My Geisha* and Gillian as a scholar at the beginning of "An American Geisha," their geisha masquerade may conjure up for the female viewer (who may or may not be a self-identified lesbian) a homoerotic fantasy at the point where the transvestite mask of pseudomasculinity meets the artificial femininity of the geisha. This would certainly help to explain the nearly asexual girlishness of many of the geisha as well as the emphasis on the conventlike atmosphere of the geisha house in "An American Geisha." Since the heterosexual relationships in that film remain somewhat problematic, the mask of geisha femininity may imaginatively conjure up a lesbian fantasy of a self-contained female utopia.

This can be felt particularly in the scene in "An American Geisha" in which Gillian solidifies her bond to Kohana in a ceremony attended exclusively by the women of the geisha house. Dressed for the last time in kimono, Gillian is further eroticized by the diffuse lighting and slightly soft focus cinematography used in the scene. In contrast to these visuals that bear a striking similarity to the way in which the heterosexual love scenes are photographed, Gillian's pseudoreligious invocation of "true womanhood" masks any hints of a lesbian eroticism underlying the innocence of the sisterhood: "I honor the dignity of women that survives all tragedy and disaster. I honor the kinship of women that takes precedence over personal desire. I honor the art of women which is grace and peace and harmony. I honor the sacrifices of women to the higher good of all." Gillian leaves behind her geisha masquerade and its pleasures with references to the suppression of personal desire and sacrifices for the "higher good." That these references may go beyond her decision to break up with Konguro alludes to a different sort of pleasure afforded by the geisha masquerade, one that may be barely hinted at, to female spectators.

The White Madame Butterfly

It must be remembered that the geisha masquerade is not only a fantasy that underscores questions of gender; it is also, despite whatever narrative mechanisms come into play to try to suppress it, a fantasy about race. The white geisha makeup both hides and highlights racial differences. By crossing the racial boundaries demarcated by white America, the heroines pay a price added to the toll exacted for their transgression of gender lines. In fact, although issues of race are downplayed, questions of race and gender constantly echo one another throughout both films. Race and gender seem to unite around the sacrifices each heroine makes to solidify her revised identity by the conclusion of both films.

In *My Geisha*, this sacrifice expressly parallels the fictional role of Cho-Cho San that Lucy plays in the film. In "An American Geisha," the specter of *Madame Butterfly* indirectly haunts the telefilm. Although both heroines must relinquish their geisha identity at the conclusion of each narrative, they still retain the masochistic, self-effacing aspect of their feminine masquerade. Just as Cho-Cho San commits suicide at the end of *Madame Butterfly*, both Lucy and Gillian kill off their geisha alter egos so as to emerge as "true" women ready to submerge their own wills and identities for the sake of their men.

In *My Geisha*, Lucy's real instruction as a geisha, which goes beyond mimicking dress, accent, and movement, comes from her husband Paul. In a series of reverse shots in which Lucy/Yoko kneels at the feet of a seated Paul, Lucy must patiently listen to her husband's confessional remarks to the geisha Yoko. Her contained gestures and unassertive posture contrast sharply with Lucy's expansive, energetic, and "unladylike" movements.

Paul begins: "The Western woman is no match for the Japanese woman. . . . The Western woman can learn a lot from you in the observance of the homely virtues." In the middle of the conversation, Lucy/Yoko gets up and begins to massage Paul's neck. Paul continues by confessing he wanted to make a film without his wife to prove his masculinity: "I was Mrs. Lucy Dell. . . . That couldn't happen to a Japanese man. He is born a big man to his wife. In the Western world, a man must be a big man to his wife, too, but often this is difficult. I think the Western world is wrong, and your world is right." He reveals that he wanted his film to be successful mostly so he "could be the man, [and] so she [Lucy] could be the woman."

Later, Lucy gets her second instruction in Japanese womanhood from Katsume. At the Tokyo premiere of Paul's film, Lucy goes backstage to change into her geisha costume for the publicity stunt that would reveal her true identity. Katsume helps her dress. The scene intercuts the dressing room discussion with shots of the audience in the auditorium and Cho-Cho San's death scene on screen. To underscore the parallels between Lucy's dilemma and Cho-Cho San's, this suicide scene is actually shown twice in *My Geisha*—once during its filming and this second time during the film's premiere.

While Lucy dresses, Katsume gives her a memento, a fan inscribed with a Japanese proverb, "No one before you, my husband, not even I." As the meaning of the proverb sinks in, a close-up of Lucy's face in the dressing room mirror, one eye with a brown contact lens and the other blue, underscores her own identity problems. She uses a fan to cover part of her face, exposing her blue eye and brown eye in turn. Her racial and gender identities both become problematic. If she adopts geisha dress and appears on stage as Yoko only to lift her wig and reveal Lucy, she indulges, paradoxically, her "Western," "liberated" self, which has been criticized as overbearing, emasculating, selfish, and unappealing. If, however, she "kills off" Yoko and appears as Lucy, she internalizes the "lesson" she learned from being a Japanese woman—that she should always submit completely to the will of men.

Lucy decides on the latter course, and, after Cho-Cho San kneels before her altar and commits hara-kiri, Lucy appears on stage to tell the world that Yoko has retired to a Buddhist convent. Any threat that either Paul would lose himself in his interest in Japan or that Lucy would lose herself in her feminine masquerade is obliterated as the values of traditional marriage and male domination assert themselves over the initial excesses of female independence and an "unnatural" masculinity.

In "An American Geisha," the ideological connections made between female sacrifice and racial separation play a far more overt and significant role. Without confronting its own racist assumptions that a Westerner should have the power to go to Japan and do as he or she pleases under the cloak of study, adventure, or instruction, "An American Geisha" makes it quite clear that Gillian oversteps her role as a woman and not as an "Orientalist" who defines and disciplines the racial other in the name of "science." Her feminine identity and sexuality, not her academic interests, pose the problems explicitly dealt with in the telefilm. Thus, racial divisions, cloaked behind a veil of high-toned, liberal sentiments, reestablish themselves as Gillian discovers her "true" womanhood.

Unlike Lucy, Gillian encounters actual hostility when she takes on her geisha identity as well as her Japanese lover. Beginning with her American boyfriend, the majority of the characters question her interest in geisha: a number of men involved in the geisha trade; Konguro, who wonders why a "liberated" woman should be interested in a social anachronism; and the *okasan*, who is baffled by Gillian's desire to be Japanese. This hostility reaches its peak when her assertive fellow geisha, Yoshiko, chastises Gillian for "experimenting" with geisha life. Complaining that Gillian interferes with the other geisha's abilities to conduct their affairs because of her popularity, Yoshiko challenges Gillian's selfishness: "We geisha are sisters. To us, happiness is duty, loyalty, obligation to each other. . . . You will never be sister to any of us."

Gillian encounters a similar hostility toward her romantic interest in Konguro. Her fellow geisha warn that Konguro's traditional Kabuki family would never accept her. Confirming this, Konguro's mother angrily asks, "What do you want? What is missing in your culture that you search for in ours? In my son?" Later, she reminds Gillian of the failings of her American culture: "Your culture values romance, but not unselfish love." Although Ann comforts Gillian by reminding her that she is "building a bridge between cultures so that others can cross," that "bridge" seems rather unsteady.

Like Lucy, Gillian eventually destroys her Japanese identity in order to absorb into her American self the supposedly "Japanese" values of self-sacrifice and duty. She gives up her geisha masquerade to dress in her "masculine" American pants to free Tanaka to pursue Kohana, sacrificing her identity as Korin so that she can be accepted as a "sister" before she begins her trip back to the United States. Similarly, she puts her pretensions to become a Japanese wife to Konguro aside only after he has "taught" her how to submit to a man's desires. Any threat that an American woman would "lose" herself in a non-white world to an Asian man is squelched at the same time that Gillian's supposedly "selfish American" (i.e., self-assertive, intelligent, and independent) identity softens as she becomes a wife and mother back home. Once again, the geisha mask is stripped away to reveal a "true" femininity modeled on Cho-Cho San's masochistic self-sacrifice for the "greater good" of her American ex-husband and their son.

Both *My Geisha* and "An American Geisha" seem to move relentlessly toward a final closure that ends any possible resurfacings of female independence or rebelliousness. These films also close off any possibility that their independent heroines would lose themselves in their Japanese roles and turn their backs on American culture and, more specifically, white American men.

However, although it has been argued that ideological and narrative closure do go hand-in-hand in classical realist fiction, both *My Geisha* and "An American Geisha" represent slightly different cases. Although both display to a large degree the typical markers of realism—stylistic transparency, temporal clarity and logic, and closure—associated with classical Hollywood fiction, neither *My Geisha*'s movie world self-consciousness nor "An American Geisha's" somewhat nostalgic reworking of the classical "woman's film" place either unquestioningly in the category of classical realist fiction.

Moreover, each film deals with the fantasies that make explicit the potentially radical notion of femininity as a masquerade. Not only does this open up possibilities of looking at gender as a cultural and historical construction that can be consciously changed but it also conjures up the possibility of a lesbian eroticism. An ironic distance from the feminine role, made possible by the "exaggerated" femininity of the geisha mask, offers the female spectator the possible pleasure of indulging in a fantasy of self-definition and the paradoxical power this put-on femininity has in the male world.

Even though they are domesticated by the end of the films, these heroines still represent a certain spirit of adventure and self-possession associated with the world traveler. They symbolize the possibility, if not the realization, of the freedoms afforded women who dare put their usual roles aside, choose to encounter an alien culture, and fall in love with a different race.

10

Conclusion

The Postmodern Spectacle of Race and Romance in *Year of the Dragon*

In his seminal essay on contemporary culture, "Postmodernism and Consumer Society," Fredric Jameson lists *Chinatown* (Roman Polanski, 1974) as an example of the "nostalgia film" or *la mode retro* (retrospective styling). Like other postmodern instances of pastiche, its uncritical evocation of classical Hollywood films of the 1930s and 1940s points to

> a world in which stylistic innovation is no longer possible, all that is left is to imitate dead styles, to speak through the masks and with the voices of the styles in the imaginary museum. But this means that contemporary or postmodernist art is going to be about art itself in a new kind of way; even more, it means that one of its essential messages will involve the necessary failure of art and the aesthetic, the failure of the new, the imprisonment in the past.[1]

Unlike earlier aesthetic styles, which could hope to deal, at least symbolically, with actual social and cultural contradictions, postmodernism relieves art of this ideological function. Postmodern art acts as spectacle—outside the discursive functions of narrative. Beyond the realist notion that film can accurately depict the material world as well as the modernist conception of art as intervention, postmodernism accepts the image as a fabrication, as part of a commodity culture where no depth exists beyond the surface of the marketplace.

Thus, *Chinatown* does not even pretend to try to evoke an actual place, but, rather, it conjures up an image, an imaginary construct of past representations from other mass-mediated sources. In fact, bits and pieces of anachronistic representations of Chinatown figure prominently in many postmodern films.[2] Removed from their original historical contexts and drained of meaning, "yellow peril" clichés coexist with antiracist discourses, anachronistic opium peddlers interact with urban reformers. Chinatown functions as pure style with neon dragons, pop songs, lion dances, and displays of martial artistry, forming a part of postmodern popular iconography.

Interracial sexuality becomes an element of this stylistic mélange, a contrast in color, rather than either a liberal call for reform or a conservative demand for exclusionism. Indeed, any given film may voice a number of political positions, leveling these discourses, too, by draining them of any potentially meaningful (i.e., socially critical or offensive) substance. Portions of Hollywood plot formulas involving interracial romances between Asian and Caucasian characters resurface and recombine into different patterns that evoke earlier rape, seduction, captivity, salvation, sacrifice, or assimilation patterns.

Just as earlier Hollywood films used the interracial romance to explore issues of identity—crises in the social construction of race, class, ethnicity, and gender—postmodern narratives use these romantic plots as a shorthand for the mercurial nature of identity. Indeed, a tacit acceptance of the illusory nature of identity itself is one of the principal markers of postmodernism as a style. Jameson sees this psychic borderlessness as part of an acknowledged "schizophrenic" loss of "self" occasioned by the contemporary acceptance of the death of the Cartesian subject. Although it may be tempting to look at postmodern identity as a celebration of cultural plurality, multiethnicity, liberation from traditional gender roles, and freedom to cross various social boundaries at will, there is a price to be paid for the death of even the illusion of the individual subject. As Jameson observes,

> The schizophrenic . . . is not only "no one" in the sense of having no personal identity; he or she also does nothing, since to have a project means to be able to commit oneself to a certain continuity over time. The schizophrenic is thus given over to an undifferentiated vision of the world in the present, a by no means pleasant experience.[3]

Like pastiche, this postmodern sense of schizophrenia robs the film of its sense of history and, consequently, its critical ability to allude to the possibility of change. In the Chinatown of postmodern Hollywood, this loss of identity enables the viewer to accept the most outrageous stereotype and the most complex characterization on the same level, as equally valid and equally superficial. Political change and social action become part of the spectacle; critical thinking dies with the notion of the centered subject.

As pure style and as spectacle, Chinatown fulfills a commercial hunger for a domesticated otherness that can represent both the fulfillment of the American myth of the melting pot and play with the dangers of the exotic. *Year of the Dragon* (Michael Cimino, 1985) represents simply one example of this postmodern use of Chinatown as spectacle in contemporary Hollywood cinema.

Spectacle and Identity in *Year of the Dragon*

Like many postmodern films, *Year of the Dragon* tells a very simple story basic to Hollywood cinema, evoking a sense of recognition or nostalgia for older generic forms.[4] An uncorrupted lawman, Stanley White (Mickey Rourke), is assigned to clean up a corrupt town—in this case, Chinatown. His principal adversary is a young gangster on the way up, Joey Tai (John Lone).

As in many action-adventure narratives, the hero and the villain are quite similar. In this case, both men find themselves on the outside. They are set apart from their colleagues, their families, their communities. Stanley rails against a police force that refuses to do anything about corruption in Chinatown, and Joey Tai shakes up his sluggish criminal organization by using youth gangs to move in on Italian and Southeast Asian drug trafficking. Both are identified as flamboyant, violent, impatient with the "older generation," rebellious, and desirous of making good in mainstream American society. In addition, both are ethnic: Stanley White has changed his Polish surname to whitewash his ethnicity, while Tai exploits his Chinese ethnicity to rise within the underworld.

As in most narratives of this type, the main plot line revolves around the hero's attempt to prove himself different from the villain, in other words, justified in his violence and supportive of the white, Anglo-Saxon mainstream. He sees himself as having the moral right to eradicate the villain, since someone foreign represents a threat to the racial and ethnic status quo. Much of the ideological tension of this sort of plot revolves around who can and cannot be assimilated into American society. The hero must prove his ability to melt into the mainstream by drawing a line between himself and the villain, thereby coming to grips with his own ethnicity. *Year of the Dragon* begins with a fundamental ideological contradiction revolving around ethnicity and American identity. Melting into America is acceptable only if a white, male, Anglo-Saxon definition of identity is taken as the ideal. White meets this definition; Tai does not.

Figure 26. In Year of the Dragon (1985), Stanley White (Mickey Rourke) embodies ethnic, racial, and sexual identity crises. His name conjures up questions of ethnic and racial identity, while his foppish attention to dress (indicated by his careful coiffure and stylish suit and tie) signal the possibility of a sexual identity crisis. Still courtesy of Jerry Ohlinger.

In addition, similar ethnic and racial tensions are played out in a romance between the hero and a Chinese American woman. Although married, White finds himself attracted to a young Chinese newswoman, Tracy Tzu (Ariane). Their romance parallels both White's unrelenting push to rid Chinatown of gang influence and Tai's bid to become undisputed boss of the underworld. The romance also toys with similar tensions in what can and cannot constitute American identity. Through her involvement with White, Tzu renounces her Chinese ethnicity and subordinates herself to White's championing of mainstream ideals.

Year of the Dragon takes up issues related to race, gender, class, and ethnicity and then eases any contradictions these may raise by eradicating the villain and allowing romance to triumph. However, this similarity to other Hollywood films does not necessarily mean that *Year of the Dragon* can be looked at as simply another interracial romance played out within the genre of the *policier*, like *The Crimson Kimono*, for example. Rather, a certain irony pervades the film. Unlike the irony characteristic of modernist works, however, this irony has no critical bite. Rather, the distance the film places between its characters and its viewers (e.g., the antihero as the protagonist and the allure of the villain) simply functions as part of the style, vaguely conjuring up earlier images of heroic white knights and diabolical Fu Manchus not as parody, but as pastiche. The viewer may take these figures seriously or view the film as "campy" and enjoy it as pure style.

The film's exploitation of spectacle helps to mark it as postmodern. *Year of the Dragon* begins with a moment of spectacle, with images of Chinese New Year being celebrated in the streets of Chinatown. This sets a pattern that operates throughout the course of the film, which is punctuated with displays of violence, sexuality, ritual, or sheer exoticism, which have little, if any, narrative importance.

The film begins with a high-angle shot of a ceremonial lion head and pulls back to show the lion dancing, along with firecrackers and drums, which characterize Chinese New Year celebrations. At first, emphasis is placed on the exotic aspect of Chinatown, on the allure and charm of its foreign rituals. Quickly, however, the dancing turns into a riot as rival lions begin to fight, and the young men under them toss their costumes aside and begin to brawl. Although this gang rivalry and the lion brawl are never explained clearly, the next scene, depicting the bloody execution of the Chinese gangster, Jackie Wong, clarifies the link between the exotic and the dangerous. Later, during Wong's elaborate funeral, the Chinese youth gangs strike again and kill a Caucasian shopkeeper who refuses to pay protection money. A pattern surfaces. Each moment of spectacle—whether it is a festival, funeral, banquet,

Figure 27.   Tracy Tzu (Ariane), as a television newscaster, both creates and functions as a spectacle for public surveillance. Still from Year of the Dragon *courtesy of the Museum of Modern Art/Film Stills Archive.*

or bedroom scene—has a threatening edge. Underneath a picturesque veneer, Chinatown hides its violence and corruption.

Spectacle tends to be contradictory. It both attracts and repulses, encouraging viewer identification while keeping that involvement at a distance. Moments of spectacle that feature ethnic and racial differences can define and reinforce the boundaries between ethnic and racial groups to keep the dominant culture's own power intact. However, these moments also often include violent eruptions that challenge the dominant culture's ability to define those differences and boundaries. Violence bursts forth against the racial and ethnic status quo, and the viewer may identify with this antiestablishment aspect of the spectacle as well as with its ostensible condemnation.

In *Year of the Dragon*, the importance of spectacle is also emphasized by making Tracy Tzu, the protagonist's love interest, a news reporter (a reference to Connie Chung and the Asian women who have appeared as newscasters since her national debut). Both a creator of spectacle and an object on display herself, Tzu provides the perfect rationalization of the film's voyeuristic treatment of Chinatown. Stanley White quickly convinces a reluctant Tzu to expose Chinatown as decadent, corrupt, and threatening, after a gangland attack occurs in

Figure 28.   Surrounded by the kitsch opulence of a Chinatown restaurant, Stanley and Tracy are on display for the viewer. Still from Year of the Dragon *courtesy of Jerry Ohlinger.*

the restaurant in which they are meeting for dinner. By using a Chinese character as the point of identification for the contemplation of the spectacle, the film does the same thing the fictitious White does in the narrative. That is, the film hides its own racism by using a non-white character to focus attention on the racial and ethnic other as a threat to the status quo.

Beyond this function, however, Tracy Tzu also operates as a specular object in her own right. When she enters the large, lavishly decorated Chinatown establishment to dine with Stanley White, for example, the camera dollies to follow her as she almost regally ascends a flight of stairs to join her dinner companion. Thin and elegantly dressed, her body always carefully framed and followed by the camera, Tzu provides the white male viewer with an image of racial, ethnic, and gender difference that may both titillate and disturb.

Like all moments of spectacle in *Year of the Dragon*, this moment leads to violence. During an assault on this restaurant, Tracy Tzu's elegance and composure crumble as bullets fly, fish tanks burst, and White saves the hysterical Tzu from harm. In fact, all displays of Tzu's body in *Year of the Dragon* are coupled with moments of violence. For

Figure 29.   Gangland violence legitimizes White's desire to bring a white patriarchal sense of order to Chinatown by saving Tzu from her own people and the supposedly menacing excesses of Asian culture. Still from Year of the Dragon *courtesy of Jerry Ohlinger.*

example, during their love scenes together, White slaps and verbally assaults Tzu. In another scene, the camera follows the elegantly dressed Tzu into her apartment where a group of thugs lie in wait to rape her.

In *Year of the Dragon*, the spectacle subsumes all manner of racial, ethnic, and gender differences. If Chinatown is exotic, then so too is Stanley White's working-class Polish neighborhood. Filled with Eastern European church domes, Catholic icons and rituals, it can also be looked at as exotic from the standpoint of the mainstream Anglo-American viewer. Similarly, the film depicts Little Italy as a definitely Caucasian community also overrun by organized crime and having a similarly alien flavor.

As in many postmodern Hollywood films, the central hero no longer represents an ethnic, racial, class, gender, ethical, moral, or psychological point of identification for the viewer. In films like *The World of Suzie Wong, Japanese War Bride*, or *Sayonara*, the narratives, despite their ideological gaps and complications, always seem to put forward the promise that any identity crisis the hero might suffer would ultimately be solved. However, *Year of the Dragon* makes its antiheroic protagonist so suspect in terms of ethnicity, class, sexuality, and morality that it precludes any adequate resolution through narrative closure. Thus, there appears to be a "schizophrenic" breakdown in boundaries between mainstream "self" and ethnic, class, or sexual "other."

For example, White's ethnic self-identity is shown in crisis, since he anglicizes his Polish name and tries to move away from his ethnic roots. This ethnic identity crisis, too, is associated with his class standing, since the film makes it clear that White links his upward mobility with a move away from his working-class community. Moreover, this crisis of ethnic identity is linked to a similar crisis of sexual identity. The film presents White as having marital problems with his wife, Connie (Caroline Cava), because he is unable to impregnate her (for whatever reason—impotence, sterility, simple lack of interest in sex). Thus, Stanley's identity is in doubt both because of his ethnicity and because of his masculinity. The fact that White is a Vietnam veteran further questions his identity as a potent hero able to perform this task, since this marks him as a "loser," an "outsider," as a potentially explosive, frustrated soldier without a real war.

Many of these identity issues play themselves out within moments of spectacle in which characters' physical presences take on particular significance. Thus, Stanley White's identity crises are made concrete in terms of spectacular displays in which Stanley confronts his racial and ethnic and sexual foils—Joey Tai and Tracy Tzu. In fact, Stanley encounters both Tracy Tzu and Joey Tai for the first time at the funeral of Jackie Wong, Tai's father-in-law. The film depicts both characters in remarkably similar ways. If Tzu's body is displayed as spectacle, then Tai also functions as an object of sexual contemplation. Both are elegantly dressed in tailored suits and long coats; both are lean and lithe, similarly shaped; both have similar facial features and move in a highly dramatic way that betrays John Lone's Chinese opera training and Ariane's background in modeling. Certainly, these visual parallels, coupled with the narrative's insistence that both be conquered by the hero, place a further strain on White's identity as a heterosexual male. Moreover, Tzu's career as a newswoman and single life-style and Tai's nearly absent family and close association with other men (e.g., his black bodyguard) tie the threat of racial and ethnic difference to the threat of homosexuality, loss of male power and privilege, and the weakening of gender boundaries.

In the case of Joey Tai, *Year of the Dragon* merges the myth of the Asian man as a sexual threat with the image of the eunuch. Presented as effeminate in the film, Tai does not safely drop out of sight as

Figure 30. Year of the Dragon's *showdown between White and Joey Tai (John Lone) in which Tai submits masochistically to White's offer of an "honorable" death. Still from* Year of the Dragon *courtesy of Jerry Ohlinger.*

a passive buddy figure (the role fulfilled by Herbert Kuang [Dennis Dun] in the film), but instead becomes more of a threat to Stanley's identity by bringing into play a homosexual subtext.

In the climactic scene in which the beaten Tai lies at White's feet on a railway trestle and Stanley opts to give Tai a pistol to commit suicide rather than face trial, an extensive Freudian analysis is certainly unnecessary to understand the scene as sexually charged. Not only does White give Tai the phallic means to his own end but Tai accepts this end, masochistically submits to it and to White's domination. His suicide is the ultimate confirmation of his subordinate, feminized position, and Stanley's role in it allows him to symbolically do away with the threat Tai represents to the hero's identity as white, male, and decidedly heterosexual.

Interestingly, this moment of violent spectacle also opens the film up to alternative, ironic, camp readings. It is a pastiche of the Western gunfight. White and Tai play the classic roles of villain and hero. However, in addition to the possible homosexual undertones mentioned above, the gunfight can be looked at as juggling other possible readings, too. Thus, the attractive villain ironically dies at the hands of the suspect White. The villain accepts his end and dies with "grace" and a certain panache. Although punished violently for his hubris, Tai, like the American gangster heroes before him, must also be respected for his ability to climb so far, for the assertion of his individualism despite the pressures to keep it contained. Tai represents the ambivalence at the root of the gangster mythos; he is both condemned and applauded for being a good capitalist.

In fact, class seems to be the last significant way in which issues of identity are complicated in the film. If *Year of the Dragon* can be looked at as an ironic postmodern entertainment, part of what it incorporates is a standard Hollywood working-class fantasy that allows the viewer the satisfaction of seeing bourgeois characters controlled by a working-class cop. Tai falls because he has risen above his station in his desire to fulfill the American Dream illegally through drug running. He represents capitalism out of control, and his death may have a particular appeal to the working-class viewer suspicious of the power that wealth brings.

Similarly, part of Stanley's desire to dominate Tracy comes from a voiced class antagonism. At one point, for example, Stanley remarks, "I hated you before I even met you. I hated you on TV. I hated you in Vietnam . . . Most of all, I hate rich kids." Thus, Stanley may want to dominate Tracy because she challenges gender roles (through her profession), or because of her race and ethnicity (the challenge her exotic allure poses to heterosexual identity and the nuclear family), or because of her class standing (not only is she successful at her profession but she also comes from a wealthy family). Charges of racism or sexism can fall by the wayside as the viewer focuses on the character's class standing and roots for the "rich kid" to get her comeuppance.

In fact, the homosexual subtext that puts Stanley's identity in doubt in his relationship with Joey Tai also operates in a similar way in Stanley's relationship with Tracy. In this case, Tracy poses a threat to Stanley not only because she represents the nonwhite seductress whose exotic allure draws the white male away from hearth and home but because she also embodies a threat to gender boundaries by her independence, active pursuit of a career, and boyish short hair and slender physique. Throughout *Year of the Dragon*, plot events and the actions of the hero himself both serve to tighten the gender boundaries Tracy at first seems to loosen. Not only does Stanley take away Tracy's independence by moving in and telling her how to run her career but he also verbally abuses her and strikes her. Moreover, plot events like the attack on the Chinatown restaurant and the assault in her apartment force Tracy to depend more and more on Stanley's protection. By taking away her independence, the film domesticates Tracy, places her under male control, forces her to side with Stanley against the Chinese community. Although she objects to this throughout the film, by the end she happily accepts Stanley's embrace.

In fact, through this romance, *Year of the Dragon* promises a narrative resolution reminiscent of Hollywood classicism. Both as a woman and as an Asian, Tracy has submitted to Stanley's authority, and, through their romance, the film legitimizes Stanley's right to dominate her as a woman and as a Chinese American. The consummation of their romance erases doubts about Stanley's potency and identity. He has affirmed white, male, American dominance over nonwhite, feminized, foreign threats. White transforms Tzu from the seductive "Dragon Lady" into the passive, loyal, and subservient "China Doll." The shift from one to the other marks White's personal conquest and assimilation of the foreign into the domestic mainstream, thereby assuring his own identity, his own right also to be a part of that American melting pot.

However, this romance, like White's relationship with Tai, has its contradictory aspects. If Stanley has legitimized white male power over a nonwhite woman, he has also fulfilled the working-class fantasy of possessing wealth magically through romance and dominating it through sexuality. Thus, desire for class equality obscures the film's otherwise too obvious racism and sexism. Moreover, the film's concluding romantic embrace can be read symbolically as a liberal call for racial understanding and harmony. Stanley's romance with Tracy can be looked at as the way the character comes to grips with and over-comes his own racism by falling in love. In this case, the myth of romantic love can be seen as not only the cure-all for crises of male identity but also an antidote for the film's rather open racism. According to this reading, the containment of Tracy's possible sexual threat through heterosexual romance can be seen as a function of her gender rather than her race or ethnicity, so the film can use sexism to mask its racism if this interpretation is pursued. In fact, as this line of reasoning indicates, *Year of the Dragon* operates as a mélange of competing discourses vying for authority.

Many of these conflicting discourses come together in scenes featuring Stanley White's Chinese "buddy," Herbert Kuang. Kuang acts as a eunuch figure, nonthreatening, sexless, totally under the domination of the hero who is both boss and "best friend." Taken straight from the police academy to assure his anonymity for his undercover work in Chinatown, Kuang, at first, appears as an innocent dupe who can barely drive a car, speaks the accented English of a recent immigrant, and is concerned only about making enough money to send home to China. If Joey Tai and Tracy Tzu, in their own ways, pose a threat to the hero because of their ethnic exoticism, Kuang simply functions, by agreeing to work with White, as the "good" Asian legitimizing White's mission to clean up Chinatown. Also, in terms of class, Kuang functions as a "good" working-class Chinese. Like other working-class Chinese who dot the film to provide atmosphere, Kuang is seen as a victim of capitalism out of control in his own community. Once again, class relations are used to hide what otherwise could only be read as racism in the film. Only the rich are villainous among the Chinese; the Chinese workers may be ignorant, passive, and impotent, but the film can cling to its liberalism by showing them as decidedly not villainous.

Kuang, however, only reluctantly accepts this buddy role. Although Tracy taunts Stanley with his racism as part of their sexual gaming, Kuang accuses White of racism in earnest. At one point he challenges the way Stanley treats him by saying, "You make us all die for you. I'm not going to kill myself for you, Captain White. No more 'China-man Joe.' Those days are over." Still, even after Kuang complains that he cannot die for White because his family counts on him for income, he does precisely that, and his death becomes another rationalization of White's right to control Chinatown.

In yet another moment of spectacle, which has an excessive, almost operatic, quality, Kuang is riddled with bullets as he tries to run to Stanley with information on Tai's drug trafficking. Eventually, Kuang dies, bleeding grotesquely in White's arms; his last words give Stanley the location of Tai's next drug shipment. Clearly, this moment places Kuang's earlier speech in a new light. No longer the unwitting dupe, Kuang here willingly gives his life for Stanley's cause, choosing this white American mission over the well-being of his Chinese family. He has become "Chinaman Joe" again, placing his life and his loyalty firmly within Stanley's camp.

Prefiguring Tai's suicide, Kuang's death functions in a similar way as spectacle. In fact, these moments of violence featuring Asians dying in the arms or at the feet of the white hero stand outside the narrative as images of ethnic and racial relations that seem to go beyond the parameters of the film itself. Outside the implied history that the temporal dimension of narrative must assure at some level, spectacle reifies images and places them beyond history. It also mythologizes social relations. Ironically, however, it makes concrete the racial and gender hierarchies that may have been hidden in other parts of the film. Although still vibrating with the contradictions that the film raises and then abandons, spectacle assures that these moments of violent domination of the ethnic other are somehow justified, correct, proper, and even inevitable. Functioning as spectacle, race, ethnicity, and gender exist as ahistorical, set, preordained, and unchangeable. Spectacle provides those exaggerated moments in which the social boundaries are most clearly demarcated. Within postmodern culture, spectacle assures that the film commodity will not attempt to threaten the social order with any critical significance. It levels discourse, incorporating all voices within a visual image that signifies nothing.

However, in these moments of spectacular display, the viewer may refuse to identify with the hero in the bedroom or in a brawl. Then, that viewer may realize that she or he has not been drawn into the ideological workings of the film, and the possibility of resistance can begin to surface.[5]

Beyond the Text: Confronting the Image

In addition to its use of spectacle, fractured identities, and exploitation of contending social discourses to present a contradictory mixture of both liberal and conservative interpretative possibilities, a disclaimer has been affixed to *Year of the Dragon* to complicate its discourse even further:

> This film does not intend to demean or to ignore the many positive features of Asian-Americans and specifically Chinese-American communities. Any similarity between the depiction in this film and any associations, organizations, individuals or Chinatowns that exist in real life is accidental.[6]

This disclaimer further removes the film from any engagement with an actual social or political environment. If the film exploits Chinatown commercially as an image, as spectacle, it denies any association that image may have with actual ethnic communities or racial groups. The film pleads its own case as a commodity begging to be consumed. It makes no attempt to ask to be understood as discourse, looked at as a representation, or taken as a possible intervention within the ideological realm.

MGM-UA added this disclaimer because of protests from a coalition of Asian American associations and media groups that picketed theaters and organized other types of protests against the film.[7] Despite a postmodern absorption of liberal, radical, and conservative positions within its textual operation, the existence of *Year of the Dragon* still could provoke public protest and debate.

In her 1987 video documentary, *Slaying the Dragon*, Deborah Gee analyzes the media's use of Connie Chung, clearly the principal, figurative inspiration for the look and style of the Tzu character in *Year of the Dragon*. For many in the Asian American community, this figure of the successful female newscaster has come to embody a new bent on racist representations of Asian Americans as the "model minority." To allay any guilt the dominant culture may feel toward its appalling treatment of nonwhites, the media celebrates the achievements of Asian Americans as exemplars of how to be successful in white America despite racism. Not only does this mask the continuing problems faced by Asian Americans in terms of immigration, employment, housing, education, and other areas in which discrimination is still strikingly apparent, but the myth of the "model minority" also potentially weakens Asian Americans politically by separating them from other minority groups with similar concerns. Moreover, by making the representative of the "model minority" female, a continuing specular fascination with Asian women can be coupled with the promotion of this image as both an advance for gender as well as racial liberalization. *Slaying the Dragon*'s deconstruction of this image and its historical and cultural context stands as a corrective to *Year of the Dragon*'s exploitation of Chinatown as spectacle.

In fact, beyond Hollywood's continuing exploitation of Asia and the Asian American community, there exists a fertile Asian American filmmaking presence that has consistently turned a critical eye on the dominant media's representation of racial and ethnic others. Many of these films have taken up the theme of interracial sexual relations from a specifically Asian American point of view (*Mississippi Triangle*[8] [Chris Choy, Worth Long, and Alan Seigel, 1983], *Family Gathering* [Lise Yasui and Ann Tegnell, 1988], *West Is West* [David Rathod,

1988], *Juxta* [Hiroko Yamazaki, 1989], *Two Lies* [Pam Tom, 1989], and *Sally's Beauty Spot* [Helen Lee, 1990], to name just a few recent examples). They include documentaries, experimental shorts, and fiction features, and all attempt to use the cinema to explore aspects of interracial relations seldom broached by Hollywood. Some focus specifically on Asian American women, others treat Asian and African American romances, while some others deal with parent-child issues seldom addressed by Hollywood.

It should come as little surprise that Asian American filmmakers, many of whom are women, have been drawn to interracial romance and sexuality as subject matter for their work. By adopting the Hollywood narrative as a taken-for-granted part of the dominant culture's figuration of Asia and the Asian American community, these filmmakers have been able to use these accepted images as part of their own critique of the media. As I hope this book has demonstrated, Hollywood narratives broach the issues of racism, sexism, ethnic assimilation, national identity, and economic inequality in ways that make the ideological contradictions with which they deal often quite difficult to contain. Since many of these Hollywood films address women specifically, a recognition of gender and the role sexuality plays within race relations also makes these narratives attractive springboards for the critical work attempted by many Asian American filmmakers.[9]

Summation: Grand Narratives, Tall Tales, and Romantic Stories

In *The Postmodern Condition: A Report on Knowledge*, Jean-Francois Lyotard develops an epistemological theory based on the legitimation of knowledge through reference to what he calls "grand narratives." He defines the "modern" as

> any science that legitimates itself with reference to a metadiscourse
> . . . making an explicit appeal to some grand narrative, such as the dialectics of Spirit, the hermeneutics of meaning, the emancipation of the rational or working subject, or the creation of wealth.[10]

The "postmodern," then, can be defined as

> incredulity toward metanarratives. . . . The narrative function is losing its functors, its great hero, its great dangers, its great voyages, its great goal.[11]

Year of the Dragon represents one of these instances of narrative crisis. While ostensibly presenting itself as "progressive" in its treatment of racial relations and gender politics, the death of the villain and the union of the couple at the conclusion no longer can rid the film of either its racist or sexist underpinnings. Even though the film attempts to be a narrative about the emancipation of Chinatown and the spiritual cleansing of its hero's psyche, the tale it tells pales next to its extravagant use of spectacle and the extratextual critique of its obvious exploitation of hackneyed stereotypes.

This book has been an exploration of the relationship between narratives and ideas. The contradictions within these narratives have pointed to gaps in the foundations of many of those popularly accepted ideas about race, gender, sexuality, ethnicity, and American identity. While all the plot formulae dealt with here do not have the weight or the "grandeur" of Lyotard's metanarratives, they are part of the ideological fabric that makes up the "modern" narratives of emancipation and progress he does discuss. Whether liberal or conservative in nature, they are now, in a postmodern age, part of a crisis in understanding. While Lyotard, in this pragmatic and skeptical era, may cast a suspicious eye on the protests against films like *Year of the Dragon*, as he would on the film itself, the fact that Hollywood's little narratives about the emancipatory nature of heterosexual romance or the healing of social ills through intimate interpersonal understanding should ring hollow indicates that the ideological foundations of these tales may indeed be crumbling.

All the narratives discussed in this book have dealt with the same fundamental crisis of Anglo-American culture desperately trying to reconcile its credo of "liberty and justice for all" with its insistence on white, male, bourgeois domination of the public sphere. Although the films dealing with white knights may provide the clearest examples, all the films treated here are fundamentally narratives of salvation. They all attempt to "save" the Anglo-American, bourgeois, male establishment from any threats to its hegemony by saving the white woman from sexual contact with the racial other, rescuing the nonwhite woman from the excesses of her own culture, or spiritually saving the couple from a living death by allowing them to be symbolically assimilated into the American mainstream through their romance.

In *The Cheat*, Edith is literally saved from the "yellow peril" embodied by the villain. In *Broken Blossoms*, Lucy is physically saved by Cheng Huan while the narrative "saves" her purity with its deadly conclusion. Megan, in *The Bitter Tea of General Yen*, is saved from a loveless marriage by the warlord Yen, while his suicide, once again but with less certainty, saves her virtue. Similarly, in *Shanghai Express*, captivity saves Lily from licentious contact with men of presumably many races by sending her back into the protective arms of Doc.

In *Lady of the Tropics*, Manon "saves" herself spiritually by sacrificing herself physically for her husband's honor. Similarly, all the
Madame Butterfly heroines, including the white Madame Butterflies in
My Geisha and "An American Geisha," remain sympathetic because
of their desire to sacrifice themselves for the sake of their lovers. Mark
Elliott "saves" Han Suyin in *Love Is a Many-Splendored Thing* by
allowing her to sacrifice her career for their affair. The transcendent
nature of their romance saves the couples in *Sayonara*, *The Crimson
Kimono*, *Japanese War Bride*, *Bridge to the Sun*, and *The World of
Suzie Wong* from the spiritual vacuum of a life without bourgeois,
heterosexual romance and marriage.

By following this master narrative that links personal salvation and
romantic love with social emancipation and progress, all these films
seem to tell one story about American identity as both superficially
liberal and deeply conservative with respect to racial and ethnic differences. All place limits on both the progressive elements in their discourses that call for understanding as well as their racist aspects that
insist on either absolute exclusionism or the subordination of the nonwhite partner to the Anglo-American.

These narratives of salvation, moreover, rely on heterosexual romance and traditional gender roles as their ideological anchor while
they test the limits of permissible interracial intimacy. The "independent" woman "asks for trouble" and is punished by rape, abduction, or
death and is saved by the love of the "right" man. The supposedly excessive nature of Asian sexuality, which is manifested by a predatory
femininity and a brutal or effeminate masculinity, similarly can only be
contained by intimate contact with a white love object. Racial difference becomes sexual excess, and romantic love acts as both personal
salvation and social corrective.

Thus, all the narratives examined here function discursively in nearly identical ways. Only in *Year of the Dragon* does the metanarrative
of social progress and individual salvation through romantic love begin
to crumble within the film itself as spectacle, style, and surface drain it
of significance. However, even this postmodern film refers to this
metanarrative, and its continuing cultural resonance cannot be denied.

An attempt has been made here to seriously take these narratives
involving race and sexuality, to look at them historically, and critique
their ideology. However, questions remain: Does the postmodern crisis of narrative knowledge preclude the possibility of a different kind of
narrative of emancipation? Is this critique of these Hollywood films as
hopelessly anachronistic as the films themselves? Does the emptiness
of *Year of the Dragon*'s spectacle have more significance than the fer-
vent protests against its exploitation of the living community of China-

town, New York? However, abandoning all connections between the film and ideology may ultimately mean relinquishing any hope of social change through media work. This would make any criticism of the kind found in this study pointless.

I hope that this book points in new directions for future work rather than marking a critical cul-de-sac within postmodernism. While quite a bit of theoretical work on the representation of racial and ethnic differences in the mass media has appeared, most has grown out of the concerns of African Americans and the experiences of the African diaspora.[12] More thought needs to be devoted to the way in which "race" as a social category, implying a hierarchy of power, works across different ethnic and cultural boundaries. The different ways in which African Americans, Asian Americans, Native Americans, Hispanics, among others, are grouped together, separated, classified, labeled, and set against each other need to be better understood theoretically in order to dismantle the existing inequitable social order. Given that the media play a critical ideological role in all this, much more needs to be done to critique the ways in which "race" exists as a category in Hollywood as well as in other popular art forms.

Moreover, important theoretical work on race and gender by feminist scholars like bell hooks, Gayatri Spivak, Trinh T. Minh-ha needs to be absorbed into film studies more completely.[13] As Jane Gaines has pointed out in her essay, "White Privilege and Looking Relations: Race and Gender in Feminist Film Theory," the isolation of gender relations from the issues of race, ethnicity, and class blinds feminist film criticism to other forms of oppression:

> Since it has taken gender as its starting point in the analysis of oppression, feminist theory has helped to reinforce white middle-class values, and to the extent that it works to keep women from seeing other structures of oppression, it functions ideologically . . . .The dominant feminist paradigm actually encourages us *not to think* in terms of any oppression other than male dominance and female subordination.[14]

This book has attempted to provide one way of rethinking gender and race as it exists in Hollywood. Going a step beyond the identification of stereotypes, this look at the ideological configuration of popular narratives sheds some light on the complexities of these discourses. Much more still needs to be done on these films' reception among diverse audiences within the United States and abroad, their relationship to other types of narratives involving Asians and Asian Americans, and their relationship to other popular fictions involving interracial sexuality.

Beyond this, there exists outside Hollywood an entire world of film and television that deals with Asian and Asian American culture. These works need to be given careful attention and looked at in relation to Hollywood as an alternative voice providing a different perspective on this subject matter. Another volume could be devoted to Asian American, Asian, and other filmmakers who have depicted interracial sexual relations in dramatically different ways than found in the films analyzed here. Undoubtedly, the methods employed in this study would have to be rethought or discarded in order to properly understand these other films. This examination of Hollywood can only be a starting point, a critical look at a minuscule corner of the vast cultural fabric that includes the highly volatile issues of gender, race, sexuality, and American identity.

Notes

1: Introduction

1. Eugene Franklin Wong, *On Visual Media Racism: Asians in the American Motion Pictures* (New York: Arno Press, 1978); Dorothy B. Jones, *The Portrayal of China and India on the American Screen, 1896–1955* (Cambridge: Center for International Studies, Massachusetts Institute of Technology, 1955).

2. For more information on the "yellow peril," see John W. Dower, *War Without Mercy: Race and Power in the Pacific War* (New York: Pantheon, 1986); Harold R. Isaacs, *Scratches on Our Minds: American Images of China and India* (New York: John Day Co., 1958); H. Brett Melendy, *The Oriental Americans* (New York: Hippocrene, 1972); Stuart Creighton Miller, *The Unwelcome Immigrant: The American Image of the Chinese, 1785–1882* (Berkeley and Los Angeles: University of California Press, 1969).

3. Gary Hoppenstand, "Yellow Devil Doctors and Opium Dens: A Survey of the Yellow Peril Stereotypes in Mass Media Entertainment," in *The Popular Culture Reader*, 3d ed., ed. Christopher D. Geist and Jack Nachbar (Bowling Green, Ohio: Bowling Green University Popular Press, 1983): 174. For an overview of "yellow peril" stereotypes specifically in the cinema, see Richard A. Oehling, "The Yellow Menace: Asian Images in American Film," in *The Kaleidoscopic Lens: How Hollywood Views Ethnic Groups*, ed. Randall M. Miller (Englewood, N.J.: Jerome S. Ozer, 1980): 182–206.

4. Wong, *On Visual Media Racism*.

5. Jones, *Portrayal of China and India*, 18.

6. Noted in Kevin Brownlow, *Behind the Mask of Innocence* (New York: Alfred A. Knopf, 1990).

7. For more information on the representation of Asians in film, see Wong, *On Visual Media Racism*; Jones, *Portrayal of China and India*; Brownlow, *Be-*

hind the Mask of Innocence; Oehling, "The Yellow Menace"; as well as the following: Christine Choy, "Cinema as a Tool of Assimilation: Asian Americans, Women, and Hollywood," in *In Color: Sixty Years of Images of Minority Women in the Media, 1921–1981*, ed. Pearl Bowser (New York: Third World Newsreel, 1983): 23–25; Christine Choy, "Images of Asian-Americans in Films and Television," in *Ethnic Images in American Film and Television*, ed. Randall M. Miller (Philadelphia: Balch Institute, 1978): 145–155; and Renee Tajima, "Asian Women's Images in Film: The Past Sixty Years," in Bowser, *In Color*, 26–29.

For bibliographic listings on minorities in Hollywood, see Allen L. Woll and Randall M. Miller, *Ethnic and Racial Images in American Film and Television: Historical Essays and Bibliography* (New York: Garland, 1987). For an updated look at minorities in Hollywood, see Lester D. Friedman, ed., *Unspeakable Images: Ethnicity in the American Cinema* (Urbana: University of Illinois Press, 1991).

For a fascinating filmography of minority women in Hollywood, see Maryann Oshana, *Women of Color: A Filmography of Minority and Third World Women* (New York: Garland, 1985). This listing provided an invaluable starting point for the selection of texts included for analysis in this study.

8. For a discussion of the MPAA production code, see Garth Jowett, *Film: The Democratic Art* (Boston: Little, Brown and Co., 1976).

9. Michel Foucault, *The History of Sexuality, Vol. 1: An Introduction*, trans. Robert Hurley (New York: Vintage, 1980).

10. This decline in population was due to exclusionary laws and other methods of discouraging immigration. See Ronald Takaki, *Strangers from a Different Shore: A History of Asian Americans* (New York: Penguin, 1989).

11. The presence of Asian American filmmakers in Hollywood is still minimal. However, the success of filmmakers like Wayne Wang, Peter Wang, and Shirley Sun in finding commercial releases for their productions may portend a change in the future. For a list of Asian-American film productions, see Bill Gee, ed., *Asian American Media Reference Guide*, 2d ed. (New York: Asian CineVision, 1990). See also Russell Leong, ed., *Moving the Image: Independent Asian Pacific American Media Arts* (Los Angeles: UCLA Asian American Studies Center and Visual Communications, Southern California Asian American Studies Central, Inc., 1991).

12. For more on the basic myths that form the fabric of much of American culture, see Leslie A. Fiedler, *Love and Death in the American Novel* (New York: Dell Publishing, Inc., 1960); and Richard Slotkin, *Regeneration Through Violence: The Mythology of the American Frontier, 1600–1860* (Middletown, Conn: Wesleyan University Press, 1973).

13. Edward W. Said, *Orientalism* (New York: Vintage Books, 1979): 3.

14. Diane MacDonell, *Theories of Discourse: An Introduction* (New York: Basil Blackwell, 1986).

15. Antonio Gramsci, *Selections from the Prison Notebooks*, ed. and trans. Quintin Hoare and Geoffrey Nowell-Smith (New York: International Publishers, 1971).

The discussion of ideology and popular culture here owes a great debt to work done under the auspices of the Birmingham School of cultural studies. For more on this approach, see Stuart Hall, Dorothy Hobson, Andrew Lowe, and Paul Willis, eds., *Culture, Media, Language* (London: Hutchinson and Centre for Contemporary Cultural Studies, University of Birmingham, 1980). For an excellent introduction to the use of this approach for the analysis of classical Hollywood cinema, see Jackie Byers, *All That Hollywood Allows: Rereading Gender in 1950s Melodrama* (Chapel Hill: University of North Carolina Press, 1991). For a general overview, see Patrick Brantlinger, *Crusoe's Footprints: Cultural Studies in Britain and America* (New York: Routledge, 1990). For a collection of feminist scholarship produced by cultural studies researchers, see *Women Take Issue: Aspects of Women's Subordination* (London: Hutchinson, 1978). For further discussion of cultural studies and textual analysis, see Richard Johnson, "What Is Cultural Studies Anyway?" *Social Text*, no. 16 (Winter 1986–1987): 38–80.

16. Fredric Jameson, *The Political Unconscious: Narrative as a Socially Symbolic Act* (Ithaca: Cornell University Press, 1981): 76.

17. Claude Levi-Strauss, *Structural Anthropology*, trans. Claire Jacobson and Brooke Grundfest Schoepf (New York: Basic Books, 1963).

18. Jameson, *The Political Unconscious*, 79.

19. Roland Barthes, "Myth Today," in *Mythologies*, trans. and ed. Annette Lavers (New York: Hill and Wang, 1972): 143.

20. For more on this point, see Charles Eckert, "The Anatomy of a Proletarian Film: Warner's *Marked Woman*," in *Movies and Methods*, vol. 2, ed. Bill Nichols (Berkeley and Los Angeles: University of California Press, 1985), 407–429; Bill Nichols, *Ideology and the Image: Social Representation in the Cinema and Other Media* (Bloomington: Indiana University Press, 1981); Robert B. Ray, *A Certain Tendency of the Hollywood Cinema, 1930–1980* (Princeton: Princeton University Press, 1985); Peter Steven, ed., *Jump Cut: Hollywood, Politics and Counter-Cinema* (New York: Praeger, 1985).

2: The Rape Fantasy: *The Cheat* and *Broken Blossoms*

1. For further discussion of race and the rape fantasy in Hollywood, see Ella Shohat, "Gender and Culture of Empire: Toward a Feminist Ethnography of the Cinema," *Quarterly Review of Film Studies* 13, nos. 1–3 (May 1991): 45–84

2. Arnold Hauser, *The Social History of Art*, vol. 3 (New York: Vintage, 1957): 84.

3. Peter Brooks, *The Melodramatic Imagination: Balzac, Henry James, Melodrama and the Mode of Excess* (New Haven: Yale University Press, 1976): 20. Certainly, the fact that women were encouraged to become literate to improve their ability to function as proper mothers and spiritual guides within the family has a great deal to do with melodrama's interest in moral instruction. This point is not emphasized by Brooks.

4. For more information on the rise of the bourgeois family, see Frederick

Engels, *The Origin of the Family, Private Property, and the State* (New York: International Publishers, 1942); and Eli Zaretsky, *Capitalism, the Family, and Personal Life* (New York: Harper and Row, 1976).

5. Chuck Kleinhans, "Notes on Melodrama and the Family under Capitalism," *Film Reader*, no. 3 (February 1978): 45.

6. Geoffrey Nowell-Smith, "Minnelli and Melodrama," in *Home Is Where the Heart Is: Studies in the Melodrama and the Woman's Film*, ed. Christine Gledhill (London: British Film Institute, 1987): 74.

7. Many scholars have commented on women's role in the melodrama. See Gledhill, *Home Is Where the Heart Is*, and Tania Modleski, *Loving with a Vengeance: Mass-Produced Fantasies for Women* (New York: Methuen, 1982).

8. Some recent articles have addressed issues of race and sexuality in the domestic melodrama. See, for example, Marina Heung, "'What's the Matter with Sara Jane?': Daughters and Mothers in Douglas Sirk's *Imitation of Life*," *Cinema Journal* 26, no. 3 (Spring 1987): 21–43; Michael E. Selig, "Contradiction and Reading: Social Class and Sex Class in *Imitation of Life*," *Wide Angle* 10, no. 4 (1988): 13–23; Jane Gaines, "*Scar of Shame*: Skin Color and Caste in Black Silent Melodrama," *Cinema Journal* 26, no. 4 (Summer 1987): 3–21.

9. Northrop Frye, *Anatomy of Criticism: Four Essays* (Princeton: Princeton University Press, 1957): 47.

10. Quoted in Marshall Deutelbaum, "*The Cheat*," in *The Rivals of D. W. Griffith: Alternate Auteurs 1913–1918*, ed. Richard Koszarski (Minneapolis: Walker Art Center, 1976): 44. From *Moving Picture World*, 25 Dec. 1915, 2384.

11. Sumiko Higashi, "Ethnicity, Class, and Gender in Film: DeMille's *The Cheat*," in *Unspeakable Images: Ethnicity and the American Cinema*, ed. Lester D. Friedman (Urbana: University of Illinois Press, 1991): 130.

12. Thomas F. Gossett, *Race: The History of an Idea in America* (New York: Schocken Books, 1965): 269–270.

13. Gossett, *Race*, 271.

14. Jacquelyn Dowd Hall, "'The Mind that Burns in Each Body': Women, Rape, and Racial Violence," in *Powers of Desire: The Politics of Sexuality*, ed. Ann Snitow, Christine Stansell, and Sharon Thompson (New York: Monthly Review Press, 1983): 335.

15. Susan Brownmiller, *Against Our Will: Men, Women, and Rape* (New York: Bantam Books, 1975): 281. Although Brownmiller attempts to be evenhanded as in the passage quoted here, she has also been criticized by black feminists for her insensitivity to racial issues. For example, see Angela Y. Davis, *Women, Race, and Class* (New York: Vintage, 1981).

16. Higashi, "Ethnicity, Class, and Gender in Film," 130.

17. For more information, see Kevin Brownlow, *Behind the Mask of Innocence* (New York: Alfred A. Knopf, 1990); Ronald Takaki, *Strangers from a Different Shore: A History of Asian Americans* (New York: Penguin, 1989); Eugene Franklin Wong, *On Visual Media Racism: Asians in the American Motion Pictures* (New York: Arno Press, 1978).

18. The so-called Rembrandt or Lasky lighting in the film creates a chiar-

oscuro effect and has been discussed in detail by film historians. For example, see David Bordwell, Janet Staiger, and Kristin Thompson, *The Classical Hollywood Cinema: Film Style and Mode of Production to 1960* (New York: Columbia University Press, 1985): 225.

19. As Higashi points out in her essay, the temple gate of Tori's brand has the same sound, "torii," as the character's name.

20. See Wong, *On Visual Media Racism*.

21. A great deal has been written on the appeal of rape fantasies for women. For an overview, see Brownmiller, *Against Our Will*.

22. Higashi, "Ethnicity, Class, and Gender in Film," 131.

23. DeWitt Bodeen, "Sessue Hayakawa," *Films in Review* (April 1976): 193. Quoted in Brownlow, *Behind the Mask of Innocence*, 193.

24. Miriam Hansen, "Pleasure, Ambivalence, Identification: Valentino and Female Spectatorship," *Cinema Journal* 25, no. 4 (Summer 1986): 21.

25. Nick Browne, "American Film Theory in the Silent Period: Orientalism as an Ideological Form," *Wide Angle* 11, no. 4 (Oct. 1989): 29.

26. Lary May, *Screening Out the Past: The Birth of Mass Culture and the Motion Picture Industry* (Chicago: University of Chicago Press, 1980).

27. Stuart Ewen and Elizabeth Ewen, *Channels of Desire: Mass Images and the Shaping of American Consciousness* (New York: McGraw-Hill, 1982).

28. May, *Screening Out the Past*, 31.

29. For more on DeMille and social history, see Ewen and Ewen, *Channels of Desire*; Higashi, "Ethnicity, Class, and Gender in Film"; and May, *Screening Out the Past*.

30. Sumiko Higashi, "Cecil B. DeMille and the Lasky Company: Legitimating Feature Film as Art," *Film History* 4 (1990): 181–197.

31. See Gayle Rubin, "The Traffic in Women: Notes on the 'Political Economy' of Sex," in *Toward an Anthropology of Women*, ed. Rayna R. Reiter (New York: Monthly Review Press, 1975). For a discussion of the exchange of Edith as an object in *The Cheat*, see Judith Mayne, *The Woman at the Keyhole: Feminism and Women's Cinema* (Bloomington: University of Indiana Press, 1990).

32. See Charles Eckert, "The Anatomy of a Proletarian Film: Warner's *Marked Woman*," in *Movies and Methods: An Anthology*, vol. 2, ed. Bill Nichols (Berkeley and Los Angeles: University of California Press, 1985).

33. For information on United States, British, and Chinese relations see James C. Thomson, Jr., Peter W. Stanley, and John Curtis Perry, *Sentimental Imperialists: The American Experience in East Asia* (New York: Harper Colophon Books, 1981).

34. See contemporary reviews of the film anthologized in George C. Pratt, *Spellbound in Darkness: A History of the Silent Film* (Greenwich, Conn: New York Graphic Arts Society, 1973): 250–251; and the critics cited in Lewis Jacobs, *The Rise of the American Film: A Critical History* (New York: Teachers College Press, Columbia University, 1968): 389–390.

35. See Harry M. Geduld, *Focus on D. W. Griffith* (Englewood Cliffs, N.J.: Prentice-Hall, Inc., 1971).

36. Charles Affron, *Star Acting: Gish, Garbo, Davis* (New York: E. P. Dutton, 1977): 12–36.

37. See Vance Kepley, Jr., "Griffith's *Broken Blossoms* and the Problem of Historical Specificity," *Quarterly Review of Film Studies* 3, no. 1 (Winter 1978): 37–47; Dudley Andrew, "*Broken Blossoms*: The Art and Eros of a Perverse Text," *Quarterly Review of Film Studies* 6, no. 1 (Winter 1981): 81–90.

38. For example, see Bordwell, Staiger, and Thompson, *The Classical Hollywood Cinema*, 287.

39. Robert Lang, *American Film Melodrama: Griffith, Vidor, Minnelli* (Princeton: Princeton University Press, 1989); Nick Browne, "Griffith's Family Discourse: Griffith and Freud," in *Home Is Where the Heart Is: Studies in Melodrama and the Woman's Film*, ed. Christine Gledhill (London: British Film Institute, 1987): 223–234.

40. Brownlow, *Behind the Mask of Innocence*; Dorothy B. Jones, *The Portrayal of China and India on the American Screen, 1896–1955*; Wong, *On Visual Media Racism*. In "Chinky: The Uneasy Other of *Broken Blossoms*" (unpublished paper presented at the 1991 Society for Cinema Studies Conference at the University of Southern California), Phoebe Chao discusses the film's depiction of race in relation to the original Burke short story. For a discussion of the film's depiction of race in relation to the work of photographer Arnold Genthe, see John Kuo Wei Tchen, "Modernizing White Patriarchy: Re-viewing D. W. Griffith's *Broken Blossoms*," in *Moving the Image: Independent Asian Pacific American Media Arts*, ed. Russell Leong (Los Angeles: UCLA Asian American Studies Center and Visual Communications, Southern California Asian American Studies Central, Inc. 1991): 133–143.

41. Sumiko Higashi, *Virgins, Vamps, and Flappers: The American Silent Movie Heroine* (Montreal: Eden Press, 1978); Julia Lesage, "Artful Racism, Artful Rape: Griffith's *Broken Blossoms*," in *Home Is Where the Heart Is*, ed. Christine Gledhill (London: British Film Institute, 1987): 235–254; Marjorie Rosen, *Popcorn Venus* (New York: Avon, 1973).

42. See Lesage, "Artful Racism, Artful Rape"; Andrew, "*Broken Blossoms*"; and Browne, "American Film Theory in the Silent Period." Also, Angela Carter, *The Sadeian Woman and the Ideology of Pornography* (New York: Harper and Row, 1978): 60.

43. Lesage, "Artful Racism, Artful Rape," 242–243.

44. Ronald Pearsall, *The Worm in the Bud: The World of Victorian Sexuality* (New York: Penguin, 1969).

45. Noted in Brownlow, *Behind the Mask of Innocence*.

46. Lang, *American Film Melodrama*, 99. This discussion of sadism, fetishism, narrative, and spectacle is based on Laura Mulvey, "Visual Pleasure and Narrative Cinema," *Screen* 16, no. 3 (Autumn 1975): 6–18.

47. Browne, "American Film Theory in the Silent Period," 225–226.

48. Lesage, "Artful Racism, Artful Rape," 243. Although Burrows did know about the relationship between Cheng Huan and Lucy at this point in the narrative, it was certainly not general knowledge as this title implies.

49. Point made by Brownlow as well as Wong.

3: The Threat of Captivity: *The Bitter Tea of General Yen* and *Shanghai Express*

1. Gayle Rubin, "The Traffic in Women: Notes on the 'Political Economy' of Sex," in *Toward an Anthropology of Women*, ed. Rayna R. Reiter (New York: Monthly Review Press, 1975): 177. See also Simone de Beauvoir, "Early Tillers of the Soil," *The Second Sex*, trans. H. M. Parchley (New York: Vintage, 1974); 74–91, and Juliet Mitchell, "Patriarchy, Kinship and Women as Exchange Objects," *Psychoanalysis and Feminism* (New York: Vintage, 1975): 370–376.

2. See Richard Slotkin, *Regeneration Through Violence: The Mythology of the American Frontier, 1600–1860* (New York: Dell, 1960).

3. Glenda Riley, *Women and Indians on the Frontier, 1825–1915* (Albuquerque: University of New Mexico Press, 1984).

4. For a fascinating journalistic account of China in the 1930s, see Agnes Smedley, *China Correspondent* (London: Pandora Press, 1984). First published in 1943 as *Battle Hymn of China*.

5. Frank Capra, *The Name Above the Title* (New York: Macmillan, 1971). Although a great deal of critical material exists on Capra's oeuvre, *The Bitter Tea of General Yen* has received far less attention than Capra's better-known comedies. There is an extensive discussion of plot and style of *The Bitter Tea of General Yen* in Leland Poague, *The Cinema of Frank Capra* (Cranbury, N.J.: A. S. Barnes, 1975). Ellen Draper, "Historical Context for Gender Roles in *The Bitter Tea of General Yen*," unpublished paper presented at the 1990 Society for Cinema Studies Conference, Washington, D.C., provides useful historical information.

6. For an account of women missionaries in China, see Jane Hunter, *The Gospel of Gentility: American Women Missionaries in Turn-of-the-Century China* (New Haven: Yale University Press, 1984). For more on the socio-cultural background that motivated this missionary impulse, see Ann Douglas, *The Feminization of American Culture* (New York: Avon Books, 1977).

7. Frank Krutnik, "*The Shanghai Gesture*: The Exotic and the Melodrama," *Wide Angle* 4, no. 2 (1980): 36. For more on von Sternberg's style, see John Baxter, *The Cinema of Josef von Sternberg* (London: A. S. Barnes, 1971) and Andrew Sarris, *The Films of Josef von Sternberg* (New York: The Museum of Modern Art and Doubleday and Co., 1966). For the director's own account of his interest in China, see Josef von Sternberg, *Fun in a Chinese Laundry: An Autobiography* (New York: Collier Books, 1965).

8. Elliot Rubenstein, "*Shanghai Express*," *The International Dictionary of Films and Filmmakers: Volume I. Films*, ed. Christopher Lyon (Chicago: St. James Press, 1984): 423.

9. Much has been written on Marlene Dietrich's ambiguous sexuality and its appeal; see, for example, Claire Whitaker, "Hollywood Transformed: Interviews with Lesbian Viewers," in *Jump Cut: Hollywood, Politics, and Counter-Cinema*, ed. Peter Steven (New York: Praeger, 1985): 106–118.

10. It is interesting to note that over thirty years after *Shanghai Express*, John Ford, the director of *Stagecoach*, among other well-known films, also

used a captivity narrative in his last film, *Seven Women* (1966). Set in China, the film explores the theme of lesbianism and the threat it poses to Western Christianity to maintain its sense of superiority over the heathen "other." However, Ford's conservative treatment of the issue differs greatly from *Shanghai Express*'s ambivalent treatment of lesbianism.

4: Passport Seductions: *Lady of the Tropics*

1. Edward W. Said, *Orientalism* (New York: Random House, 1979): 118.
2. Ella Shohat, "Gender and the Culture of Empire: Toward a Feminist Ethnography of the Cinema," *Quarterly Review of Film and Video* 13, nos. 1–3 (May 1991): 57.
3. Even in the 1990s, Eurasian characters, almost invariably played by white performers, still appear in popular entertainments. The 1991 Broadway production of the London musical, *Miss Saigon*, with a leading Eurasian character played by a white actor, provides simply one example.
4. Eugene Franklin Wong, *On Visual Media Racism: Asians in the American Motion Pictures* (New York: Arno, 1978). Wong discusses the use of Eurasian characters in Hollywood films in some detail.
5. Donald Bogle, *Toms, Coons, Mulattoes, Mammies and Bucks: An Interpretative History of Blacks in American Films*, 2d ed. (New York: Continuum, 1989).
6. For an extensive discussion of race and sexuality in Sirk's *Imitation of Life*, see Marina Heung, "'What's the Matter with Sara Jane?': Daughters and Mothers in Douglas Sirk's *Imitation of Life*," *Cinema Journal* 26, no. 3 (Spring 1987): 21–43.
7. E. Ann Kaplan, ed., *Women in Film Noir* (London: British Film Institute, 1978).
8. Given the prominence of the film's scriptwriter, Ben Hecht, it comes as little surprise that so much of *Lady of the Tropics*' dramatic exposition should be based on the dialogue.
9. Milton Osborne, "Fear and Fascination in the Tropics: A Reader's Guide to French Fiction in Indo-China," in *Asia in Western Fiction*, ed. Robin W. Winks and James R. Rush (Honolulu: University of Hawaii Press, 1990): 167.

5: The Scream of the Butterfly: *Madame Butterfly, China Gate*, and "The Lady from Yesterday"

1. Lyric from "The Soft Parade," by The Doors.
2. Endymion Wilkinson, *Japan Versus the West: Image and Reality* (London: Penguin, 1990): 113.
3. For an analysis of Mary Pickford and sexuality, see Lary May, *Screening Out the Past: The Birth of Mass Culture and the Motion Picture Industry* (Chicago: University of Chicago Press, 1983).
4. Quoted in Edward Wagenknecht, *The Movies in the Age of Innocence* (New York: Ballantine Books, 1971): 135.

5. For details, see Sumiko Higashi, *Virgins, Vamps, and Flappers: The American Silent Movie Heroine* (Montreal: Eden Press, 1978).

6. Denis de Rougemont, *Love in the Western World*, trans. Montgomery Belgion (New York: Schocken Books, 1983).

7. Simone de Beauvoir, *The Second Sex*, trans. and ed. H. M. Parchley (New York: Vintage, 1974); 713–714. For an interesting application of de Beauvoir's observations to the cinema, see Lucy Fischer, *Shot/Countershot: Film Tradition and Women's Cinema* (Princeton: Princeton University Press, 1989): chap. 4.

8. John Luther Long, *Madame Butterfly, Purple Eyes, Etc.* (New York: Garrett Press, 1969): 59, 8.

9. Long, *Madame Butterfly*, 80.

10. de Beauvoir, *Second Sex*, 739–740.

11. Philip Young, "The Mother of Us All: Pocahontas Reconsidered," *Kenyon Review* 24 (Summer 1962): 391–415.

12. Rayna Green, "The Pocahontas Perplex: The Image of Indian Women in American Culture," *Massachusetts Review* 16 (1975): 714.

13. Mary V. Dearborn, *Pocahontas's Daughters: Gender and Ethnicity in American Culture* (New York: Oxford University Press, 1986): 103.

14. Leslie Fielder, *The Return of the Vanishing American* (New York: Stein and Day, 1968). For more on Pocahontas, see Werner Sollors, *Beyond Ethnicity: Consent and Dissent in American Culture* (New York: Oxford University Press, 1986). For a historical account of Pocahontas, see Grace Steele Woodward, *Pocahontas* (Norman: University of Oklahoma Press, 1969.)

15. Rick Berg, "Losing Vietnam: Covering the War in an Age of Technology," in *From Hanoi to Hollywood: The Vietnam War in American Film*, ed. Linda Dittmar and Gene Michaud (New Brunswick, N.J.: Rutgers University Press, 1990): 53. Albert Auster and Leonard Quart, *How the War Was Remembered: Hollywood and Vietnam* (New York: Praeger, 1988), also point out that Hollywood made several other films about Americans in Indochina during the Franco-Viet war. One of the more notable, *The Quiet American* (directed by Joseph Mankiewicz, 1957), based on a novel by Graham Greene, also uses an interracial love triangle as a metaphor for Vietnamese politics.

16. For more on the use of Eurasian characters in Hollywood films, see Eugene Franklin Wong, *On Visual Media Racism: Asians in the American Motion Picture* (New York: Arno Press, 1978).

17. Sarah Kozloff, *Invisible Storytellers: Voice-Over Narration in American Fiction Film* (Berkeley and Los Angeles: University of California Press, 1988): 80. As Kozloff points out, too, the voice-over often stands in for the director's voice in Hollywood films. Certainly, the Cold War political rhetoric in *China Gate* is common to many other Fuller films. For more on Fuller's oeuvre, see Nicholas Garnham, *Samuel Fuller* (London: British Film Institute, 1971).

18. For another reading of this episode of "Miami Vice," see Lynne Joyrich, "Critical and Textual Hypermasculinity," in *Logics of Television: Essays in Cultural Criticism*, ed. Patricia Mellencamp (Bloomington: Indiana University Press, 1990).

19. For more on Hollywood melodramas on the Vietnam War, see Andrew Martin, "Vietnam and Melodramatic Representation," *East-West Film Journal*

4, no. 2 (June 1990): 54–67. For an analysis of American fiction on Vietnam and the contemporary gender crisis, see Susan Jeffords, *The Remasculinization of America: Gender and the Vietnam War* (Bloomington: Indiana University Press, 1989) .

20. See Laurie Schulze, "The Made-for-Movie: Industrial Practice, Cultural Form, Popular Reception," in *Hollywood in the Age of Television*, ed. Tino Balio (Boston: Unwin Hyman, 1990): 351–376.

21. Here, "Lady from Yesterday" alludes to several well-publicized incidents in which Vietnamese fisherman were actually harrassed by whites in Texas. Louis Malle's feature film, *Alamo Bay*, also dealt with these incidents.

6: White Knights in Hong Kong: *Love Is a Many-Splendored Thing* and *The World of Suzie Wong*

1. For an interesting view of Hong Kong film critics' perspectives on Hollywood's depiction of Hong Kong, see *Changes in Hong Kong Society Through Cinema* (Hong Kong: Hong Kong International Film Festival, 1988).

2. Barbara Sichtermann, *Femininity: The Politics of the Personal*, trans. John Whitlam, ed. Helga Geyer-Ryan (Minneapolis: University of Minnesota Press, 1986): 81. Emphasis in the original.

3. See Robert B. Ray, *A Certain Tendency of the Hollywood Cinema, 1930–1980* (Princeton: Princeton University Press, 1985).

4. S. N. Ko, "Under Western Eyes," *Changes in Hong Kong Society Through Cinema*, 66.

5. Of course, Han Suyin's real-life story differs considerably. See Amy Ling, *Between Worlds: Women Writers of Chinese Ancestry* (Riverside, N.J.: Pergamon, 1990). It is also interesting to note the ways in which Hollywood chose to change Han Suyin's original novel, in which Mark is a British national and no adopted refugee orphan exists: Han Suyin, *A Many-Splendored Thing* (Boston: Little, Brown and Co., 1953).

For a discussion of the ways in which reporters figure ideologically in Hollywood films about the Third World, see Claudia Springer, "Comprehension and Crisis: Reporter Films and the Third World," in *Unspeakable Images: Ethnicity and the American Cinema*, ed. Lester Friedman (Urbana: University of Illinois Press, 1991): 167–189.

6. Mary V. Dearborn, *Pocahontas's Daughters: Gender and Ethnicity in American Culture* (New York: Oxford University Press, 1986).

7. Edward W. Said, *Orientalism* (New York: Vintage, 1979): 3.

7: Tragic and Transcendent Love: *Sayonara* and *The Crimson Kimono*

1. Another interracial relationship between Captain Bailey (James Garner) and Fumiko (Reiko Kuba) is also featured in *Sayonara*; however, it is not in any way a significant part of the plot.

2. Roland Barthes, *S/Z* (New York: Hill and Wang, 1974). For an example of the use of Barthes' methodology in film criticism, see Julia Lesage, "*S/Z* and *Rules of the Game*," *Jump Cut* 12–13 (1976): 45–51; also anthologized in Bill Nichols, ed., *Movies and Methods*, vol. 2 (Berkeley: University of California Press, 1985): 476–500.

3. For more on the Korean War, see Bruce Cumings, *The Origins of the Korean War* (Princeton: Princeton University Press, 1981).

4. The Editors, *Cahiers du Cinema*, "John Ford's *Young Mr. Lincoln*," in Bill Nichols, ed., *Movies and Methods*, vol. 2 (Berkeley: University of California Press, 1976): 493–529.

5. Brian Henderson, "*The Searchers*: An American Dilemma," *Film Quarterly* 34, no. 2 (Winter 1980–81): 9–23; also anthologized in Bill Nichols, ed., *Movies and Methods*, vol. 2 (Berkeley and Los Angeles: University of California Press, 1985): 429–449.

6. See, for example, Kate Millett, *Sexual Politics* (New York: Avon, 1969). See the discussion of this issue in chapter 5 of this study as well.

7. John W. Dower, *War Without Mercy: Race and Power in the Pacific War* (New York: Pantheon, 1986).

8. Ian Buruma, *Behind the Mask* (New York: Meridian, 1984).

9. Nicholas Garnham, *Samuel Fuller* (London: British Film Institute, 1971): 15–16.

10. Colin McArthur, *Underworld USA* (London: British Film Institute, 1972): 144.

11. For information on the internment of the Japanese during World War II, see Ronald Takaki, *Strangers from a Different Shore: A History of Asian Americans* (New York: Penguin, 1989).

8: Japanese War Brides: Domesticity and Assimilation in *Japanese War Bride* and *Bridge to the Sun*

1. Although *Bridge to the Sun* has a French director and was produced by the French company, Cité Films Production, it is included here as a "Hollywood" film because it has a Hollywood distributor, MGM, features well-known Hollywood actors, and is scripted entirely in English, based on a book written by an American woman.

2. For more on the social problem film, see Peter Roffman and Jim Purdy, *The Hollywood Social Problem Film: Madness, Despair, and Politics from the Depression to the Fifties* (Bloomington: Indiana University Press, 1981); and on the social melodrama, see John G. Cawelti, *Adventure, Mystery, and Romance: Formula Stories as Art and Popular Culture* (Chicago: University of Chicago Press, 1976).

3. Anselm L. Strauss, "Strain and Harmony in American-Japanese War-Bride Marriages," in *The Blending of America: Patterns of Intermarriage*, ed. Milton L. Barron (Chicago: Quadrangle Books, 1972): 280. Reprinted from *Marriage and Family Living* 16, no. 2 (May 1954): 99–106.

4. J. E. Smith and W. L. Worden, "They're Bringing Home Japanese

Wives," *Saturday Evening Post* 224, no. 29 (19 January 1952). Cited in Strauss, "Strain and Harmony in American-Japanese War-Bride Marriages."

5. Gwen Terasaki, *Bridge to the Sun* (Newport, Tenn.: Wakestone Books, 1985).

6. David N. Rodowick, "Madness, Authority and Ideology: The Domestic Melodrama of the 1950s," in *Home Is Where the Heart Is: Studies in Melodrama and the Woman's Film*, ed. Christine Gledhill (London: British Film Institute, 1987): 270–271.

7. Thomas Elsaesser, "Tales of Sound and Fury: Observations on the Family Melodrama," in Gledhill, *Home Is Where the Heart Is*, 62.

8. Geoffrey Nowell-Smith, "Minnelli and Melodrama," in Gledhill, *Home Is Where the Heart Is*, 73.

9. For more on the domestic space in the Hollywood melodrama, see Roger D. McNiven, "The Middle-Class American Home of the Fifties: The Use of Architecture in Nicholas Ray's *Bigger than Life* and Douglas Sirk's *All That Heaven Allows*," *Cinema Journal* 22, no. 4 (Summer 1983): 38–57. For a discussion of ideology, women's fantasies and domestic space, see Julia Lesage, "The Hegemonic Female Fantasy in *An Unmarried Woman* and *Craig's Wife*," *Film Reader* 5 (1982): 83–94.

10. Eli Zaretsky, *Capitalism, the Family, and Personal Life* (New York: Harper & Row, 1976): 39.

11. Zaretsky, *Capitalism, the Family, and Personal Life*, 39.

12. Elsaesser, "Tales of Sound and Fury," 62.

9: The Return of the Butterfly: The Geisha Masquerade in *My Geisha* and "An American Geisha"

1. Frantz Fanon, *Black Skin, White Masks*, trans. Charles Lam Markmann (New York: Grove Press, 1967). For more on contemporary theories of the sociopsychological construction of racial categories, see Henry Louis Gates, Jr., ed., *"Race," Writing, and Difference* (Chicago: University of Chicago Press, 1985); and David Theo Goldberg, ed., *Anatomy of Racism* (Minneapolis: University of Minnesota Press, 1990).

2. For more information on the geisha in Japanese art and society, see Liza Dalby, *Geisha* (New York: Vintage, 1985; originally published by the University of California Press in 1983). For more on how the geisha is viewed within the context of Japanese attitudes toward sexuality, see Ian Buruma, *Behind the Mask: On Sexual Demons, Sacred Mothers, Transvestites, Gangsters and Other Japanese Cultural Heroes* (New York: Pantheon, 1984).

3. Richard Meyers, *Movies on Movies: How Hollywood Sees Itself* (New York: Drake, 1978).

4. This film is reviewed in Harold S. Williams, *Shades of the Past: Indiscreet Tales of Japan* (Rutland, Vt.: Charles E. Tuttle Co., 1958).

5. The Westmore family of makeup artists was responsible for Shirley MacLaine's transformation in *My Geisha*, which took much longer than the few minutes devoted to it in the film. See Frank Westmore and Muriel Davidson,

The Westmores of Hollywood (New York: J. B. Lippincott Co., 1976). For more on this and other instances of racial cosmetology, see Eugene Franklin Wong, *On Visual Media Racism* (New York: Arno, 1978).

6. This concept is discussed in *Cahiers du Cinema,* "John Ford's *Young Mr. Lincoln,*" in *Movies and Methods,* ed. Bill Nichols (Berkeley and Los Angeles: University of California Press, 1976): 493–529.

7. I am grateful to Sumiko Higashi for pointing this out in a presentation she made on *Toll of the Sea* at the 1988 Asian American Film Festival in Washington, D.C.

8. Edward Branigan, "Color and Cinema: Problems in the Writing of History," in *Movies and Methods,* vol. 2, ed. Bill Nichols (Berkeley and Los Angeles: University of California Press, 1985): 121–143. David L. Parker, "'Blazing Technicolor,' 'Stunning Trucolor,' and 'Shocking Eastmancolor,'" in *The American Film Heritage: Impressions from the American Film Institute Archives* (Washington, D.C.: Acropolis Books, 1972): 19–27.

9. Dana Polan, "A Brechtian Cinema? Towards a Politics of Self-Reflexive Film," in Nichols, *Movies and Methods,* 2: 661–672. Reprinted from *Jump Cut* 17 (1978): 29–32.

10. Barbara Klinger, "'Cinema/Ideology/Criticism' Revisited: The Progressive Genre," in *Film Genre Reader,* ed. Barry Keith Grant (Austin: University of Texas Press, 1986). Reprinted from *Screen* 25 (January–February 1984): 30–44.

11. Dalby, *Geisha.*

12. Molly Haskell, *From Reverence to Rape: The Treatment of Women in the Movies* (New York: Penguin, 1974).

13. Julia Lesage, "The Hegemonic Female Fantasy in *An Unmarried Woman* and *Craig's Wife,*" *Film Reader* 5 (1982): 83–94. B. Ruby Rich, "In the Name of Feminist Film Criticism," in Nichols, *Movies and Methods,* 2: 340–358. Charlotte Brunsdon, "A Subject for the Seventies . . . ," *Screen* 23, nos. 3–4 (September–October 1982): 20–38.

14. Jane Gaines, "Introduction: Fabricating the Female Body," in *Fabrications: Costume and the Female Body,* ed. Jane Gaines and Charlotte Herzog (New York: Routledge, 1990): 1–27.

15. Laura Mulvey, "Visual Pleasure and Narrative Cinema," *Screen* 16, no. 3 (Autumn 1975). For a discussion of race, gender, and visual pleasure involving a different sort of Asian masquerade, see Eric Smoodin, "The Oriental Dame and the Mixed-Race Romance in *Footlight Parade,*" *Balcones* 1 (Spring 1987): 53–56.

16. Laura Mulvey, "Afterthoughts . . . Inspired by *Duel in the Sun,*" *Framework* (Summer 1981): 12–15.

17. For a summary of this perspective, see John Fletcher, "Versions of Masquerade," *Screen* 29, no. 3 (Summer 1988): 43–70.

18. Claire Johnston, "Femininity and the Masquerade: *Anne of The Indies,*" in *Jacques Tourneur,* ed. Claire Johnston and Paul Willemen (Edinburgh: Edinburgh Film Festival, 1975): 41.

19. Mary Ann Doane, "Film and the Masquerade—Theorizing the Female Spectator," *Screen* 23, nos. 3–4 (September–October 1982): 81–82.

20. Gaylyn Studlar, "Masochism, Masquerade, and the Erotic Metamorphoses of Marlene Dietrich," in *Fabrications: Costume and the Female Body*, ed. Gaines and Herzog, 229–277.

21. Christine Holmlund, "I Love Luce: The Lesbian, Mimesis and Masquerade in Irigaray, Freud, and Mainstream Film," *New Formations* 9 (Winter 1989): 105–123.

10: Conclusion: The Postmodern Spectacle of Race and Romance in *Year of the Dragon*

1. Fredric Jameson, "Postmodernism and Consumer Society," in Hal Foster, ed. *The Anti-Aesthetic: Essays on Postmodern Culture* (Port Townsend, Wash: Bay Press, 1983): 115–116.

2. *Blade Runner* (1982) provides simply one example of this exploitation of Asian American communities in the postmodern text. See Giuliana Bruno, "Ramble City: Postmodernism and *Blade Runner*," *October*, no. 41 (Summer 1987): 61–74.

3. Jameson, "Postmodernism and Consumer Society," 119–120.

4. In many ways, *Year of the Dragon* resembles the revised genre film discussed in Robert B. Ray, *A Certain Tendency of the Hollywood Cinema, 1930–1980* (Princeton: Princeton University Press, 1985).

5. For a different view of *Year of the Dragon*, see Robin Wood, "Hero/Anti-Hero: The Dilemma of *Year of the Dragon*," *CineAction!*, no. 6 (August 1986): 57–61.

6. Actually the novel and the film both refer to actual instances that occurred in New York's Chinatown. For more information, see Peter Kwong, *The New Chinatown* (New York: Noonday Press, 1987).

7. For more on these protests, see Martha Gever, "Dragon Busters," *The Independent* 8, no. 8 (October 1985): 8–9.

8. For a discussion of this film, see Gina Marchetti, "Ethnicity, the Cinema and Cultural Studies," *Unspeakable Images: Ethnicity and the American Cinema*, ed. Lester Friedman (Urbana: University of Illinois Press, 1991): 277–307.

9. For an overview of Asian American filmmaking, see Russell Leong, ed., *Moving the Image: Independent Asian Pacific American Media Arts* (Los Angeles: UCLA Asian American Studies Center and Visual Communications, Southern California Asian American Studies Central, Inc., 1991).

For a discussion of contemporary media representations of minority groups, including Asian Americans, see Michael Omi, "In Living Color: Race and American Culture," in Ian Angus and Sut Jhally, eds., *Cultural Politics in Contemporary America* (New York: Routledge, 1989): 111–122.

10. Jean-Francois Lyotard, *The Postmodern Condition: A Report on Knowledge*, trans. Geoff Bennington and Brian Massumi (Minneapolis: University of Minnesota Press, 1984): xxiii.

11. Ibid., xxiv.

12. For an overview of current thought on the cultural construction of "race," see Henry Louis Gates, Jr., ed., *"Race," Writing and Difference*

(Chicago: University of Chicago Press, 1986); and David Theo Goldberg, ed., *Anatomy of Racism* (Minneapolis: University of Minnesota Press, 1990).

13. For more on race and feminist theory, see Elizabeth V. Spelman, *Inessential Woman: Problems of Exclusion in Feminist Thought* (Boston: Beacon Press, 1988); and Chandra Talpade Mohanty, Ann Russo, and Lourdes Torres, *Third World Women and the Politics of Feminism* (Bloomington: Indiana University Press, 1991).

14. Jane Gaines, "White Privilege and Looking Relations—Race and Gender in Feminist Theory," *Cultural Critique*, no. 4 (Fall 1986): 61, 66. Reprinted in *Screen* 29, no. 4 (Autumn 1988): 12–27.

Bibliography

Affron, Charles. *Star Acting: Gish, Garbo, Davis*. New York: E. P. Dutton, 1977.

Andrew, Dudley. *"Broken Blossoms:* The Art and Eros of a Perverse Text." *Quarterly Review of Film Studies* 6, no. 1 (Winter 1981): 81–90.

Auster, Albert, and Leonard Quart. *How the War Was Remembered: Hollywood and Vietnam*. New York: Praeger, 1988.

Barthes, Roland. *S/Z*, trans. Richard Miller. New York: Hill and Wang, 1974.

——— "Myth Today." In *Mythologies*, trans. and ed. Annette Lavers. New York: Hill and Wang, 1972.

Baxter, John. *The Cinema of Josef von Sternberg*. London: A. S. Barnes, 1971.

Berg, Rick. "Losing Vietnam: Covering the War in an Age of Technology." In *From Hanoi to Hollywood: The Vietnam War in American Film*, ed. Linda Dittmar and Gene Michaud. New Brunswick: Rutgers University Press, 1990, 41–68.

Bodeen, DeWitt. "Sessue Hayakawa." *Films in Review* 27 (April 1976): 193.

Bogle, Donald. *Toms, Coons, Mulattoes, Mammies and Bucks: An Interpretative History of Blacks in American Films*, 2d ed. New York: Continuum, 1989.

Bordwell, David, Janet Staiger, and Kristin Thompson. *The Classical Hollywood Cinema: Film Style and Mode of Production to 1960*. New York: Columbia University Press, 1985.

Branigan, Edward. "Color and Cinema: Problems in the Writing of History." In *Movies and Methods*, vol. 2. Berkeley and Los Angeles: University of California Press, 1985, 121–143. Reprinted from *Film Reader* 4 (1979): 16–34.

Brantlinger, Patrick. *Crusoe's Footprints: Cultural Studies in Britain and America*. New York: Routledge, 1990.

Brooks, Peter. *The Melodramatic Imagination: Balzac, Henry James, Melodrama and the Mode of Excess*. New Haven: Yale University Press, 1976.

Browne, Nick. "Orientalism as an Ideological Form: American Film Theory in the Silent Period." *Wide Angle* 11 no. 4 (October 1989): 23–31.

———— "Griffith's Family Discourse: Griffith and Freud." In *Home Is Where the Heart Is: Studies in Melodrama and the Woman's Film*, ed. Christine Gledhill. London: British Film Institute, 1987, 223–234.

Brownlow, Kevin. *Behind the Mask of Innocence*. New York: Alfred A. Knopf, 1990.

Brownmiller, Susan. *Against Our Will: Men, Women, and Rape*. New York: Bantam Books, 1975.

Bruno, Giuliana. "Ramble City: Postmodernism and *Blade Runner*." *October* 41 (Summer 1987): 61–74.

Brunsdon, Charlotte. "A Subject for the Seventies . . . ." *Screen* 23, nos. 3–4 (September–October 1982): 20–38.

Buruma, Ian. *Behind the Mask: On Sexual Demons, Sacred Mothers, Transvestites, Gangsters and Other Japanese Cultural Heroes*. New York: Pantheon, 1984.

Byers, Jackie. *All That Hollywood Allows: Rereading Gender in 1950s Melodrama*. Chapel Hill: University of North Carolina Press, 1991.

Capra, Frank. *The Name Above the Title*. New York: Macmillan, 1971.

Carter, Angela. *The Sadeian Woman and the Ideology of Pornography*. New York: Harper & Row, 1978.

Cawelti, John G. *Adventure, Mystery, and Romance: Formula Stories as Art and Popular Culture*. Chicago: University of Chicago Press, 1976.

Changes in Hong Kong Society Through Cinema. Hong Kong: Hong Kong International Film Festival, 1988.

Chao, Phoebe. "Chinky: The Uneasy Other of *Broken Blossoms*." Unpublished paper presented at the 1991 Society for Cinema Studies Conference at the University of Southern California.

Choy, Christine. "Cinema as a Tool of Assimilation: Asian Americans, Women, and Hollywood." In *In Color: Sixty Years of Images of Minority Women in the Media, 1921–1981*, ed. Pearl Bowser. New York: Third World Newsreel, 1983, 23–25.

———— "Images of Asian-Americans in Films and Television." In *Ethnic Images in American Film and Television*, ed. Randall M. Miller. Philadelphia: Balch Institute, 1978, 145–155.

Cumings, Bruce. *The Origins of the Korean War*. Princeton: Princeton University Press, 1981.

Dalby, Liza. *Geisha*. New York: Vintage, 1985. Originally published by the University of California Press in 1983.

Davis, Angela Y. *Women, Race, and Class*. New York: Vintage, 1981.

de Beauvoir, Simone. *The Second Sex*, trans. H. M. Parchley. New York: Vintage, 1974.

de Rougemont, Denis. *Love in the Western World*, trans. Montgomery Belgion. New York: Schocken Books, 1983.

Dearborn, Mary V. *Pocahontas's Daughters: Gender and Ethnicity in American Culture*. New York: Oxford University Press, 1986.

Deutelbaum, Marshall. *"The Cheat."* In *The Rivals of D. W. Griffith: Alternate Auteurs 1913–1918*, ed. Richard Koszarski. Minneapolis: Walker Art Center, 1976.

Doane, Mary Ann. "Film and the Masquerade—Theorizing the Female Spectator." *Screen* 23, nos. 3–4 (September–October 1982): 81–82.

Douglas, Ann. *The Feminization of American Culture*. New York: Avon Books, 1977.

Dower, John W. *War Without Mercy: Race and Power in the Pacific War*. New York: Pantheon, 1986.

Draper, Ellen. "Historical Context for Gender Roles in *The Bitter Tea of General Yen*." Unpublished paper presented at the 1990 Society for Cinema Studies Conference, Washington, D.C.

Eckert, Charles. "The Anatomy of a Proletarian Film: Warner's *Marked Woman*." In *Movies and Methods*, vol. 2, ed. Bill Nichols. Berkeley and Los Angeles: University of California Press, 1985, 407–429. Reprinted from *Film Quarterly* 27, no. 2 (Winter 1973–1974): 10–24.

Elsaesser, Thomas. "Tales of Sound and Fury: Observations on the Family Melodrama." In *Home Is Where the Heart Is: Studies in Melodrama and the Woman's Film*, ed. Christine Gledhill. London: British Film Institute, 1987, 43–69. Reprinted from *Monogram* 4 (1972): 2–16.

Engels, Frederick. *The Origin of the Family, Private Property, and the State*. New York: International Publishers, 1942.

Ewen, Stuart, and Elizabeth Ewen. *Channels of Desire: Mass Images and the Shaping of American Consciousness*. New York: McGraw-Hill, 1982.

Fanon, Frantz. *Black Skin, White Masks*, trans. Charles Lam Markmann. New York: Grove Press, 1967.

Fiedler, Leslie A. *Love and Death in the American Novel*. New York: Dell Publishing, Inc., 1960.

Fielder, Leslie. *The Return of the Vanishing American*. New York: Stein and Day, 1968.

Fischer, Lucy. *Shot/Countershot: Film Tradition and Women's Cinema*. Princeton: Princeton University Press, 1989.

Fletcher, John. "Versions of Masquerade." *Screen* 29, no. 3 (Summer 1988): 43–70.

Foucault, Michel. *The History of Sexuality, Volume 1: An Introduction*, trans. Robert Hurley. New York: Vintage, 1980.

Friedman, Lester D., ed. *Unspeakable Images: Ethnicity in the American Cinema*. Urbana: University of Illinois Press, 1991.

Frye, Northrop. *Anatomy of Criticism: Four Essays*. Princeton: Princeton University Press, 1957.

Gaines, Jane. "Introduction: Fabricating the Female Body." In *Fabrications: Costume and the Female Body*, ed. Jane Gaines and Charlotte Herzog. New York: Routledge, 1990, 1–27.

——— "White Privilege and Looking Relations—Race and Gender in Feminist Film Theory." *Cultural Critique* 4 (Fall 1986): 59–79. Reprinted in *Screen* 29, no. 4 (Autumn 1988): 12–27.

———— "*Scar of Shame*: Skin Color and Caste in Black Silent Melodrama." *Cinema Journal* 26, no. 4 (Summer 1987): 3–21.

Garnham, Nicholas. *Samuel Fuller*. London: British Film Institute, 1971.

Gates, Henry Louis, Jr., ed. *"Race," Writing, and Difference*. Chicago: University of Chicago Press, 1986.

Geduld, Harry M. *Focus on D. W. Griffith*. Englewood Cliffs, N.J.: Prentice-Hall, 1971.

Gee, Bill, ed. *Asian American Media Reference Guide*, 2d ed. New York: Asian CineVision, 1990.

Gever, Martha. "Dragon Busters." *The Independent* 8, no. 8 (October 1985): 8–9.

Goldberg, David Theo, ed. *Anatomy of Racism*. Minneapolis: University of Minnesota Press, 1990.

Gossett, Thomas F. *Race: The History of an Idea in America*. New York: Schocken Books, 1965.

Gramsci, Antonio. *Selections from the Prison Notebooks*, ed. and trans. Quintin Hoare and Geoffrey Nowell-Smith. New York: International Publishers, 1971.

Green, Rayna. "The Pocahontas Perplex: The Image of Indian Women in American Culture." *Massachusetts Review* 16 (Autumn 1975): 698–714.

Hall, Jacquelyn Dowd. "'The Mind That Burns in Each Body': Women, Rape, and Racial Violence." In *Powers of Desire: The Politics of Sexuality*, ed. Ann Snitow, Christine Stansell, and Sharon Thompson. New York: Monthly Review Press, 1983, 328–349.

Hall, Stuart, Dorothy Hobson, Andrew Lowe, and Paul Willis, eds. *Culture, Media, Language*. London: Hutchinson and Centre for Contemporary Cultural Studies, University of Birmingham, 1980.

Han Suyin. *A Many-Splendored Thing*. Boston: Little, Brown and Co., 1953.

Hansen, Miriam. "Pleasure, Ambivalence, Identification: Valentino and Female Spectatorship." *Cinema Journal* 25, no. 4 (Summer 1986): 6–32.

Haskell, Molly. *From Reverence to Rape: The Treatment of Women in the Movies*. New York: Penguin, 1974.

Hauser, Arnold. *The Social History of Art*, vol. 3. New York: Vintage, 1957.

Henderson, Brian. "*The Searchers*: An American Dilemma." *Film Quarterly* 34, no. 2 (Winter 1980–81): 9–23. Anthologized in Bill Nichols, ed., *Movies and Methods*, vol. 2. Berkeley and Los Angeles: University of California Press, 1985, pp. 429–449.

Heung, Marina. "'What's the Matter with Sara Jane?': Daughters and Mothers in Douglas Sirk's *Imitation of Life*." *Cinema Journal* 26, no. 3 (Spring 1987): 21–43.

Higashi, Sumiko. "Ethnicity, Class, and Gender in Film: DeMille's *The Cheat*." In *Unspeakable Images: Ethnicity and the American Cinema*, ed. Lester D. Friedman. Urbana: University of Illinois Press, 1991, 112–139.

———— "Cecil B. DeMille and the Lasky Company: Legitimating Feature Film as Art." *Film History* 4 (1990): 181–197.

——— *Virgins, Vamps, and Flappers: The American Silent Movie Heroine.* Montreal: Eden Press, 1978.

Holmlund, Christine. "I Love Luce: The Lesbian, Mimesis and Masquerade in Irigaray, Freud, and Mainstream Film." *New Formations* 9 (Winter 1989): 105–123.

Hoppenstand, Gary. "Yellow Devil Doctors and Opium Dens: A Survey of the Yellow Peril Stereotypes in Mass Media Entertainment." In *The Popular Culture Reader*, 3d ed., ed. Christopher D. Geist and Jack Nachbar. Bowling Green, Ohio: Bowling Green University Popular Press, 1983, 171–185.

Hunter, Jane. *The Gospel of Gentility: American Women Missionaries in Turn-of-the-Century China.* New Haven: Yale University Press, 1984.

Isaacs, Harold R. *Scratches on Our Minds: American Images of China and India.* New York: John Day Co., 1958.

Jacobs, Lewis. *The Rise of the American Film: A Critical History.* New York: Teachers College Press, Columbia University, 1968.

Jameson, Fredric. "Postmodernism and Consumer Society." In *The Anti-Aesthetic: Essays on Postmodern Culture*, ed. Hal Foster. Port Townsend, Washington: Bay Press, 1983, 111–125.

——— *The Political Unconscious: Narrative as a Socially Symbolic Act.* Ithaca: Cornell University Press, 1981.

Jeffords, Susan. *The Remasculinization of America: Gender and the Vietnam War.* Bloomington: Indiana University Press, 1989.

Johnson, Richard. "What Is Cultural Studies Anyway?" *Social Text* 16 (Winter 1986–1987): 38–80.

Johnston, Claire. "Femininity and the Masquerade: *Anne of the Indies.*" In *Jacques Tourneur*, ed. Claire Johnston and Paul Willemen. Edinburgh: Edinburgh Film Festival, 1975, 36–44.

Jones, Dorothy B. *The Portrayal of China and India on the American Screen, 1896–1955.* Cambridge, Massachusetts: Center for International Studies, Massachusetts Institute of Technology, 1955.

Jowett, Garth. *Film: The Democratic Art.* Boston: Little, Brown and Co., 1976.

Joyrich, Lynne. "Critical and Textual Hypermasculinity," In *Logics of Television: Essays in Cultural Criticism*, ed. Patricia Mellencamp. Bloomington: Indiana University Press, 1990.

Kaplan, E. Ann, ed. *Women in Film Noir.* London: British Film Institute, 1978.

Kepley, Vance, Jr. "Griffith's *Broken Blossoms* and the Problem of Historical Specificity." *Quarterly Review of Film Studies* 3, no. 1 (Winter 1978): 37–47.

Kleinhans, Chuck. "Notes on Melodrama and the Family under Capitalism." *Film Reader* 3 (February 1978): 40–47.

Klinger, Barbara. "'Cinema/Ideology/Criticism' Revisited: The Progressive Genre." In *Film Genre Reader*, ed. Barry Keith Grant. Austin: University of Texas Press, 1986, 74–90. Reprinted from *Screen* 25, no. 1 (January–February 1984): 30–44.

Ko, S. N. "Under Western Eyes." *Changes in Hong Kong Society Through Cinema*. Hong Kong: Hong Kong International Film Festival, 1988, 64–67.

Kozloff, Sarah. *Invisible Storytellers: Voice-Over Narration in American Fiction Film*. Berkeley and Los Angeles: University of California Press, 1988.

Krutnik, Frank. "*The Shanghai Gesture*: The Exotic and the Melodrama." *Wide Angle* 4, no. 2 (1980): 36–42.

Kwong, Peter. *The New Chinatown*. New York: Noonday Press, 1987.

Lang, Robert. *American Film Melodrama: Griffith, Vidor, Minnelli*. Princeton: Princeton University Press, 1989.

Leong, Russell, ed. *Moving the Image: Independent Asian Pacific American Media Arts*. Los Angeles: UCLA Asian American Studies Center and Visual Communications, Southern California Asian American Studies Central, Inc., 1991.

Lesage, Julia. "Artful Racism, Artful Rape: Griffith's *Broken Blossoms*." In *Home Is Where the Heart Is: Studies in Melodrama and the Woman's Film*, ed. Christine Gledhill. London: British Film Institute, 1987, 235–254. Reprinted from *Jump Cut* 26 (1981): 51–55.

———— "*S/Z* and *Rules of the Game*." *Jump Cut* 12–13 (1976): 45–51. Anthologized in Bill Nichols, ed. *Movies and Methods*, vol. 2. Berkeley and Los Angeles: University of California Press, 1985, 476–500.

———— "The Hegemonic Female Fantasy in *An Unmarried Woman* and *Craig's Wife*." *Film Reader* 5 (1982): 83–94.

Levi-Strauss, Claude. *Structural Anthropology*, trans. Claire Jacobson and Brooke Grundfest Schoepf. New York: Basic Books, 1963.

Ling, Amy. *Between Worlds: Women Writers of Chinese Ancestry*. Riverside, New Jersey: Pergamon, 1990.

Long, John Luther. *Madame Butterfly, Purple Eyes, Etc.* New York: Garrett Press, 1969.

Lyotard, Jean-Francois. *The Postmodern Condition: A Report on Knowledge*, trans. Geoff Bennington and Brian Massumi. Minneapolis: University of Minnesota Press, 1984.

McArthur, Colin. *Underworld USA*. London: British Film Institute, 1972.

MacDonell, Diane. *Theories of Discourse: An Introduction*. New York: Basil Blackwell, 1986.

McNiven, Roger D. "The Middle-Class American Home of the Fifties: The Use of Architecture in Nicholas Ray's *Bigger than Life* and Douglas Sirk's *All That Heaven Allows*." *Cinema Journal* 22, no. 4 (Summer 1983): 38–57.

Marchetti, Gina. "Ethnicity, the Cinema and Cultural Studies." In *Unspeakable Images: Ethnicity and the American Cinema*, ed. Lester Friedman. Urbana: University of Illinois Press, 1991, 277–307.

Martin, Andrew. "Vietnam and Melodramatic Representation." *East-West Film Journal* 4, no. 2 (June 1990): 54–67.

May, Lary. *Screening Out the Past: The Birth of Mass Culture and the Motion Picture Industry*. Chicago: University of Chicago Press, 1983.

Mayne, Judith. *The Woman at the Keyhole: Feminism and Women's Cinema*. Bloomington: University of Indiana Press, 1990.

Melendy, H. Brett. *The Oriental Americans*. New York: Hippocrene, 1972.

Meyers, Richard. *Movies on Movies: How Hollywood Sees Itself.* New York: Drake, 1978.

Miller, Stuart Creighton. *The Unwelcome Immigrant: The American Image of the Chinese, 1785–1882.* Berkeley and Los Angeles: University of California Press, 1969.

Millett, Kate. *Sexual Politics.* New York: Avon, 1969.

Mitchell, Juliet. *Psychoanalysis and Feminism.* New York: Vintage, 1975.

Modleski, Tania. *Loving with a Vengeance: Mass-Produced Fantasies for Women.* New York: Methuen, 1982.

Mohanty, Chandra Talpade, Ann Russo, and Lourdes Torres. *Third World Women and the Politics of Feminism.* Bloomington: Indiana University Press, 1991.

Mulvey, Laura, "Afterthoughts . . . Inspired by *Duel in the Sun.*" *Framework* (Summer 1981): 12–15.

——— "Visual Pleasure and Narrative Cinema." *Screen* 16, no. 3 (Autumn 1975): 6–18.

Nichols, Bill. *Ideology and the Image: Social Representation in the Cinema and Other Media.* Bloomington: Indiana University Press, 1981.

Nowell-Smith, Geoffrey. "Minnelli and Melodrama." In *Home Is Where the Heart Is: Studies in the Melodrama and the Woman's Film,* ed. Christine Gledhill. London: British Film Institute, 1987, 70–74. Reprinted from *Screen* 18, no. 2 (Summer 1977): 113–118.

Oehling, Richard A. "The Yellow Menace: Asian Images in American Film." In *The Kaleidoscopic Lens: How Hollywood Views Ethnic Groups,* ed. Randall M. Miller. Englewood, N.J.: Jerome S. Ozer, 1980, 182–206.

Omi, Michael. "In Living Color: Race and American Culture." In *Cultural Politics in Contemporary America,* ed. Ian Angus and Sut Jhally. New York: Routledge, 1989, 111–122.

Osborne, Milton. "Fear and Fascination in the Tropics: A Reader's Guide to French Fiction in Indo-China." In *Asia in Western Fiction,* ed. Robin W. Winks and James R. Rush. Honolulu: University of Hawaii Press, (1990), 159–174.

Oshana, Maryann. *Women of Color: A Filmography of Minority and Third World Women.* New York: Garland, 1985.

Parker, David L. "'Blazing Technicolor,' 'Stunning Trucolor,' and 'Shocking Eastmancolor.'" In *The American Film Heritage: Impressions from the American Film Institute Archives.* Washington, D.C.: Acropolis Books, 1972, 19–27.

Pearsall, Ronald. *The Worm in the Bud: The World of Victorian Sexuality.* New York: Penguin, 1969.

Poague, Leland. *The Cinema of Frank Capra.* Cranbury, N.J.: A. S. Barnes, 1975.

Polan, Dana. "A Brechtian Cinema? Towards a Politics of Self-Reflexive Film." In *Movies and Methods,* vol. 2, ed. Bill Nichols. Berkeley and Los Angeles: University of California Press, 1985, 661–672. Reprinted from *Jump Cut* 17 (1978): 29–32.

Pratt, George C. *Spellbound in Darkness: A History of the Silent Film.* Greenwich, Conn: New York Graphic Arts Society, 1973.

Ray, Robert B. *A Certain Tendency of the Hollywood Cinema, 1930–1980*. Princeton: Princeton University Press, 1985.

Rich, B. Ruby. "In the Name of Feminist Film Criticism." In *Movies and Methods*, vol. 2, ed. Bill Nichols. Berkeley: University of California Press, 1985, 340–358. Reprinted from *Jump Cut* 19 (1978): 9–14.

Riley, Glenda. *Women and Indians on the Frontier, 1825–1915*. Albuquerque: University of New Mexico Press, 1984.

Rodowick, David N. "Madness, Authority and Ideology: The Domestic Melodrama of the 1950s." In *Home Is Where the Heart Is: Studies in Melodrama and the Woman's Film*, ed. Christine Gledhill. London: British Film Institute, 1987, 268–280. Reprinted from *The Velvet Light Trap* 19 (1982): 40–45.

Roffman, Peter, and Jim Purdy. *The Hollywood Social Problem Film: Madness, Despair, and Politics from the Depression to the Fifties*. Bloomington: Indiana University Press, 1981.

Rosen, Marjorie. *Popcorn Venus*. New York: Avon, 1973.

Rubenstein, Elliot. "*Shanghai Express*." In *The International Dictionary of Films and Filmmakers: Volume I-Films*, ed. Christopher Lyon. Chicago: St. James Press, 1984, 423.

Rubin, Gayle. "The Traffic in Women: Notes on the 'Political Economy' of Sex." In *Toward an Anthropology of Women*, ed. Rayna R. Reiter. New York: Monthly Review Press, 1975, 157–210.

Said, Edward W. *Orientalism*. New York: Vintage Books, 1979.

Sarris, Andrew. *The Films of Josef von Sternberg*. New York: The Museum of Modern Art and Doubleday and Co., Inc., 1966.

Schulze, Laurie. "The Made-for-TV-Movie: Industrial Practice, Cultural Form, Popular Reception." In *Hollywood in the Age of Television*, ed. Tino Balio. Boston: Unwin Hyman, 1990, 351–376.

Selig, Michael E. "Contradiction and Reading: Social Class and Sex Class in *Imitation of Life*." *Wide Angle* 10, no. 4 (1988): 13–23.

Shohat, Ella. "Gender and Culture of Empire: Toward a Feminist Ethnography of the Cinema." *Quarterly Review of Film and Video* 13, nos. 1–3 (May 1991): 45–84.

Sichtermann, Barbara. *Femininity: The Politics of the Personal*, trans. John Whitlam, ed. Helga Geyer-Ryan. Minneapolis: University of Minnesota Press, 1986.

Slotkin, Richard. *Regeneration Through Violence: The Mythology of the American Frontier, 1600–1860*. New York: Dell, 1960, and Middletown, Conn.: Wesleyan University Press, 1973.

Smedley, Agnes. *China Correspondent*. London: Pandora Press, 1984. First published in 1943 as *Battle Hymn of China*. London: Gollancz, 1943.

Smith, J. E. and W. L. Worden. "They're Bringing Home Japanese Wives." *Saturday Evening Post* 224, no. 29, January 19, 1952.

Smoodin, Eric. "The Oriental Dame and the Mixed-Race Romance in *Footlight Parade*." *Balcones* 1, no. 1 (Spring 1987): 53–56.

Sollors, Werner. *Beyond Ethnicity: Consent and Dissent in American Culture*. New York: Oxford University Press, 1986.

Spelman, Elizabeth V. *Inessential Woman: Problems of Exclusion in Feminist Thought.* Boston: Beacon Press, 1988.

Springer, Claudia. "Comprehension and Crisis: Reporter Films and the Third World." In *Unspeakable Images: Ethnicity and the American Cinema*, ed. Lester Friedman. Urbana: University of Illinois Press, 1991, 167–189.

Steven, Peter, ed. *Jump Cut: Hollywood, Politics and Counter-Cinema.* New York: Praeger, 1985.

Strauss, Anselm L. "Strain and Harmony in American-Japanese War-Bride Marriages." In *The Blending of America: Patterns of Intermarriage*, ed. Milton L. Barron. Chicago: Quadrangle Books, 1972, 268–281. Reprinted from *Marriage and Family Living* 16, no. 2 (May 1954): 99–106.

Studlar, Gaylyn. "Masochism, Masquerade, and the Erotic Metamorphoses of Marlene Dietrich." In *Fabrications: Costume and the Female Body*, ed. Jane Gaines and Charlotte Herzog. New York: Routledge, 1990, 229–277.

Tajima, Renee. "Asian Women's Images in Film: The Past Sixty Years." In *In Color: Sixty Years of Images of Minority Women in the Media, 1921–1981*, ed. Pearl Bowser. New York: Third World Newsreel, 1983, 26–29.

Takaki, Ronald. *Strangers from a Different Shore: A History of Asian Americans.* New York: Penguin, 1989.

Tchen, John Kuo Wei. "Modernizing White Patriarchy: Re-viewing D. W. Griffith's *Broken Blossoms*." In *Moving the Image: Independent Asian Pacific American Media Arts*, ed. Russell Leong. Los Angeles: UCLA Asian American Studies Center and Visual Communications, Southern California Asian American Studies Central, Inc., 1991, 133–143.

Terasaki, Gwen. *Bridge to the Sun.* Newport, Tenn.: Wakestone Books, 1985.

The Editors, *Cahiers du Cinema.* "John Ford's *Young Mr. Lincoln*." In *Movies and Methods*, ed. Bill Nichols. Berkeley and Los Angeles: University of California Press, 1976, 493–529.

Thomson, James C., Jr., Peter W. Stanley, and John Curtis Perry. *Sentimental Imperialists: The American Experience in East Asia.* New York: Harper Colophon Books, 1981.

von Sternberg, Josef. *Fun in a Chinese Laundry: An Autobiography.* New York: Collier Books, 1965.

Wagenknecht, Edward. *The Movies in the Age of Innocence.* New York: Ballantine Books, 1971.

Westmore, Frank, and Muriel Davidson. *The Westmores of Hollywood.* New York: J. B. Lippincott Co., 1976.

Whitaker, Claire. "Hollywood Transformed: Interviews with Lesbian Viewers," In *Jump Cut: Hollywood, Politics, and Counter-Cinema*, ed. Peter Steven. New York: Praeger, 1985, 106–118.

Wilkinson, Endymion. *Japan Versus the West: Image and Reality.* London: Penguin, 1990.

Williams, Harold S. *Shades of the Past: Indiscreet Tales of Japan.* Rutland, Vt.: Charles E. Tuttle Co., 1958.

Woll, Allen L., and Randall M. Miller. *Ethnic and Racial Images in American Film and Television: Historical Essays and Bibliography.* New York: Garland, 1987.

Women Take Issue: Aspects of Women's Subordination. London: Hutchinson, 1978.

Wong, Eugene Franklin. *On Visual Media Racism: Asians in the American Motion Pictures*. New York: Arno Press, 1978.

Wood, Robin. "Hero/Anti-Hero: The Dilemma of *Year of the Dragon*." *CineAction!* 6 (August 1986): 57–61.

Woodward, Grace Steele. *Pocahontas*. Norman: University of Oklahoma Press, 1969.

Young, Philip. "The Mother of Us All: Pocahontas Reconsidered." *Kenyon Review* 24 (Summer 1962): 391–415.

Zaretsky, Eli. *Capitalism, the Family, and Personal Life*. New York: Harper & Row, 1976.

Index

Designer: U.C. Press Staff
Compositor: Asco Trade Typesetting Ltd.
Text: 10/12 Times Roman
Display: Helvetica
Printer: BookCrafters
Binder: BookCrafters